T0212190

Lecture Notes in Computer Science   9707

Commenced Publication in 1973
Founding and Former Series Editors:
Gerhard Goos, Juris Hartmanis, and Jan van Leeuwen

More information about this series at http://www.springer.com/series/7408

Thierry Lecomte · Ralf Pinger
Alexander Romanovsky (Eds.)

Reliability, Safety, and Security of Railway Systems

Modelling, Analysis, Verification, and Certification

First International Conference, RSSRail 2016
Paris, France, June 28–30, 2016
Proceedings

 Springer

Editors
Thierry Lecomte
ClearSy
Aix en Provence
France

Alexander Romanovsky
Newcastle University
Newcastle upon Tyne
UK

Ralf Pinger
Siemens AG
Braunschweig
Germany

ISSN 0302-9743 ISSN 1611-3349 (electronic)
Lecture Notes in Computer Science
ISBN 978-3-319-33950-4 ISBN 978-3-319-33951-1 (eBook)
DOI 10.1007/978-3-319-33951-1

Library of Congress Control Number: 2016938374

LNCS Sublibrary: SL2 – Programming and Software Engineering

Printed on acid-free paper

This Springer imprint is published by Springer Nature
The registered company is Springer International Publishing AG Switzerland

Preface

Welcome to the proceedings of the International Conference on Reliability, Safety and Security of Railway Systems: Modelling, Analysis, Verification, and Certification (RSSRail 2016). We are very pleased that RSSRail 2016 is taking place in Paris during June 28–30, 2016.

This is the first international conference focusing on the reliability, safety, and security of railway systems. The conference is hosted by RATP (Régie Autonome des Transports Parisiens) and held in the main auditorium at their head office in Paris, adjacent to the Gare de Lyon railway station. The conference aims to bring together researchers and engineers interested in building critical railway applications and systems. This is a working conference in which research advances are discussed and evaluated by both researchers and engineers, focusing on their potential to be deployed in industrial settings.

Our aim is to hold a conference that will contribute to a range of key objectives. We feel that there is a pressing need to bring together researchers and developers working on railway system reliability, security, and safety to discuss how these requirements can be met in an integrated way. It is also vital to ensure that all advances in research (both in academia and industry) are driven by real industrial needs. This can help ensure that such advances are followed by industrial deployment. Another particularly important objective is to integrate research advances into the current development processes, and make them usable and scalable. Finally, a key goal is to develop advanced methods and tools that will ensure that the systems meet the requirements imposed by the standards and in building the arguments.

We hope that this conference will successfully contribute to all of these objectives.

The conference covers topics related to all aspects of reliability, safety, and security engineering for railway systems and networks, including:

- Safety in development processes and safety management
- Combined approaches to safety and security
- System and software safety analysis
- Formal modelling and verification techniques
- System reliability
- Validation according to the standards
- Safety and security argumentation
- Fault and intrusion modelling and analysis
- Evaluation of system capacity, energy consumption, costs, and their interplay
- Tool and model integration, and tool chains
- Domain-specific languages and modelling frameworks
- Model reuse for reliability, safety, and security

RSSRail 2016 attracted 36 submissions from 14 countries. Fifteen papers were accepted after a rigorous review process with each paper receiving at least three reviews. These include nine technical papers, three industrial experience reports, and three PhD students' papers. They cover a number of topics, including failure analysis, interlocking verification, formal system specification and refinement, security analysis of ERTMS, safety verification, formalisation of requirements, proof automation, operational security, railway system reliability, risk assessment for ERTMS, and verification of EN-50128 safety requirements.

Three prominent researchers working on railway engineering — Robin Bloomfield from Adelard/City University (UK), Denis Sabatier from ClearSy, and Jan Peleska from University of Bremen/Verified Systems — kindly agreed to deliver keynote talks. The papers describing the research presented in the keynote talks are also included in this volume.

We would like to thank the Program Committee members and the additional reviewers for all their efforts. We are indebted to RATP for hosting our event in Maison de la RATP in Paris. We would like to acknowledge the help of Newcastle University staff: Joan Atkinson, Tom Anderson, Wayne Smith, and Dee Carr. We are grateful to Alfred Hofmann from Springer for supporting the publication of these proceedings in the LNCS series. But, most of all, our thanks go to all the contributors and the attendees of the conference for making this conference a success.

March 2016

Ralf Pinger
Thierry Lecomte
Alexander Romanovsky

Organization

Conference Chairs

Thierry Lecomte   ClearSy, France
Ralf Pinger   Siemens Mobility, Germany
Alexander Romanovsky   Newcastle University, UK

Program Committee

Mark Behrens   DLR, Germany
Andrea Bondavalli   University of Florence, Italy
David Bonvoisin   RATP, France
Stephane Callet   SNCF, France
Simon Collart-Dutilleul   IFFSTAR, France
Veronique Delebarre   SafeRiver, France
Alessandro Fantechi   University of Florence, Italy
Francesco Flammini   Ansaldo STS, Italy
Wan Fokkink   Vrije University, The Netherlands
Stefania Gnesi   ISTI, Italy
Michael Jastram   Formal Mind, Germany
Alexei Iliasov   Newcastle University, UK
Tim Kelly   University of York, UK
Hironobu Kuruma   Hitachi, Japan
Michael Leuschel   University of Düsseldorf, Germany
Jean Marc Mota   Thales R&T, France
Odd Nordland   SINTEF, Norway
Yiannis Papadopoulos   Hull University, UK
Andras Pataricza   BUTE University, Hungary
Peter Popov   City University, UK
Etienne Prun   ClearSy, France
Joris Rehm   ClearSy, France
Aryldo Russo   CERTIFER, France
Kenji Taguchi   AIST, Japan
Ina Schaefer   TU Braunschweig, Germany
Reiner Schmid   Siemens CT Munich, Germany
Walter Schon   University of Technology Compiegne, France
Laurent Voisin   Systerel, France
Kirsten Winter   University of Queensland, Australia

Additional Reviewers

Dominik Hansen	University of Düsseldorf, Germany
Anne E. Haxthausen	TU Denmark, Denmark
Sebastian Krings	University of Düsseldorf, Germany
Sentot Kromodimoeljo	University of Queensland, Australia
Marco Paolieri	University of Florence, Italy
Steve Schneider	University of Surrey, UK
Daisuke Souma	AIST, Japan
Enrico Vicario	University of Florence, Italy
David M. Williams	Thales, UK
Shunsuke Yatabe	JR-West, Japan

Sponsors

AdaCore

ClearSy

Newcastle
University

RATP

Siemens

Systerel

Contents

XII   Contents

Verification and Validation

Keynote Talks

The Risk Assessment of ERTMS-Based Railway Systems from a Cyber Security Perspective: Methodology and Lessons Learned

Robin Bloomfield[1]([⊠]), Marcus Bendele[1], Peter Bishop[1],
Robert Stroud[1], and Simon Tonks[2]

[1] Adelard LLP, London, UK
{reb,mmb,pgb,rjs}@adelard.com
[2] Porterbrook Leasing Company, Derby, UK
simon.tonks@porterbrook.co.uk

Abstract. The impact that cyber issues might have on the safety and resilience of railway systems has been studied for more than five years by industry specialists and government agencies. This paper presents some of the work done by Adelard in this area, ranging from an analysis of potential vulnerabilities in the ERTMS specifications through to a high-level cyber security risk assessment of a national ERTMS implementation and detailed analysis of particular ERTMS systems on behalf of the GB rail industry. The focus of the paper is on our overall methodology for security-informed safety and hazard analysis. Lessons learned will be presented but of course our detailed results remain proprietary or sensitive and cannot be published.

Keywords: Security assessment · Safety-critical systems · Security-informed safety · ERTMS · Railway signaling systems

1 Introduction

The European Railway Traffic Management System (ERTMS) is a major industrial project that aims to replace the many different national train control, command and signaling systems in Europe with a standardized system. In Great Britain, Network Rail are preparing to introduce ERTMS as part of the upgrade of the signaling and communications systems running on Britain's rail infrastructure. This upgrade has the potential to increase the risk of an electronic attack on the rail infrastructure, as it brings more systems under centralized control. Government and railway stakeholders identified a need to understand the security implications of the new technology more than five years ago and there have been a number of studies by industry specialists and government agencies of the impact that cyber issues might have on the safety and resilience of railway systems.

This paper presents some of the work done by Adelard in this area, ranging from an analysis of potential vulnerabilities in the ERTMS specifications through to a high-level cyber security risk assessment of a national ERTMS implementation and detailed

© Springer International Publishing Switzerland 2016
T. Lecomte et al. (Eds.): RSSRail 2016, LNCS 9707, pp. 3–19, 2016.
DOI: 10.1007/978-3-319-33951-1_1

analysis of particular ERTMS systems on behalf of the GB rail industry. The focus of the paper is on our overall methodology for security-informed safety and hazard analysis. Lessons learned will be presented but of course our detailed results remain proprietary or sensitive and cannot be published.

2 Railway Security Requirements

Traditionally, computer security deals with threats to confidentiality, integrity, and availability, but here we are concerned with train movements rather than information, so our primary concern is integrity, then availability, and finally confidentiality. Loss of integrity could result in accidents or collisions, whereas loss of availability would bring the railway system to a halt. Loss of confidentiality is less of an immediate threat, but might result in the leak of sensitive operational information. Reliability is also important, since an unreliable train service will result in a loss of public confidence in the railway operators.

Thus, the hazards or potential failures or undesirable outcomes to be avoided are:

- a collision involving multiple trains;
- an accident such as derailment involving a single train;
- widespread disruption of train services over a large area;
- disruption to individual trains, or trains within a local area;
- creation of a situation that leads to panic and potential loss of life (e.g., an emergency stop and uncontrolled evacuation onto the track);
- creation of a situation that leads to passenger discomfort and dissatisfaction (e.g., stopping a train indefinitely in a tunnel);
- loss of public confidence in the railway system due to intermittent low-level problems affecting the reliability of the service;
- leak of sensitive information (e.g., movements of hazardous cargoes or VIPs).

The ERTMS safety analysis considers the effect of potentially catastrophic events on the integrity of the system. Faults that could result in an accident need to be considered in both a safety and security analysis, regardless of the underlying cause of the fault (accidental, deliberate or malicious).

3 Security Analysis of ERTMS Specifications

The starting point for our ERTMS work was a security analysis of the ERTMS specifications that we were commissioned to perform on behalf of key UK railway stakeholders and UK government about five years ago [1]. The aim of the study was to examine the ERTMS specifications for potential security vulnerabilities and identify systemic weaknesses in the ERTMS specifications. We were concerned with conceptual problems with the specifications rather than vulnerabilities caused by design flaws, bugs in implementations of ERTMS technology, or weaknesses in the operation or maintenance procedures for an ERTMS system. Such vulnerabilities are important but were outside the scope of our study.

Our analysis was holistic and considered whether a national deployment of ERTMS might introduce vulnerabilities into the national rail infrastructure. Our review focused on ERTMS Application Level 2, which made it possible to restrict attention to a number of core specifications, and ignore specifications for interacting with legacy train protection systems and trackside signaling equipment. We also considered the security of GSM-R and analyzed how GSM security impacts on GSM-R security. We were particularly interested in electronic attacks that could be launched remotely and would cause widespread disruption.

3.1   Methodology

Our approach was to consider the trust relationships between the various components of the overall architecture and analyze the consequence of a breach of trust. This enabled us to identify a set of potential weaknesses and vulnerabilities in the specifications. We then developed scenarios that showed how these weaknesses could be exploited by an attacker. These scenarios were refined and validated in discussion with railway stakeholders, and proved to be a very effective way of communicating the risks of an ERTMS implementation being compromised.

Analysis of Trust Relationships. ERTMS is implemented using a number of trackside and on-board sub-systems, and the ERTMS specifications describe the interfaces by which these various subsystems interact to ensure that trains move safely without exceeding their movement authority. We performed a systematic analysis of the ERTMS specifications from a security perspective by examining the on-board ETCS application, and considering its interfaces and trust relationships with other components of the ERTMS system, both trackside and on-board the train.

Development of Attack Scenarios. Having identified some potential vulnerabilities in the ERTMS specifications, we devised attack scenarios to explore the ways in which an attacker could exploit these potential weaknesses and vulnerabilities to achieve one of the undesirable outcomes identified in Sect. 2.

We devised seven attack scenarios and then analyzed each scenario in detail by considering the following questions:

- **how** is the attack performed?
- **what** vulnerabilities does the attack exploit?
- **where** can the attack be launched from?
- **what** are the possible mitigations?

We then graded each attack according to a range of criteria:

- the **type of access** required to exploit a vulnerability;
- the **level of technical sophistication** required to exploit a vulnerability;
- the **type of failure** caused by a successful attack;
- the **scale of effect** for a successful attack;
- the **scalability of the attack** from the attacker's perspective;
- the **type of impact** caused by a successful attack;

- the **types of mitigation strategy** that are possible;
- the **level of difficulty** for implementing each mitigation.

We did not attempt to rank the various attack scenarios using a weighted average of the category scores because we believe that such a ranking would be too simplistic – the relative weighting of the various categories and the ranking of the scenarios is a matter for government and industry stakeholders. Similarly, we did not attempt to estimate the likelihood of attacks being successful because this would depend on the national implementation of ERTMS and is therefore best left to the domain experts. Instead, we used color coding (HIGH, MEDIUM, Low) to highlight the issues. Using this color coding, we produced a table summarizing our grading of each attack scenario under the various headings to enable the scenarios to be easily compared.

Broadly speaking, attacks that can be launched remotely do not require a high level of sophistication and are highly scalable – however, such attacks are relatively easy to mitigate. Conversely, attacks that require local access are less scalable but also more difficult to mitigate. Hence important trade-offs need to be made by the relevant decision makers and risk managers. The advantage of the analysis and grading approach presented here is that it identifies these trade-offs and helps the stakeholders to make more informed decisions.

4   Risk Assessment of a National Implementation of ERTMS

Following on from our initial security analysis of the ERTMS specification, we were asked to provide a risk assessment for a national implementation of ERTMS.

In Great Britain, Network Rail are planning to implement an ERTMS overlay on top of the existing signaling and control system [2]. There are also plans to introduce a new traffic management system and eliminate the need for about 800 small signal boxes by centralizing traffic management into a small number of regional control centers. This centralization will require a more network-oriented architecture with remote access to local (normally unmanned) equipment rooms via Network Rail's fixed telecommunications network (FTN). The infrastructure is expected to evolve over time, with more equipment being centralized and the core FTN being updated to use IP-based protocols rather than dedicated voice and data channels.

Adelard were asked to determine on behalf of Government whether these changes represented a high-level risk to the national infrastructure. At this stage in the upgrade programme, the exact details of the planned infrastructure changes had not yet been defined, so we provided a high level assessment of the cyber security risks associated with a generic ERTMS-based railway infrastructure.

4.1   Approach

The first step of our risk assessment was to establish the system context and agree on the scope and motivation for the assessment with stakeholders. The major system assets and services were identified in order to ensure that the risk assessment was focused on high impact scenarios. Potential threat sources were identified and attack capabilities and impact levels were defined.

The next step was to perform a preliminary risk analysis, identifying potential hazards and consequences, and relevant vulnerabilities and causes, together with any intrinsic mitigations and controls. This analysis was then refined to identify specific attack scenarios, which were prioritized according to the capabilities required and the potential consequences of the attack.

The final step was to summarize the results of the risk analysis, identify areas of uncertainty, possible mitigations and controls, and present the results of the risk assessment in the following terms:

- a set of potential attacks on an ERTMS-based system
- the capabilities needed to implement these attacks
- the worst case impact of each attack

In order to quantify the actual risk, it would be necessary to combine these results with an intelligence assessment of the likelihood of a particular threat source having the necessary capabilities to perform each attack.

4.2   System Context

ERTMS is designed to be an overlay on an existing signaling infrastructure, so it is necessary to consider the underlying railway system as part of any implementation of ERTMS. Following discussions with Network Rail, we modelled the railway system as a series of layers.

Table 1 summarizes the functionality provided by each layer and the required safety integrity level (SIL).

Table 1. Railway layers

Layer	Safety Integrity Level	Functionality
Business	SIL 0	Timetable, Train Information, Operations and Maintenance
Control	SIL 2	Traffic management, Automatic Route Setting, SCADA
Safety	SIL 4	ETCS (trackside and on-board), Interlocking
Communications	SIL 0	Fixed Telecommunications Network (FTN), Radio (GSM-R)
Lineside	SIL 4	Signals, Points, Train Detection

With conventional signaling systems, the safety layer is implemented solely by trackside equipment, but the introduction of in-cab signaling and automatic train protection systems such as ERTMS means that the safety layer is now partially implemented

8   R. Bloomfield et al.

by on-board equipment. Thus, it is important to consider both trackside and on-board equipment as part of any risk assessment.

Figure 1 provides a high-level overview of the architecture of a national railway system implemented using ERTMS. The diagram illustrates the main interactions between the various layers and system components, and the criticality of each layer (SIL 0, SIL 2, SIL 4). Since railway signaling and control is a socio-technical system, the diagram includes people as well as equipment. The main roles considered include the controller, the driver, and the system maintainers.

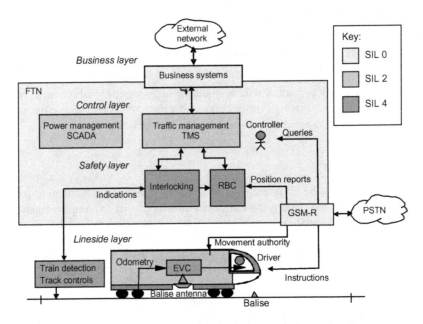

Fig. 1. Conceptual architecture of an ERTMS-enabled railway signaling system

4.3   Scope of Assessment

The focus of the risk assessment was on failures of the railway signaling and control system that could have a major national impact, namely:

- attacks that result in unsafe train movements, which could cause a train accident with considerable loss of life;
- attacks that result in loss of service, which could lead to major transport disruptions.

We chose to exclude attacks that result in the theft of information because our focus was on the integrity and safety of the rail signaling and control system; loss of confidentiality is not a major concern except for some very specific attacks (e.g., on high value passengers, hazardous or high value cargoes) and the possible knock-on effect of information theft enabling future attacks on the systems.

Moreover, as this was a security risk assessment, we only considered failures resulting from the effect of deliberate attacks. We would expect failures resulting from non-malicious causes (like fallen trees, driver error, etc.) to be covered by engineering safety assessments.

4.4 Impact Assessment

We assessed the impact of a successful attack on the railway system using a scale from 1 to 5, where 5 was the most serious.

Our risk assessment identified the capabilities that an attacker would need in order to achieve a high impact failure. Attacks were assessed with respect to the capability levels shown in Table 2.

Table 2. Attack capability levels

Capability level	Interpretation for railway systems
E	An expert in security engineering who can: • use tools specific to the domain, which may be customized for the attacks; • develop novel equipment and tools specific to the attack; • use publicly available and proprietary information on how the system works and what mitigations are in place against attacks; • develop large test beds and trials for the attack; • coordinate timing of several attacks; • influence expert insiders.
D	An expert in security engineering who can: • use tools specific to the domain, which may be customized for the attacks; • access equipment for trials and attack development; • use publicly available and proprietary information on how the system works and what mitigations are in place against attacks; • influence knowledgeable insiders.
C	Someone with a basic understanding of security engineering who can: • use tools specific to the domain but without customization; • use publicly available information on how the system works and what mitigations are in place against attacks; • influence insiders (but at routine skill level).
B	Someone with physical access to the system, for example: • an engineer who is able to plug a maintenance console into the equipment but has no specific training or authorization to access the system in this way; • an unwitting participant, using a compromised machine or device.
A	Someone without access to the system, for example: • unskilled individuals using scripts or programs developed by others to attack computer systems and networks; • someone who has been co-opted into scaling a distributed denial of service attack; • an enterprise IT user.

Although our risk assessment was mainly concerned with cyber attacks, we also considered the effect of physical attacks on cyber assets because the infrastructure is geographically distributed and is therefore more open to such attacks. We used a similar set of criteria (skills, resources, equipment, etc.) to grade the capability needed for physical attacks on cyber equipment.

Evaluation of the likely attack frequencies and capabilities of specific threat sources is outside the assessment scope and would normally be undertaken by government agencies.

4.5   Risk Analysis

In this section we describe each step of our risk analysis, which considered possible attack scenarios that could compromise railway assets to cause either:

- unsafe movements;
- no movement when it is safe to proceed.

Preliminary Fault Tree Analysis. The initial stage of risk analysis was to construct fault trees in order to identify possible attacks on operational assets that could lead to the top events (unsafe movements and no movement). The fault trees systematically considered:

- attacks on messages sent between systems, typically by:
  - blocking transmission;
  - modifying / inserting messages;

- attacks on the systems themselves, typically via compromises of:
  - system firmware;
  - system configuration data.

The fault trees considered the effect of application-level attacks and only dealt with the consequence of these attacks, not their technical difficulty or potential impact.

Attack Vectors and Capabilities. The next stage of analysis was to consider what capabilities (as defined in Table 2) were needed to implement each attack scenario. The scale ranges from A (little skill required) to E (capabilities usually possessed only by nation states).

The preliminary risk analysis identified a number of possible attack vectors, so attack capabilities were estimated for each of these attack vectors. The primary attack vectors considered were:

- physical attacks;
- cyber intrusion;
- data preparation / installation;

- software maintenance;
- network attacks.

The estimated attack capabilities took account of the safety integrity level (SIL) of the system being attacked because we would expect the vulnerabilities and defenses to differ between SIL 0 and SIL 4 systems. However, because our analysis was based on a generic system architecture for a national implementation of an ERTMS-based signaling system, our estimates of attack capability were necessarily quite broad. For a more precise assessment, we would need to have detailed knowledge of the actual system architecture.

Attack Scenarios. Using the fault trees and attack capabilities required for each attack vector, we developed a series of potential attack scenarios. Each scenario identifies the target asset, the potential attack vectors, and the capability required for the attack. These capability estimates were fairly broad to accommodate uncertainties in the security features present in the systems and the maintenance processes.

We also considered the immediate effect and the potential scale of each attack, which we used to inform the impact assessment.

Impact Assessment. Our criticality scale distinguishes between loss of service and loss of life, so we make this distinction in our impact assessment.

Loss of Life. It is credible that an attack that resulted in "unsafe movement" could cause an accident with 100 or more deaths in the worst case. The Eschede [3] and Amagasaki [4] train accidents exceeded this level while the Santiago de Compostela [5] accident was just below it. One could envisage multiple attacks causing multiple accidents and several hundred deaths, but it is likely that rail operators would respond to multiple accidents by shutting down the network.

However, we also need to consider the associated disruption. For a physical attack, we estimate that the disruption would be localized to a particular part of the network and would last for about a week until the physical repairs were completed. In contrast, if the accident was shown to be due to a systemic cyber security problem within the safety, communications, or lineside layer, the disruption could be far greater. To respond to a systemic cyber problem:

- all assets of the same type within the rail infrastructure would need to be assessed in order to determine if they were vulnerable to the same attack;
- operational changes would need to be put in place to minimize the risk. This would imply degraded service levels for all vulnerable parts of the network;
- systems will need to be updated and validated before normal service can be restored.

In the worst-case scenario, the resulting disruption could be nationwide and last several weeks.

Loss of service. There are many attacks that could result in a wide-scale loss of service, particularly at the business, control and communications layers.

Cyber attacks on the business and control layers (for example, attacks on the timetable or traffic management system) would be a cause for concern, but it might be easier to accept systemic vulnerabilities in these layers if the attacks could be detected and rapidly corrected (e.g., by restoring systems from secure backup storage). Given rapid system restoration, a recovery to normal service might take 1 or 2 days. However, the impact might be increased by repeat attacks if the vulnerability could not easily be addressed.

Successful physical attacks could also have a widespread effect at the business and control layers but again recovery would be fairly rapid (a few days) unless there were repeated attacks.

Loss of service could also be achieved by physical attacks on the safety and lineside layers but the effect would be localized and physical repairs would only take a few days, so the impact would be low. Repetition of attacks is possible but the impact would still be fairly low.

In practice, it is difficult to be too specific about the impact from loss of service as this depends on the resilience built into the system architecture. In particular, the impact of a cyber attack depends on the recovery process and could be reduced by switching to a fallback mechanism.

Impact vs Capability Summary. We combined the capabilities needed for the attacks on specific layers to obtain an overall capability range and assigned a worst-case impact based on the rationale outlined in the previous section. We then summarized our results graphically, as shown in Fig. 2. The lines plot the range of impact and likelihood for the different layers, attacks and impacts. The figure identifies the highest impact and lowest capability attack for each layer and shows the scope for driving the risks down by reducing the impact or increasing the capability for each attack.

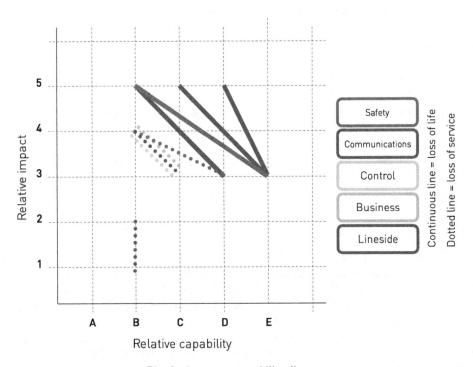

Fig. 2. Impact vs. capability diagram

Further information about the implementation would enable us to develop more precise capability estimates. Similarly, we could reduce our impact estimates if the implementation included features to limit the level of disruption caused by a successful attack.

Although our analysis identified cases where relatively low capability attacks could have a high impact, this is partly due to our uncertainty about the actual capability needed to perform cyber attacks.

The capability required for physical attacks is easier to assess and relatively modest capabilities can have quite significant effects.

For cyber attacks on the network, the capability needed at the communications layer to cause loss of life depends critically on the protection provided at the endpoint subsystems in the safety and lineside layers, which in turn depends on whether the network is considered to be open or closed. A cyber attack on the connection between the interlocking and lineside equipment is currently difficult. However, this may change as newer technology (like IP) is introduced. If the communications layer is always regarded as untrusted and the endpoints are protected, the capability needed for a successful cyber attack rises from C-E to D-E.

The other low capability-high criticality attacks relate to attacks on the data used to configure SIL 4 systems in the safety layer. Our capability B assessment is at the low end of the capability range and might be overly pessimistic.

5   Cyber Security Risk Assessments of ETCS On-board Systems

As part of the ERTMS upgrade programme, the companies that own the trains (Rolling Stock Operating Companies or ROSCOs) are in the process of tendering for 'first-in-class' fitments of ETCS on-board systems for each class of locomotive that will be used on ERTMS-enabled infrastructure. In the light of concerns about the security of ERTMS, Adelard and MWR InfoSecurity were commissioned by Porterbrook on behalf of the National Joint ROSCO Programme (NJRP) to provide advice and guidance on any additional security requirements that might need to be included in the contract. Adelard have expertise in risk assessment whilst MWR InfoSecurity have expertise in security testing.

Each risk assessment was informed by our generic research into ERTMS security issues, the results of a security-focused Hazop workshop that was held with the suppliers, subsequent analysis of the system by Adelard, and the results of security testing performed by MWR InfoSecurity at each supplier's test facility.

5.1   Security-Informed Hazop Methodology

A series of workshops was held to study the security risks associated with each system. The workshops took the form of security-informed Hazard and Operability (Hazop) studies, and were attended by experts from each supplier.

A Hazop study is a structured approach to the identification of potential hazards and deviations from design and operating intention. The technique is qualitative, and aims to stimulate the imagination of participants to identify potential hazards and operability problems.

The study is based on the architecture of the system and involves a multi-disciplinary team of experts. Each element of the system is reviewed systematically, using a set of guidewords to prompt the experts to identify potential hazards. The experts are asked to identify

- causes of a potential malfunction
- potential consequences of the malfunction
- any system features that can detect or mitigate the malfunction
- any follow-up activities

Each study was based on a simplified architecture diagram that was intended to capture the most relevant components and interfaces of the ETCS on-board system from a cyber security perspective. Adelard created this diagram after reviewing the various documents provided by the supplier.

The goal of each Hazop study was to identify potential attacks on the ETCS on-board system that could be investigated further during the security testing, and to suggest some additional controls and assurance activities that would provide confidence that the system was protected against such attacks.

The workshops also provided an opportunity to clarify the system architecture and the test environment available for the security testing, and identify particular areas of concern to be the focus of the security testing.

The findings of each workshop were systematically recorded as a series of Hazop tables, and recommendations were categorized and numbered to ensure consistency. Each study resulted in a detailed analysis of possible attack scenarios, potential hazards, existing protections, and recommendations for additional security controls.

5.2   Security Testing

In this section, we describe our general approach to security testing and the specific objectives of the security testing that was performed on each supplier's system by a team of experienced penetration testers from MWR InfoSecurity.

General Approach to Security Testing. An ETCS on-board system can be attacked externally via interfaces that are required for ERTMS interoperability or internally via interfaces that are proprietary to the system. Attacks can be at the application level, network level, or platform level. In particular, the underlying platform might be built using commercial off-the-shelf components that contain security vulnerabilities or expose additional services that are not required for the application.

At the application level, security weaknesses in the ERTMS specifications allow a variety of attacks that are not described here for obvious reasons.

At the network level, security testing should include robustness testing of all the major interfaces, both external and internal, in order to probe whether the system is robust against deliberately crafted messages that pass the integrity checks but are invalid at the application level.

Testing should also challenge closed network assumptions. This requires investigating the security of the network used to connect together components of the ETCS on-board system and assessing the damage that could be done to the system by an attacker with access to these networks.

Security Testing Objectives. The overall goal of the security testing is to explore this range of attack vectors and determine whether any of the attacks are feasible. In practice, depending on the test environment, it may not be possible to perform the full range of tests, so the aim is to achieve broad coverage of the possible attack vectors.

More specifically, the security testing objectives can be broken down as follows:

- explore the feasibility of attacks allowed by the ERTMS specifications and discover whether the driver receives any notification if something unexpected happens;
- determine whether the ETCS implementation is robust against malformed messages or whether it is possible to crash the system or cause it to behave in an arbitrary way;
- investigate whether the closed network assumption is valid and determine what damage could be done by an attacker with access to the network and some inside knowledge;
- perform a security audit of the underlying platform and any third-party components.

Some of the test results exposed anomalies or ambiguities in the ERTMS specifications. Although these anomalies do not raise any safety or security concerns, it is important to resolve any ambiguities in the ERTMS specifications in order to remove the potential for an attacker to exploit differences in behavior between implementations.

5.3 Recommendations

Our final set of recommendations were divided into four categories:

1. technical or procedural controls that would improve the security of the ETCS on-board system;
2. assurance activities to improve confidence in the security of the ETCS on-board system;
3. recommendations for the national implementation of ERTMS;
4. suggested changes to the ERTMS specifications.

Unfortunately, we cannot publish any of our recommendations here because they implicitly identify potential vulnerabilities in the systems.

6 Discussion/Lessons Learned

6.1 Context

There is a growing awareness that safety and security can no longer be considered in isolation and that a system cannot be considered to be safe unless it has also been shown to be secure. However, there is currently a lack of underpinning analysis to demonstrate how and whether cyber security issues can be integrated in to hazard and risk analyses, and hence a lack of consensus about the best way to integrate safety and security. In particular, there are no clear guidelines about methodology, and standards in this area are still evolving. As a result of the work on security-informed safety that Adelard and others have been doing in the railway industry, this situation is changing within the UK. The Department of Transport has recently published guidance on Rail Cyber Security [6] and commissioned work to develop a code of practice for the railway industry on how best to develop security-informed safety cases. Adelard has been active in this area and worked with the Railway Safety and Standards Board (RSSB) to develop a security-informed safety case as an exemplar for the railway industry. However, security-informed safety is not just a concern for the railway industry – Adelard was a partner in the SESAMO project [7], which was concerned with security and safety modelling for embedded systems across a wide range of industrial domains, including avionics, automotive, industrial control, medical, smart grid as well as rail. There is now a much greater awareness of the need to consider cyber security in the design of safety-critical systems, and the focus has shifted from raising awareness to developing guidance, standards and worked examples.

6.2 Strategy

Adopting a phased approach towards cyber security assessment has proved to be an effective strategy. We started by performing a security audit of the ERTMS specifications, which enabled us to identify a number of systemic vulnerabilities in the specification and potential areas of concern. These were refined by developing specific attack scenarios, which proved to be an excellent way of communicating and engaging with railway stakeholders because the attacks became real rather than theoretical and abstract.

The next stage was to conduct a high-level risk assessment of a national implementation of ERTMS, which was used to inform the national risk register. Focusing on the potential risks at a national level gave our risk assessment a sense of proportionality and perspective.

In practice, the worst-case impact in terms of loss of life or loss of service depends on many implementation factors (including provisions for resilience) that have not yet determined at this stage in the upgrade programme. Thus, our assessment will need to be revisited as the upgrade progresses and more operational experience is gained. However, we believe that our main findings are robust.

Our risk assessment of a national ERTMS implementation was based on a generic system architecture with little specific information about the vulnerabilities and defenses that might exist in the actual system. In contrast, our risk assessment of ETCS on-board systems from each of the major suppliers looked at real systems in detail and took into account the results of security testing and vulnerabilities discovered in the configuration of each system. These assessments were performed on behalf of the rolling stock operating companies (ROSCOs), who wished to purchase ETCS on-board systems for new and existing trains and needed to have some reassurance that their assets would be robust against cyber attack. The results of the assessments were used to inform the procurement process for the 'first-in-class' fitment programme to install ETCS on each class of locomotive, and the recommendations from each assessment were written into the contract with each supplier. The assessments were beneficial to both the purchasers and the suppliers because they enabled the purchasers to reduce their risk whilst providing guidance to the suppliers on how to improve the security of their products.

6.3   Where Next?

Over the last few years, government and industry have been mobilizing and commissioning research and support for developing cyber security strategies and guidance and there is now a plethora of groups working in this area. It is important to develop a coherent strategy that clearly identifies roles and responsibilities at different levels of governance (project, industry, government) and identifies gaps where further research and development of standards and guidance is necessary.

Railway-Specific Issues. In the railway context, management of cyber risk is complicated by the divided responsibilities for maintaining safety in an ERTMS-based signaling system. Responsibility for the safety layer is split between the trackside and the train, which are owned and managed by different organizations. Security needs to be embedded in the processes used by all stakeholders in order to maintain the overall safety and integrity of the signaling system.

Another complicating factor is the widespread use of legacy systems that were designed in a different age to protect against different threats. Closed network assumptions are no longer valid but it is not always possible to add security features to legacy systems, so alternative approaches are needed.

At a more general level, we need to consider if there is adequate oversight for the introduction and operation of new technology like ERTMS and whether there are sufficient technical resources available to the regulator.

Incident Reporting. It is important to ensure that we can learn from incidents, so that safety issues with the new technology can be identified and rectified. Ideally, incident reporting should be undertaken by all ERTMS users and suppliers. We recommend the introduction of policies for the collection, analysis and sharing of cyber incident information, even when such incidents have no safety impact.

Resilience Requirements. There is currently a lack of any clear definition of resilience requirements from a policy perspective. While safety is governed by existing legislation, there do not appear to be any system level resilience requirements. Governance and business models should be established to ensure that sufficient resilience is provided by the system as a whole. Incentives may need to be provided for diversity that is justified from wider societal considerations rather than from an infrastructure owner's business case.

Secure by Design. There is also clearly a need for industry guidance on methodology and guidance for developing and assessing systems that are intended to be both safe and secure. Suppliers need guidance on how to build security into their products, and purchasers need to be informed about cyber security and be given tools to help them assess whether a product is adequately secure for its intended use. This is particularly important during the procurement phase of a large railway project, where there is an opportunity to influence both the generic product and a specific application of the product to the GB context.

There are already a number of sources of guidance available, including:

- 20 Critical Controls for Effective Cyber Security Defense;
- DHS Cyber Security Procurement Language;
- Trustworthy Software Initiative;
- Cyber Essentials;
- BSIMM, OWASP, Microsoft SDL, SafeCode;
- Common Criteria.

These need to be customized and adapted for the railway sector.

Standards and Legislation. In Europe, any significant changes to a mainline railway system must be assessed in accordance with the Common Safety Method. This is a legal requirement. Similarly, the ERTMS specifications form part of the Technical Specification for Interoperability, which is mandated by European law. This makes it difficult for GB concerns about cyber security within the railway industry to be addressed at a national level, and makes it necessary to engage at a European level to influence the development of these standards to ensure that they include adequate provision and protection against cyber attacks.

Risk and Uncertainty. A risk assessment should be a living document and needs to be revisited periodically during the system life cycle. Risks can change during the development of the system and also during its operation, so it is important to understand the risks and the mitigations in place at every stage of the life cycle. This is particularly true for risks arising from cyber security threats – security decays faster than safety.

Our risk assessments of ETCS on-board systems were assessments of real systems and were performed with the benefit of detailed design documents, access to system experts, and the opportunity to perform security testing on the actual system to determine whether potential vulnerabilities existed in reality and could be exploited. The systems were still under development but the manufacturers were receptive to our recommendations and willing to incorporate changes into the design of their systems to make them more robust and resilient against cyber attack.

In contrast, our risk assessment of a national ERTMS implementation was performed at an early stage in the upgrade programme, and was therefore based on a generic system architecture. As a result, there is significant uncertainty in the results and it is therefore important to revisit the assessment as more implementation detail is provided and more operational experience is gained. An updated risk assessment would need to address:

- the impact of the differing responsibilities of the multiple stakeholders (operators, leasing companies and the supply chain) for safety management and hence cyber risk;
- the susceptibility of data preparation and maintenance processes to cyber attack;
- the extent to which the overall system architecture is designed to limit cyber attack as the system evolves (e.g., when there are changes in network technology);
- the resilience and recovery from cyber attack provided by fallback options (both in fixed infrastructure and on board the train);
- the co-operation and security culture of the stakeholders.

7 Conclusions

The next generation of railway signaling and control systems will potentially have more risk and less resilience than the current generation of systems due to security vulnerabilities and increased connectivity. However, this increased connectivity means that the new systems could potentially be engineered with stronger controls, greater defense in depth, and improved recovery mechanisms, thus eventually presenting less risk overall and providing greater resilience. The risk assessments presented in this paper are one contribution to ensuring that this is the case.

Acknowledgements. We are grateful to our sponsors for their permission to publish this summary of our work over the last five years. We would also like to acknowledge the contribution of Richard Bloomfield and Ilir Gashi to our initial analysis of the ERTMS specifications.

References

1. Bloomfield, R., Bloomfield, R., Gashi, I., Stroud, R.: How secure is ERTMS? In: Ortmeier, F., Daniel, P. (eds.) SAFECOMP Workshops 2012. LNCS, vol. 7613, pp. 247–258. Springer, Heidelberg (2012)
2. Network Rail, Strategic Business plan for 2014/2019, January 2013
3. Wikipedia, Eschede train disaster. http://en.wikipedia.org/wiki/Eschede_train_disaster
4. Wikipedia, Amagasaki rail crash. http://en.wikipedia.org/wiki/Amagasaki_rail_crash
5. Wikipedia, Santiago de Compostela derailment. http://en.wikipedia.org/wiki/Santiago_de_Compostela_derailment
6. Department for Transport, Rail Cyber Security, Guidance to Industry, February 2016. http://www.rssb.co.uk/Library/improving-industry-performance/2016-02-cyber-security-rail-cyber-security-guidance-to-industry.pdf
7. SESAMO – Security and Safety Modelling, ARTEMIS Embedded Computing Systems Initiative 2011, Project Number 295354, May 2012

Using Formal Proof and B Method at System Level for Industrial Projects

Denis Sabatier[✉]

ClearSy, Aix-en-Provence, France
denis.sabatier@clearsy.com

Abstract. Since several years, ClearSy has driven large projects about using formal proofs at system level in the railway domain. The fundamental goal in these projects is to extract the rigorous reasoning establishing that the considered system ensures its requested properties, and to assert that this reasoning is correct and fully expressed. In this paper, we give feedback about the methodology used in all these projects, about the differences made by whether the concerned system is currently under design or already existing and about the benefits obtained. The formal proofs are performed using Event-B, with the Atelier-B toolkit.

Keywords: System level proof · Formal methods · Event-B · Atelier-B

1 Introduction

Since several years, ClearSy has driven large projects about using formal proofs at system level for railway systems in the railway domain. The fundamental goal in these projects is to *extract the rigorous reasoning* establishing that the considered system ensures its requested properties, and to *assert that this reasoning is correct* and fully expressed. At system level, this rigorous reasoning involves the properties of different kind of subsystems (from computer subsystems to operational procedures), that the formal proof shall all encompass.

It may seem that such a top-level reasoning should be very complicated, involving all details of the complex system: in reality it is often quite simple. In the case of a CBTC system (most of our system level proofs are about CBTCs), the requested properties are ensured because equipped trains determine their position correctly, because protection envelopes are determined using these correct positions, because the interlocking does so that those envelopes remain within locked routes and because equipped trains remain before their given limits. Well, it does not completely fit in a single sentence of course, but nevertheless it is fortunately simple enough to be expressed, at least independently from technical details below like track data format.

2 Role and Benefits

So contrary (and in complement to) many other methods, we start from the top level before details appear. What are the expected benefits? The system level "reasons why" properties are part of the domain knowledge. They are, however, known by domain

© Springer International Publishing Switzerland 2016
T. Lecomte et al. (Eds.): RSSRail 2016, LNCS 9707, pp. 20–31, 2016.
DOI: 10.1007/978-3-319-33951-1_2

experts in terms of complex design solutions, so the experts may not easily give the true explanations without going through all the design details. This drives the focus away from what actually ensures the properties and levels out all details as if they were of equal importance. Extracting these "reasons why" in a formal way forces one to formulate a self-sufficient and provable set of properties and assumptions: unnecessary details are eliminated thanks to assumptions optimization, and the proof ensures that all that is necessary has indeed been included.

Having a clear definition of these properties and assumptions will certainly not find hidden bugs in low level design: providing proofs at high level does not suppress the necessity to cover all the project's stages. At least we can expect that a clearer definition of what each sub-part should ensure (highlighted for important properties alone) will draw the testing /verifications toward important bugs or avoid them in the first place thanks to proper developers' focus. More precisely, we can summarize the benefits in two categories:

- Benefits thanks to a sufficient set of clear properties requested from developed sub-systems: better focus on those properties, either during development /testing (if these tasks occur during or later system level proofs) or for post verifications;
- Benefits thanks to a sufficient set of clear properties requested from context sub-systems: usually such properties or assumptions about context concern very different domains. In an industrial project each partner or company is eager to focus on its domain of expertise, even when doing so means using unclear or not well defined assumptions about context sub-systems. Important pitfalls can hide there, and they could remain undetected until the final integration phase. The system level formal proof typically helps to detect concerns that might fall in such "responsibility holes" otherwise.

3   Projects

The first project of that sort done by ClearSy is the system formal verification for the CBTC of New York subway line 7 (Flushing line system proof, see [4, 8]). New York City Transit (NYCT) has awarded THALES Toronto for the design and fitting of this CBTC (awarded in 2010, revenue service scheduled in 2016). This CBTC system is composed of an on-board computer fitted in renewed R142 cars and of field and office equipment (zone controllers and central supervision). It interfaces to the existing interlocking system, adapted with specific modifications. This system level formal verification with proofs lasted from November 2010 until December 2012 and the workload was several man years.

The second project was also for NYCT. Reusing the models developed for the Flushing line, the goal was to provide system level proofs for all CBTC complying with NYCT's Interoperability Interface Specifications (I2S). In fact, I2S based CBTCs are divided in subsystems with predefined roles: by clearly defining the required properties of each subsystem and the context assumptions a formal proof of system level properties is possible, even without knowing each possible vendor's design. ClearSy obtained such a proof; the project lasted from November 2013 to July 2015 with a workload less than half that of Flushing, thanks to reuse.

Two other projects of similar sizes and topics are currently going on concerning French railways: one for SNCF has started last summer (2015), the second one for the Paris metro operator RATP is about to start.

4   Functional or Safety Properties

Should the system proof include functional properties or be restricted to safety properties only? This question may seem straightforward, because proving as many things as possible seems natural. A closer look reveals that the proof of functional properties is often expensive or with limited benefits, even if proving only safety properties means that the proof will not give any guarantee about the system being functional at all.

Here is why functional properties are less accessible to proofs: the mechanism of a formal demonstration consists in formulating target properties, gathering assumptions and finding a logical path (i.e. using only known rules) from assumptions to target properties. But functional properties are defined in terms of performances (delays, capacity) and scenarios (typical situations where performance should be reached; in degraded situations maximum performance is not expected). So the assumptions here would be the scenarios themselves, together with all the mechanisms involved; any proof there becomes very similar to a simulation on a particular case.

Conversely safety properties should be kept whatever the scenario, using minimal assumptions about mechanisms: there a proof gives all its value by replacing testing or simulation across an unbounded set of scenarios and situations. In our case of system level proofs, we thus target global safety properties only. Of course there are cases where the notions of "safety" and "functional" merge (think for example of systems aboard planes), where keeping something functional becomes vital. Then the necessary redundancies multiply the scenarios, bringing back the value of a proof for such cases.

In railway systems and in particular in CBTCs, the safety properties remain well separated from functional ones. Typical target safety properties are:

- Impossibility of collision between trains,
- Impossibility of derailment over an unlocked switch,
- Impossibility of over-speeding.

These safety properties are found in all kind of railway systems, whether they are CTBC projects or signaling system projects. In ClearSy's system level proof projects, the top level reasoning is thus very similar despite the fact that the projects are from different contexts and different designs; however similarities decrease rapidly at more detailed levels, where the chosen design has a stronger importance.

This difference between safety properties and functional properties gives an important clue about the role of a proof in a large system project, in particular the role of a system level proof: it addresses the global safety properties that should hold whatever the scenarios and whatever the conditions. The more a property is related only to specific scenarios, the less the benefits of a proof: for such properties simulation and testing apply.

5 Methodology

5.1 Overview and Experiences

ClearSy's methodology to obtain such system level proofs is divided in two main steps:

1. Write documents explaining how the system ensures the desired properties. We call this natural language "proof", with quotes because this step is not yet a formal proof.
2. Write event-B models such that the proof performed is the formal equivalent of the natural language proof.

The first step is based on the fact that we do not use the formal method to understand why a property is ensured, but to validate that it is really ensured once the "why" is understood. We want to avoid mixing formal notation issues with domain issues, which are paramount. The second step is of course necessary to obtain a true formal proof and the correctness guarantee that comes with it. These two steps are duplicated for all topics, starting from top level properties and repeated for sub-properties down to the chosen level of details, in a hierarchical manner.

The first step "natural language proof" is deeply impacted by whether the system is already designed, ranging from a new system currently in its first stages to an existing system with legacy design. There is a paradox here: the job of the formal proof team is easier if the design is stable and well known, but then the benefits of the proof are reduced, because if pitfalls exist they will not be easily corrected and if there are no pitfalls the whole proof work seems useless. Conversely, if the design is not yet decided at all, there may be very little to prove.

In the Flushing NYCT project, the design was well known but currently under modification: THALES designers were currently adapting their CBTC design to NYCT's requirements. ClearSy had extensive contacts with the designers, so the design was easily accessible with comprehensive explanations. In the I2S project, the situation was more difficult because we had to rely only on the part of the design imposed by the interface specification: for the vendor specific part, we had to assume that the vendor's internal design would correctly establish the sub-properties taken as assumptions in the proof. ClearSy so added documents called "proof requests" (not meaning "formal" proof request) to the I2S explaining required properties and clarifying context assumptions under which these properties should hold. Besides, the design fixed with the interface was not to be changed at all, and the "reasons why" of this design was not so easily accessible. In subsequent projects we also encounter the case of a design still in its very first phases: because proving all possible solutions is not feasible, the initial task is then reduced to defining the notions in preparation for future proofs.

5.2 The Natural Language Proof

In all cases, the necessary elements to extract for the "natural language proof" are:

- Well defined target properties;
- A set of fully realistic assumptions about concerned sub-systems and context;
- An understanding of how these assumptions ensure the properties.

Defining target properties is not difficult at the system's top level because it's directly linked to what the system should obviously ensure. It is conversely *very difficult* to find the true properties from the sub-systems and the context constituting the set of assumptions cited above: the role of each subsystem is known by each domain's experts in terms of internal design details, never (or practically never) as abstract properties. Actually, it is far easier and less prone to errors to describe a subsystem using all its design details "as so" than to formulate an abstract property that sums up this subsystem. When trying such a formulation, one quickly discovers the asymptotic difference between an *almost true* property and an *always true* property for characterizing the considered subsystem!

For the proof team, it would not be realistic to expect such well-defined abstract properties from the experts or from the project documents. ClearSy uses the following method, starting from identified top properties and a first understanding of subsystem roles:

- Play scenarios trying to violate the wanted property (for instance, at top level try to play a scenario leading to a train collision), in a light and fast way, until the reasons why violating the property is impossible appear.
  - Ask feedback about those scenarios from system designers: as the desired property (for instance no collision at any time) has been their concern, they will quickly explain why the property is ensured in that case (unless there is a real pitfall!).
- Once the reasons why the property is ensured have appeared, explain those reasons, at first informally then more and more rigorously.
  - Again, ask feedback about those simplest reasons why the property is ensured from original system designers.

We repeat these steps until sufficient abstract properties for subsystems and context appear, so that the target properties seem to be ensured. Like this, close contacts with domain experts and designers ensure that the proof team manages to find the required assumptions efficiently, without illegally re-designing the system (in a way that would be incorrect compared to the real system and that would not be functional, as the proof team is not the design team).

Starting from top level target properties, we use this process to obtain the three components previously cited: target properties, context /subsystems properties, reasoning. This is done in several successive steps: the sub-properties of a step become targets properties for next steps, and so on in a hierarchical way until we reach the appropriate level of detail. Note that seen from a proof point of view, the context and subsystems properties are the assumptions for a given proof step: for this reason we call them sub-properties or assumptions indifferently. Of course, at the end of the whole process only the assumptions from all the terminal branches of the hierarchical tree will be presented as the output assumptions, to be finally validated and rechecked in case of system evolution (Fig. 1).

Key points in the methodology. Even if using "natural language" in this phase is considered necessary, it means that before the formal stage (where we use Event-B [1, 3] and Atelier-B [2]) all the ambiguities of the natural language can remain. To detect such ambiguities when first writing the properties, we use the following criterion: *in any possible scenario, it should be possible to state unambiguously whether the property is*

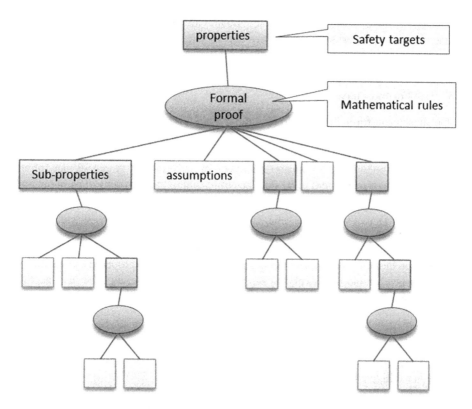

Fig. 1. Properties, sub-properties and assumptions

true or false in that case. Testing properties using this criterion leads to many questions before the formulation is satisfying. Another good test is that if an assumption or property is required from a subsystem, then we should be able to find a realistic accident scenario when removing this assumption. Such accident scenarios must be kept with the assumptions, they are their best justification.

To work in such close contact with the designers /experts, the proof team has to conform very strictly to its role:

- The proof team shall be neutral regarding the design choices;
- They should accept to go inside details with the experts, even if it means analyzing a lot of "how" to find a small amount of "why" (we say that they should accept to "plunge in the domain");
- They should do so to be a help to find and solve potential pitfalls, they should avoid at all costs any risk of discrediting the work of the designers.

Despite the fact that subsystems properties should be expressed without internal design details, to close the gap between 'almost true' and 'always true' the proof team often has to do *incursions inside the design details*. This is 'plunging into the domain' as expressed above; it is ok as long as it is done with the experts, and with the will to efficiently find the subsystems properties and to formulate them independently from these details.

5.3   The Formal Phase

In the subsequent formal phase, all the natural language proofs are rewritten in formal language. ClearSy uses Event-B and Atelier-B for this purpose: schematically, the target properties are written into top level B models, the subsystem properties are written as B refinement models in such a way so that the proof performed by Atelier-B (according to the definition of refinement in B) shall be equivalent to the reasoning done in natural language.

The formal proof in this phase is a verification, as the proof itself (the "reasons why") is found during the natural language phase. In our experience, the reasoning involved is rarely very complicated or requiring high level mathematics: most of the difficulty in the whole process resides in formulating subsystem and context properties. Once this is done for a given topic and level, the keys of the reasoning already exist because the contributing properties were revealed by examining *how the subparts actually ensure target properties*. This work is done in collaboration with the experts and the designers, so if pitfalls exist they are normally resolved (or at least discussed and mitigated) at once. Thus, this process does not produce a list of bugs to be solved at the end: if everything goes well it should finish with a proof under approved assumptions, all pitfalls resolved or mitigated.

Once found how a given target property is ensured, with context and concerned subsystems roles optimally formulated, the reasoning often seems very simple. So there is a temptation to conclude that the concerned proof step is obvious and that it is not worth rewriting in B and Atelier-B. It is almost a quality sign: the better the expression of the "reasons why", the simpler the B models and the more obvious the proof. This is particularly true for system level proofs because we remain before the complexity wall of detailed functions names, data formats or electrical interfaces.

Our experience is that rewriting in B and proving with Atelier-B *is always worth it*. With the best possible preparation, all the natural language demonstrations that we transformed into actual B models and proved were changed during this process. Very often, turning natural languages assumptions into B formulas reveals cases where the meaning is uncertain or blurry: these are typically cases where the criterion (the one defined as a key point above) does not hold, i.e. scenarios where one cannot state whether the concerned property is true or false. Less often, extra pitfalls are discovered during the proof phase; then it is usually complex cases that would probably be impossible to find without proving.

An example of this kind of complex pitfall that we discovered only in the final proof phase concerned the safe braking function of CBTC trains, in very specific cases where an initial backward movement of the train during residual traction phase could impair the correctness of the braking calculus. Real track slope values were probably such that this could not actually occur, but well, the point was not spotted and not verified before.

6   Results and Their Usage

6.1   Where to Stop

The system level proof process ends when the chosen level of detail is reached, with all the formal proofs done. This chosen level of detail is variable: one can decide to go down to actual interfaces and design of subparts (for instance down to electrical relay schematics for parts done with this technology), or to stop at a higher level. In our CBTC projects, ClearSy went down to a quite detailed level in subparts (including for instance, how slipping wheels are detected by the onboard computer), but above the level of the data formats and the actual internal design. The actual computer code was not examined; neither the data formats like the system track database. We believe that this chosen limit is suitable to solve system level problems in a sufficiently detailed way, without including the complexity of software data representation or electrical signals. Note that system interface specifications usually must go deeper, as they should dictate the message formats between subsystems.

6.2   Output Documents

After the formal proof stage, all the final assumptions (about context, about subsystems design below the chosen final level...) are expressed. In the B models this formulation is not easily readable, so we translate them back into natural language in documents called "books of assumptions".

In these documents, we give the following information:

• Target properties (explained in natural language, illustrated with examples);
• Assumptions (explained in natural language)

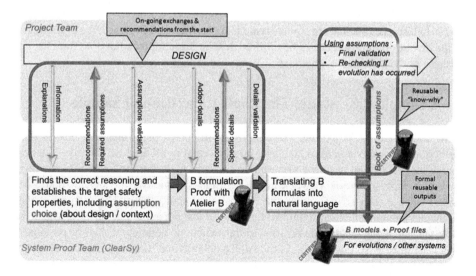

Fig. 2.   The global process with its outputs outlined.

- For each assumption, we show scenarios of what could occur if it did not hold;
- We also give information about who validated the assumption, what are the concerned teams and whether extra validation is needed (if the system is not yet ready, or in case of evolutions).

The sentences used in these documents are indeed retranslated B formulas, so they are very precise (although sometimes with a not very literary style!). Experts and designers that participated in the process are already used to the extracted notions and the agreed assumptions, however we found useful to organize several day long presentations to explain the results to a larger audience within our customers. The final results are useful only as long as they are understood and used! (Fig. 2).

6.3   Safety Cases and Standards

Besides obtaining the assurance that a formal proof could be done at system level, the benefits of this process for a given system should naturally concern the safety case, as proven target properties are basically safety properties. Standards (like EN 50126, 50129 and 50128, see [5–7] in railway domain or EN 61508 more globally) favor formal methods but more at software development level. Taking into account the extra guarantee of a system level formal proof is left to the ISA to decide upon, although it is probably in the spirit of these standards to seek 'safety proofs' in any sense.

Nevertheless, system level proofs certainly do not exempt from performing all necessary safety cycle steps (including quality, organization, verification & validation, etc.). One paramount topic is the study of possible failures and their probability. In the system proof, safety target properties are clearly meant to hold whatever the possible failures, considered at the appropriate level of probability regarding the possible accidents. So the sub-properties and assumptions that the proof relies on should also hold whatever the possible failures, considered at the appropriate level of probability. This is how the failures & probabilities studies are related to the proof.

So failure rates and hazard studies remain of paramount importance; the proof helps in the definition of properties to be ensured despite these failures but does not change this part of the safety case otherwise.

7   A Sample Case Study: The Route Cancellation Example

How exactly are the properties written, how is the proof performed and how is this methodology based on natural language proof /formal proof applied? To give a better idea of the process, let's show a very simple example. Consider the following drawing:

In this Fig. 3, there is a switch beyond a signal. Obviously the switch should be locked when a train arrives, otherwise a derailment could occur. The problem is the following: what mechanism should be installed so that when the line operator wants to close the signal and change the position of the switch, no derailment shall be possible? The usual railway solution to this is to install a delay-based route cancellation system:

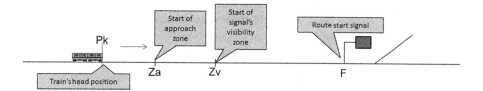

Fig. 3. The route cancel example.

- If the train is far enough (before some "approach" zone limit), the line operator can cancel the route and move the switch at once because the train has enough space and time to stop before the signal;
- If the train is already near, when the route is cancelled the signal should close but the system shall keep the switch locked for a certain time. Then the train will either stop before the signal or go beyond during this time. If the train is detected beyond the signal, the switch is maintained in locked state until the train has cleared the route.

Above is the purely informal reasoning. It is a good starting point; however it does not give the constraints between the delay and the train's stopping capabilities. Moreover, such informal clues do not provide any certainty about whether the switch is protected in all cases and under what assumptions (about train speed, braking, ...). Things become more precise when we define variables /constants /notions to denote this system. Let's not describe the possible variables here in too much detail; with obvious definitions we can sense the necessary assumptions:

- If the train is beyond F (Pk > F), then no unlocking shall be possible;
- There must be a visibility zone (Zv) such that when the train is near (Pk > Zv) and the signal is red, the train will always stop in a given maximum delay (Ts) and a given maximum distance (Ds); otherwise the train could completely ignore the signal.
- The approach zone (Za) such that the train detection inside will trigger the locking delay (T) when the route is cancelled must be larger than the worst stopping distance Ds: otherwise the train could overrun the signal after a route cancel that unlocked the switch without delay. For even more obvious reasons the visibility zone (Zv) shall be larger than Ds: the signal F would be useless otherwise.
  - Note: in the figure Za is before Zv, but this is just an example. There is no such constraint.
- The unlocking delay T shall be greater than the worst stopping time Ts: otherwise the timer may expire just before the train overruns F, thus unlocking the switch in front of the train beyond F.

At this stage, the named variables allow a far more precise description of the problem; the constraints and necessary assumptions appear thanks to the scenarios seen above. These scenarios are what we could call "otherwise" scenarios: they reveal the necessity of each assumption by showing what could occur otherwise. The target property is now easily defined: if the train is beyond the signal (Pk > F), then the switch should remain locked (using some variable named 'unlocked': unlocked = False).

We now have a strong intuition that the system is safe with only the few assumptions above (F-Zv > Ds, F-Za > Ds, T > Ts), but this is not yet a proof. Here comes the natural language proof step: finding out how we can conclude that the switch will always be locked if the train reaches it. This is a case by case reasoning:

– If the route cancel occurs when the train is not yet in the approach zone (Pk < Za), then it will stop before F (Za + Ds < F). So no question is to be asked about the switch. The same applies if the route cancel occurs when the train is not yet in the visibility zone (Pk < Zv), because the visibility zone is large enough (Zv + Ds < F).
– In the remaining case, the route cancel occurs when the train is already in the approach zone and in the visibility zone. Because the signal is directly visible, the stopping delay of the train can be counted from the route cancel event; because it is in the approach zone, the switch will remain locked during T after this route cancel event. So the switch is still locked when the final stopping of the train occurs before T; if the train is beyond F at that moment it will be detected and the switch will remain locked until the train has cleared the route.

This reasoning can be explained and checked with domain experts: this is the "natural language proof". It may seem simple, but it is now possible to carefully examine the meaning of the variables and the related assumptions: the most crucial problems are usually solved at this moment.

If we stopped here, there would be no quantifiable difference compared to an informal text explaining the system, however rigorous the previous "proof" may seem. The next step beyond is to use a computerized tool to verify this proof: we use Atelier-B with its event-B language capabilities. Constructing an event-B model such that the proof will denote the above reasoning is quite straightforward (provided enough knowledge in the event-B method of course). A single B model is suitable, with sate variables denoting Pk, time, date of the route cancellation if it occurred and so on. The target property (Pk > F => unlocked = False) can be written in the invariant, if the set of B events in the model is so that this invariant can be proven then this property is proved. Those events will be:

• Events denoting the movements of the train (in different cases: without visible red signal, with visible red signal, etc.);
• Events denoting the ground system: route cancellation, switch unlocking after the delay, etc.

The obtained B-model in this case is about 80 lines long; its proof with Atelier-B is almost fully automatic.

Such B models for system level proofs with this method are usually far simpler than B models at software level: they are often less than 1000 lines per model, and each topic is usually a single refinement chain with less than 3 or 4 refinement steps. Of course they are more complex than this toy example (80 lines, no refinements), but actually the "reasons why" at system level tend to be quite simple and so are the corresponding B models. The difficulties in this task (and the benefits) reside in *finding the correct assumptions*, and *successfully turning all explanations into a rigorous reasoning*. From a mathematical point of view we use only simple rules and results; system designs can rely on elaborated mathematical results or complex physical laws but then those central aspects are well known and covered by theories and proofs that should be taken as assumptions in the B proof.

8   Conclusion

According to ClearSy's experience today, a system level proof is feasible with manageable cost for any large system. Of course, the correct organization and the results and their usage are highly dependent on the nature of the project, and particularly on whether the design is known or under development. When driving such proof projects, the important words are adaptation, flexibility and communication rather than theoretical mathematics!

In industrial projects, the efforts to reach the required performance and to obtain the mandatory documents obviously come first. Extra efforts to reach higher levels of confidence (like actually proving properties, using formulated assumptions and logics) are always a matter of conviction. Let's hope that global experiences in more and more projects will accumulate evidence in favor of this conviction.

References

1. Abrial, J.R.: Modeling in Event-B: System and Software Engineering. Cambridge University Press, Cambridge (2010)
2. Atelier B website. http://www.atelierb.eu/
3. Abrial, J.R.: The B-Book. Cambridge University Press, Cambridge (1996)
4. Boulanger, J.L.: Formal Methods Applied to Industrial Complex Systems. Wiley-ISTE, Hoboken (2014)
5. EN50126: Railway Applications - The Specification and Demonstration of Reliability, Availability, maintainability and Safety (RAMS)
6. EN50129: Railway Applications - Communications, signaling and processing systems – Safety related electronic systems for signaling
7. EN50128: Railway Applications - Communications, signaling and processing systems
8. Sabatier, D., Burdy, L., Requet, A., Guéry, J.: Formal proofs for the NYCT line 7 (Flushing) modernization project. In: Derrick, J., Fitzgerald, J., Gnesi, S., Khurshid, S., Leuschel, M., Reeves, S., Riccobene, E. (eds.) ABZ 2012. LNCS, vol. 7316, pp. 369–372. Springer, Heidelberg (2012)

A Novel Approach to HW/SW Integration Testing of Route-Based Interlocking System Controllers

Jan Peleska$^{(\boxtimes)}$, Wen-ling Huang, and Felix Hübner

Department of Mathematics and Computer Science, University of Bremen,
Bremen, Germany
{jp,huang,felixh}@cs.uni-bremen.de

Abstract. Recent progress in bounded model checking and inductive reasoning has shown that the fully automated verification of route-based interlocking system designs of realistic "real-world" complexity is possible and ready for industrial application. In this paper, we present a new model-based testing strategy for interlocking system controllers that exploits the fact that the design has already been verified, so that it can be used as a reference model for test case and test oracle generation. Our special interest lies in the field of complete testing strategies that are able to uncover every implementation error, provided that the implementation behaviour is captured in a pre-specified fault domain. Despite their guaranteed test strength, these strategies have two well-known disadvantages: (1) applied in a naive way, they often result in an infeasible amount of test cases, and (2) the hypothesis that the real implementation behaviour is captured by a member of the fault domain can rarely be justified in a convincing way. We describe a new combination of compositional reasoning and input equivalence class generation techniques that removes problem (1). For coping with disadvantage (2), we suggest a combination of equivalence class and random testing that - while not being able to guarantee complete fault coverage for implementations outside the fault domain - results in a test strength that is significantly higher than heuristic test approaches for interlocking system controllers. Estimates are presented that show how application of this novel strategy reduces the effort for HW/SW integration testing, while simultaneously increasing the fault coverage in comparison to more conventional testing approaches.

Keywords: Interlocking systems · Model-based testing · Equivalence class partition testing · HW/SW integration testing

1 Introduction

Objectives. In this paper we suggest a new approach to safety-related HW/SW integration testing of controllers for route-based interlocking systems. This approach is based on the fact that recent advances in design verification have shown

© Springer International Publishing Switzerland 2016
T. Lecomte et al. (Eds.): RSSRail 2016, LNCS 9707, pp. 32–49, 2016.
DOI: 10.1007/978-3-319-33951-1_3

that it is possible to completely verify the safety of complex railway networks in combination with their interlocking tables and control algorithms on design level. Moreover, given a network description and a specification of the interlocking tables, the behavioural model of the associated safe route controller can be automatically generated. The design verification technique is based on bounded model checking in combination with inductive reasoning and can be fully automated [9,10].

As a consequence, we can count on the availability of reference models for safe route controller behaviours which are *a priori* known to be complete and correct. This suggests a likewise automated model-based testing approach for the route controller implementation. For such a test suite it is not necessary to elaborate a set of test cases from the safety requirements induced by the design and justify their completeness: instead, we can design a test suite that just shows the *behavioural equivalence*[1] of the system under test (SUT) and the reference model. Since the model is known to be safe, the safety of the SUT follows.

When selecting an automated test case generation approach for this purpose (see [1] for an overview of model-based testing methods available today), methods allowing full automation are of course the most attractive. At the same time, we would like these methods to come with guaranteed error detection capabilities, because this would reduce the effort to obtain certification credit for the test suite in a considerable way: the applicable standards do certainly not require test suites to uncover *every* error. They demand, however, that the test strength of test suites is assessed experimentally[2] and that test case reduction techniques like equivalence partitioning approaches are justified with respect to the trustworthiness of the reductions applied.

Complete Testing Strategies. This additional objective suggests to investigate the usability of *complete* testing strategies whose test suites are *sound* (SUT behaviours conforming to the reference model are never rejected) and *exhaustive* (non-conforming SUT behaviours are always detected by at least one test case of the suite). Completeness is usually asserted with respect to a *fault model* $\mathcal{F} = (\mathcal{S}, \leq, \mathcal{D})$ [8], expressing the hypotheses under which completeness is asserted. Here $\mathcal{S}$ denotes the reference model and $\leq$ the conformance relation – we only consider *I/O-equivalence*, that is, behavioural equivalence on the visible input/output interface and denote this by $\sim$. Set $\mathcal{D}$ denotes the *fault domain* which is a collection of models conforming or non-conforming to $\mathcal{S}$. Typically, black-box testing strategies can guarantee completeness only under the hypothesis that the true behaviour of the SUT is represented by a member of the fault domain.

---

[1] Since route controllers are deterministic and the SUT accepts all inputs in every state, it is not necessary to investigate other conformance relations, where the SUT only performs a subset of the behaviours allowed according to the reference model.

[2] This is typically achieved by applying the suite against mutants of the implementation and checking how many of them are "killed", i.e. how many injected errors are uncovered.

Though complete testing strategies were always of high interest from a theoretical point of view, they were often not considered in practical testing campaigns, because (1) they resulted in an intractable number of test cases, and (2) the hypothesis that the true SUT behaviour is reflected by a member of the fault domain is hard to justify in many cases. Recent results on complete input equivalence class testing methods, however, have shown that problem (1) can be overcome for certain classes of models by abstracting the – usually unmanageable – number of concrete input vectors to the SUT to input equivalence classes [3]. To deal with problem (2), it has been shown that a randomisation of this input equivalence class testing strategy, while preserving its completeness, results in surprisingly high test strength when applied to the test of implementations outside the fault domain: instead of using a fixed collection of representatives from input equivalence classes, one selects a random representative from the class whenever it is needed [4].

Main Contribution. The main contribution of this paper consist in the presentation of evidence showing that this approach is effective for testing controllers of route-based interlocking systems, when the integration test strategy is combined with compositional reasoning. It should be emphasised however, that we do not claim that this approach will always lead to the detection of *every* error in the SUT: interlocking systems can have a highly complex architecture involving many cooperating components; achieving 100 % fault coverage just for the route controller would not allow us to conclude that the complete interlocking system is free of any errors. Instead, our objective is to show that

1. application of this strategy exhibits significant test strength which is probably better than what can be achieved with heuristic test case design,
2. the test case generation process, including the calculation of concrete test data, can be fully automated, so that this test strength may even be reached with less effort in comparison with manual test suite development methods,
3. the number of test cases to be performed is adequate for safety critical interlocking system components and can be executed within reasonable time.

Overview. In Sect. 2 some essential facts about route-based interlocking systems are described. In Sect. 3, the case studies performed are described, and a concrete behavioural model for a route controller is presented. Using the examples from the case study for illustration purposes, the underlying testing method is described in Sect. 4. The experiments and their evaluation showing the effectiveness of the advocated approach, as well as a discussion of threats to validity are presented in Sect. 5. Section 6 contains the conclusions. References to related work are given throughout the text at the appropriate places. For a comprehensive list of references related to the underlying testing strategy see [3, Sect. 5].

Due to the usual space limitations, this paper does not contain all the details readers might be interested in. A comprehensive technical report is therefore available under [7].

2   Route-Based Interlocking Systems

The material presented in this section is based on [9,10]. We consider modern route-based interlocking systems with sequential release, as they are currently introduced, for example, for the new Danish high-speed train network designed according to the European Train Control System (ETCS) specification.

2.1   Railway Networks, Routes, and Interlocking Systems

To illustrate the terms and concepts introduced in the subsequent paragraphs, consider the small railway network in Fig. 1. It consists of linear sections (such as b10, t10, t12, ...) and points (t11, t13). These are collectively called *detection sections*, because the presence or absence of trains in these sections can be determined. Marker boards (mb10, mb11, ...), represent virtualised signals.[3] Each network portion controlled by some interlocking system has two dedicated directions UP and DOWN which are defined in relation to a fixed point (e.g. a train station at one end of the line) along the complete network. Each marker board is associated with either the UP-direction (mb10, mb13, ...) or the DOWN-direction (mb15, mb12, ...).

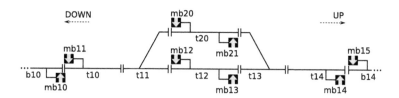

Fig. 1. Simple railway network (taken from [9]).

The network is traversed on pre-defined routes that are controlled by the interlocking system. Each route starts at a marker board pointing in train direction and ends at a neighbouring marker board pointing in the same direction: for example, the sequence of track elements t10, t11, t12 guarded at the beginning by mb10 and at the end by mb13 represents the route mb10 → mb13. The points inside a route need to be in appropriate position: for the route mb10 → mb13, point t11 has to be in *PLUS-position* (i.e. connecting t10 and t12); for the route mb10 → mb21 the *MINUS-position* connecting t10 and t20 is required. Before a train may enter the route, additional signals and points need to be switched into specific states for offering additional safety, such as flank protection or head-on collision protection. Using route mb10 → mb13, for example, requires that point t13 shall be switched into MINUS-position, so that trains travelling in DOWN direction cannot enter t12. Moreover, marker boards mb11, mb12, mb20 must be switched to HALT.

---

[3] We omit here ETCS track-side elements that are only implicitly used in this paper, such as balises or radio block centres.

The interlocking system allocates a route for a train (points and signals are switched into the appropriate states), locks it (points are fixed in their position and cannot be changed until the train has passed through), allows the train to enter the route, and detects when the route is occupied. Detection sections along the route are freed as soon as the train has passed them. The route is freed when the train has left it and entered the next route. Routes possessing common track elements – for example, routes mb10 → mb13 and mb20 → mb11 – are said to be *in conflict* with each other, because they must not be used simultaneously in order to avoid collisions. A route can only be allocated to a train if it is not in conflict with other routes currently being allocated or already locked or occupied by a train.

The sequential release principle allows for allocating a conflicting route, when the train occupying the current route has already passed the critical track elements where a collision might take place. Similarly, points and signals outside the route, offering protection to certain route portions may already be unlocked as soon as the train has traversed these portions. For example, when a train occupies route mb10 → mb13 but has already passed t10 and t11, so that it completely resides in t12, route mb20 → mb11 may already be allocated.

The route descriptions and their associated protection requirements are specified in interlocking tables; an example for the network above is given in Table 1.

Table 1. Interlocking table for the network layout in Fig. 1 (Taken from [9]; p means PLUS, m means MINUS.)

id	src	dst	Path	Points	Signals	Conflicts
1	mb10	mb13	t10;t11;t12	t11:p;t13:m	mb11;mb12;mb20	2;3;4;5;6;7
2	mb10	mb21	t10;t11;t20	t11:m;t13:p	mb11;mb12;mb20	1;3;6;7;8
3	mb12	mb11	t11;t10	t11:p	mb10;mb20	1;2;5;6;7
4	mb13	mb14	t13;t14	t13:p	mb15;mb21	1;5;6;8
5	mb15	mb12	t14;t13;t12	t11:m;t13:p	mb13;mb14;mb21	1;3;4;6;8
6	mb15	mb20	t14;t13;t20	t13:m	mb10;mb12;mb13;mb14;mb21	1;2;3;4;5;8
7	mb20	mb11	t11;t10	t11:m	mb10;mb12	1;2;3
8	mb21	mb14	t13;t14	t13:m	mb13;mb15	2;4;5;6

2.2 Route Controllers

The central component of a route-based interlocking system is the *route controller*. It is responsible for allocating requested routes to trains, for preventing simultaneous allocation of conflicting routes, performing sequential release of track elements, freeing routes after they are no longer occupied, and for reacting to cancellation commands. Moreover, the route controller supervises the validity of all safety conditions and triggers a transition to a safe state (all marker boards on HALT, no state changes for points) if one of these conditions is violated. A typical architecture for route controllers is shown in Fig. 2.

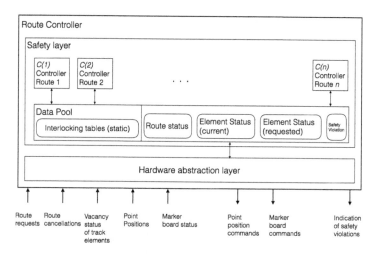

Fig. 2. Route controller interface and internal structure.

The *safety layer* manages the routes. It reads interlocking tables, route and element states from the *data pool*, and writes route state updates as well as track element commands into the data pool. Typical implementations use one controller sub-component $C(id)$ per route id. If these are scheduled sequentially, route allocations can never interfere with each other. If, however, the sub-components run concurrently, some locking mechanism (spin lock or semaphore) is needed to avoid that allocations are started for conflicting routes: each sub-component performs its evaluation whether an allocation request is in conflict with another route and records the transition into the allocating state in a critical section. For detection sections, the route controller distinguishes two Boolean attributes: the *locking status* is 1 (= **true**), when the segment has been locked – that is, specifically allocated – for a given route. The *occupancy status* is 1, if and only if a train resides (partially or completely) in the section. Safety conditions require that a segment may be locked for at most one route, and that it may only be occupied if it is also locked. Points have a third attribute denoting their *position*: in the examples below, the PLUS position is denoted by 0, and the MINUS position by 1. Marker boards only have status values (0 = HALT, 1 = GO). The current status of all these values is stored in the data pool. Route controllers send commands to points and marker boards for changing their position and their HALT/GO aspect, respectively. These commands are written by the route controller sub-components into the data pool.

The *hardware abstraction layer (HAL)* processes the hardware interfaces. On its input interface, it receives requests for routes through the network portion the route controller is responsible for. Before a route is occupied by a train, the allocation and locking process can still be aborted by means of a cancellation request. The HAL stores requests and cancellations in the data pool, to be processed by the controller sub-components residing in the safety layer. Moreover, the HAL receives status information from detection sections: the occupancy status of linear segments and points, as well as the feedback information about actual point positions and actual marker board states are also written into the data pool.

The HAL reads the output interface changes requested by the controller sub-components from the data pool. On its output interface, the HAL sends position commands to points, requesting PLUS(0) or MINUS(1) positions. To marker boards, GO(1) or HALT(0) requests are sent. Finally, safety violations are indicated (1 denotes a violation).

3   Case Studies

3.1   First Route Controller Sub-component

As will be justified below in Sect. 4.8, we can test each route controller sub-component $C(id)$ separately. Therefore, as the first part of the case study, the sub-component $C(7)$ for route id 7 (mb20 → mb11, see Table 1) in the simple railway network shown in Fig. 1 is tested. The complete route controller architecture shown in Fig. 2 induces the following component testing configuration which is depicted in Fig. 3.

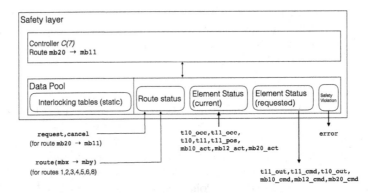

Fig. 3. Integration test configuration for $C(7)$, controlling route mb20 → mb11.

As inputs, $C(7)$ gets the Boolean request and cancel command for this specific route. Moreover, the route status of the other routes (route(mbx → mby)) influences its behaviour. The relevant track elements are t10 and t11, and their Boolean status information t10_occ and t11_occ (= 1 if occupied), t10, t11 (= 1 if locked by another route), t11_pos (= 1 if point position is MINUS), and mb10_act, mb12_act, mb20_act (= 1 if signal aspect is GO) are further inputs to the SUT. The states of all other track elements (which are also part of the data pool and available for this sub-component test) should not influence $C(7)$'s behaviour, so they are not shown in Fig. 3.

The controller for route mb20 → mb11 writes locking commands t11_out, t10_out for both track elements into the data pool. For $C(7)$, this is an output to the test environment. Moreover, requests for changing the point position are written to t11_cmd (= 1 for requested position MINUS). Requests for marker boards to change the signal aspect are written to mb10_cmd, mb12_cmd, mb20_cmd (= 1 to request signal aspect GO). Finally, the controller raises the error flag if it detects a safety violation related to its route. The outputs shown in Fig. 3 are the ones where $C(7)$ is expected to write to.

In Fig. 4, the behaviour of the route controller sub-component $C(7)$ is modelled as a state machine in SysML style. On receiving a request for this route, $C(7)$ transits into mode MARKED, where it remains until no conflicts with other routes exist. The Boolean operation no_conflicts() returns true if and only if t10 and t11 are not locked by another route (and therefore empty) and no conflicting route is in mode ALLOCATING or LOCKED.

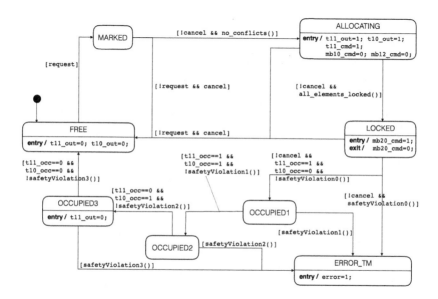

Fig. 4. Route controller state machine for route mb20 → mb11 from Fig. 1.

Note that these conditions can be directly generated from the interlocking table shown in Table 1, row id 7, columns **path** and **conflicts**. Then the controller transits into mode ALLOCATING, where elements t11, t10 are locked, the point t11 is switched into MINUS position, and the protecting marker boards mb10, mb12 are set to HALT. Note that these actions are directly generated from Table 1, row id 7, columns **path, points, signals**.

The operation all_elements_locked() returns true, if and only if the requested point position has been reached according to the feedback input t11_pos, and the feedbacks mb10_act, mb12_act from the marker boards show the requested HALT aspect. Then $C(7)$ transits into mode LOCKED, setting mb20 to GO, so that the train is free to enter the route. When the route's first segment t11 is occupied by the train, $C(7)$ transits into mode OCCUPIED1, and `mb20` is switched back to HALT. The controller sub-component now traverses the modes OCCUPIED2 and OCCUPIED3, whereafter the point `t11` is unlocked according to the sequential release principle. As soon the train has left the route, $C(7)$ reaches the mode FREE again.

While residing in modes LOCKED, OCCUPIEDx, $C(7)$ monitors the system status with respect to safety violations concerning its route. Operation `safetyViolation0()`, for example, returns `true` if and only if

```
(t11_occ == 0 && t10_occ==1) // train has not yet entered route 7, but segment t10 is
                             // occupied by an unexpected conflicting train
|| (t11_pos == 0)            // Unexpected change of point position
|| (mb10_act == 1)           // Unexpected change to aspect GO
|| (mb12_act == 1)           // Unexpected change to aspect GO
|| t10                       // t10 has been locked for another route
|| t11                       // t11 has been locked for another route
```

3.2 Second Route Controller Component

The complexity of a route controller sub-component depends on the length of the route (each track element along the route adds another OCCUPIEDx mode in the state machine described above) and on the surrounding railway network: the network layout in the vicinity of the route may induce additional flank protection requirements and offer different variants for ensuring this protection by means of points and marker boards. For this reason, a second route from a more complex network (the Lyngby train station in Denmark, see [9] for more details) has been selected as representative for the experimental evaluation of the testing strategy described in this paper. In the description of the experiments performed (Sect. 5), this sub-component reference model is denoted by C(Lyngby).

4   Model-Based Equivalence Class Partition Testing

4.1 Semantic Domain

The equivalence class partition strategy and its associated complete testing theory applied in this paper is based on the semantics of *reactive I/O state transition systems (RIOSTS)* $S = (S, \underline{s}, R)$ with state space S, initial state $\underline{s}$ and transition relation $R \subseteq S \times S$. The state space S consists of variable valuation functions $s : V \rightarrow D$ associating variables $v \in V$ with their concrete value $s(v)$ in the state s. The variable space V is partitioned into input variables (subset $I \subseteq V$), internal model variables ($M \subseteq V$), and output variables ($O \subseteq V$). It is assumed that variables from $M \cup O$ only have finite domains, so that they can be enumerated for test purposes, whereas the input variables from I can have infinite domains. We require RIOSTS state spaces to be partitioned into *quiescent states* ($S_Q \subseteq S$) and *transient states* ($S_T \subseteq S$, $S_Q \cap S_T = \varnothing$). Transitions from "stable" quiescent states can only change the values of input variables and may end up in either quiescent or transient states. Transitions from transient states must have quiescent post-states, and these transitions may affect internal model variables and outputs only. It is assumed that the SUT outputs can only be observed when it resides in quiescent states.

The semantic domain of RIOSTSs captures a wide variety of control systems, such as speed controllers in train protection systems [3], airbag controllers [4], thrust reversal controllers in aircrafts, and other systems performing discrete control decisions based on inputs from conceptually infinite domains. Various concrete modelling formalisms can be associated with RIOSTS semantics. As shown in [3], the SysML semantics of models consisting of blocks and state machines can be expressed by means of RIOSTS in a way that is consistent with the semi-formal OMG semantics[4].

Two RIOSTSs $\mathcal{S}, \mathcal{S}'$ are *I/O-equivalent* ($\mathcal{S}' \sim \mathcal{S}$), if and only if the *languages* $L(\mathcal{S}')$ and $L(\mathcal{S})$ are identical. In analogy to finite state machines, the language $L(\mathcal{S})$ of RIOSTS $\mathcal{S}$ is the set of all state traces of $\mathcal{S}$, restricted to their input/output pairs $(s(x_1), \ldots, s(x_p))/(s(y_1), \ldots, s(y_\ell))$ in the sub-sequence of quiescent states (because I/O is assumed not to be observable in transient states).

4.2 Construction of Input Equivalence Classes

Given an RIOSTS $\mathcal{S} = (S, \underline{s}, R)$, its transition relation R can be represented by specifying a proposition $\mathcal{R}$ with free variables from $V \cup V'$, $V' = \{v' \mid v \in V\}$, such that

$$R = \{(s, s') \in S \times S \mid \mathcal{R}[s(v)/v, s'(v)/v' \mid v \in V, v' \in V']\}$$

$\mathcal{R}$ is specified in such a way that $(s, s') \in R$ holds if and only if $\mathcal{R}$ evaluates to true when replacing every unprimed version of $v \in V$ by its pre-state value $s(v)$ and every primed variable symbol v' by the post-state value $s'(v)$ of v.

In [3] an algorithm is presented that allows to transform an arbitrary representation of $\mathcal{R}$ into a normalised one which is structured as

$$\underline{\mathcal{R}} \equiv \bigvee_{i \in \text{IDX}} \left(g_{i,i} \wedge (\boldsymbol{m}, \boldsymbol{y}) = (\boldsymbol{d}_i, \boldsymbol{e}_i) \wedge (\boldsymbol{m}', \boldsymbol{y}') = (\boldsymbol{m}, \boldsymbol{y}) \right) \vee$$
$$\bigvee_{(i,j) \in J} \left(g_{i,j} \wedge (\boldsymbol{m}, \boldsymbol{y}) = (\boldsymbol{d}_i, \boldsymbol{e}_i) \wedge (\boldsymbol{m}', \boldsymbol{y}') = (\boldsymbol{d}_j, \boldsymbol{e}_j) \wedge \boldsymbol{x}' = \boldsymbol{x} \right)$$

where (1) $g_{i,i}, g_{i,j}$ are propositions with free variables from I only, (2) $(\boldsymbol{m}, \boldsymbol{y})$ denotes the pair of internal state variable tuples and output variable tuples, that is, $M = \{m_1, \ldots m_k\}$ and $\boldsymbol{m} = (m_1, \ldots m_k)$, $O = \{y_1, \ldots y_\ell\}$ and $\boldsymbol{y} = (y_1, \ldots y_\ell)$, (3) $\boldsymbol{x} = (x_1, \ldots, x_p)$ denotes the tuple of input variables, $I = \{x_1, \ldots, x_p\}$, and (4) $(\boldsymbol{d}_i, \boldsymbol{e}_i), i \in \text{IDX}$ is the enumeration of reachable pairs of internal state value tuples $\boldsymbol{d}_i$ and output value tuples $\boldsymbol{e}_i$. The input conditions $g_{i,i}$ specify which input changes are possible while staying in the quiescent state class specified by $g_{i,i} \wedge (\boldsymbol{m}, \boldsymbol{y}) = (\boldsymbol{d}_i, \boldsymbol{e}_i)$. The input conditions $g_{i,j}, i \neq j$ denote propositions associated with transient state classes specified by $g_{i,j} \wedge (\boldsymbol{m}, \boldsymbol{y}) = (\boldsymbol{d}_i, \boldsymbol{e}_i)$, and leading to members of quiescent state classes specified by $g_{j,j} \wedge (\boldsymbol{m}, \boldsymbol{y}) = (\boldsymbol{d}_j, \boldsymbol{e}_j)$. Each condition $g_{i,i} \wedge (\boldsymbol{m}, \boldsymbol{y}) = (\boldsymbol{d}_i, \boldsymbol{e}_i)$ induces a state class

$$A_i = \{s \in S \mid (g_{i,i} \wedge (\boldsymbol{m}, \boldsymbol{y}) = (\boldsymbol{d}_i, \boldsymbol{e}_i))[s(v)/v \mid v \in V]\}$$

of I/O-equivalent quiescent states.

---

[4] http://www.omg.org/spec/SysML/1.4.

Example 1. For the route controller sub-component $C(7)$ shown in Fig. 4, $\boldsymbol{m}$ just denotes the actual control mode (one of FREE, MARKED, ALLOCATING, ..., interpreted as integer values in range 0,...,7), and $\boldsymbol{y}$ is the output vector

$$(\texttt{t10\_out}, \texttt{t11\_out}, \texttt{t11\_cmd}, \texttt{mb10\_cmd}, \texttt{mb12\_cmd}, \texttt{mb20\_cmd}, \texttt{error}).$$

The quiescent state class A_2 associated with control mode ALLOCATING(2), for example, is specified by

$$g_{2,2} \equiv (\texttt{request} \vee \texttt{!cancel}) \wedge \texttt{!all\_elements\_locked}()$$
$$\equiv (\texttt{request} \vee \texttt{!cancel}) \wedge (\texttt{t11\_pos} = 0 \vee \texttt{mb10\_act} = 1 \vee \texttt{mb12\_act} = 1)$$
$$(\boldsymbol{m}, \boldsymbol{y}) = (2, (1,1,1,0,0,0,0)) \qquad \qquad \Box$$

The normalised representation $\mathcal{R}$ now allows us to construct an input domain partition $\mathcal{I} = \{X_1, \ldots, X_q\}$ containing *input equivalence classes (IECs)*, so that for every $i \in \text{IDX}$ and $s_1 \in A_i$, the effect of applying a sequence $\boldsymbol{c}_1 \ldots \boldsymbol{c}_p$ of inputs to s_1, only depends on the sequence of $X_{i_1} \ldots X_{i_p}$ the $\boldsymbol{c}_1 \ldots \boldsymbol{c}_p$ reside in, but not on the concrete representatives $\boldsymbol{c}_j \in X_{i_j}$. If $\mathcal{I}$ is such an *input equivalence class partitioning (IECP)*, applying $\boldsymbol{c}_1 \ldots \boldsymbol{c}_p$ to $s_1 \in A_i$ and $\boldsymbol{c}_1' \ldots \boldsymbol{c}_p'$ to $s_2 \in A_i$ results in the same sequence of outputs, whenever $\forall j \in \{1, \ldots, p\} : \exists X \in \mathcal{I} : \boldsymbol{c}_j, \boldsymbol{c}_j' \in X$ is fulfilled. The proof of these properties and an algorithm for constructing $\mathcal{I}$ has been presented in [3]. It is easy to see that any *refinement* of the input equivalence class partitioning $\mathcal{I}$ constructed according to these rules is again an IECP of the underlying RIOSTS.

4.3   Complete Testing Theories for RIOSTS

With state equivalence classes A_i and input equivalence classes $X \in \mathcal{I}$ at hand, the RIOSTS $\mathcal{S}$ can be abstracted to a deterministic, completely specified finite state machine (DFSM) with input alphabet $\mathcal{I}$, output alphabet D_O, and state space $Q = \{A_1, A_2, \ldots\}$. The DFSM's transition relation $h \subseteq Q \times \mathcal{I} \times D_O \times Q$ is specified in such a way that

$(A_i, X, \boldsymbol{e}_j, A_j) \in h$ if and only if there exist $\mathcal{S}$-states $s \in A_i, s' \in A_j$ and an input $\boldsymbol{c} \in X$, such that RIOSTS $\mathcal{S}$ transits with input change $\boldsymbol{c}$ from s to s', and s' satisfies $(s'(y_1), \ldots, s'(y_\ell)) = \boldsymbol{e}_j$

As shown in [3], this DFSM specification is well-defined, and two deterministic RIOSTSs are I/O-equivalent if and only if their DFSM abstractions are I/O-equivalent. As a consequence, complete testing theories elaborated for DFSMs can be translated to complete theories for RIOSTSs: the input sequences $X_1 \ldots X_q, X_i \in \mathcal{I}$ to be used as DFSM test cases according to such a complete theory are translated to sequences $\boldsymbol{c}_1 \ldots \boldsymbol{c}_q$ of concrete RIOSTS input data satisfying $\boldsymbol{c}_i \in X_i$ for $i = 1, \ldots, q$, that is, each $\boldsymbol{c}_i$ is an arbitrary representative of class X_i.

The associated fault models are of the form

$$\mathcal{F} = (\mathcal{S}, \sim, \mathcal{D}(m, \mathcal{I})),$$

where the fault domain $\mathcal{D}(m, \mathcal{I})$ contains all deterministic RIOSTSs $\mathcal{S}'$ whose input equivalence partitionings coincide with the partitioning $\mathcal{I}$ of the reference model $\mathcal{S}$, and whose minimised DFSM abstractions do not have more than m states.

4.4 W-method and Wp-method

For generating the complete abstract DFSM test suites, the W-method and the Wp-method [2,6] have been applied. Both methods represent complete testing theories for completely specified DFSM and I/O-equivalence as conformance relation; the Wp-method is also applicable to nondeterministic FSMs. Test suites can be represented as sets $\mathcal{W}$ of test cases, each case consisting of a DFSM input sequence. For both methods, test cases are structured into three parts: the first part is an input sequence suitable for visiting a specific state of the DFSM reference model. The second part exercises arbitrary input sequences up to a length depending on the difference between the maximal state number expected in an implementation and the actual state number present in the reference model. The last part of each test case exercises an input sequence that helps to distinguish the expected target state reached before from other states that might have erroneously been reached due to transition faults.

The detailed algorithms for automatically generating W/Wp-test suites from DFSM reference models are described in [2,6,7]. As is shown in [7], the Wp-test suites had the same test strength as the suites based on the W-method; at the same time, application of the Wp-method resulted in considerably smaller test suites. Therefore we only refer to the Wp-method for the rest of this paper.

4.5 Discussion of Fault Hypotheses

It will be very difficult in general to prove that the estimates of m and the assumed IECP $\mathcal{I}$ are adequate for an SUT. One way to cope with this problem is to increase m and to refine $\mathcal{I}$. The test suite size, however, is increased exponentially by increasing m. Moreover, refining the IECP $\mathcal{I}$ leads to exponential growth of $\mathcal{I}$, and, consequently, again to exponential growth of the test suite size. As a consequence, it is desirable to investigate alternative methods that, while keeping the test suite size at an acceptable level, still possess superior test strength when applied against SUT whose behaviours are outside the fault domain.

4.6 Randomisation

The completeness of RIOSTS input equivalence class testing theories translated from DFSM theories as described above is preserved, if, instead of always choosing the same representative from each IEC $X \in \mathcal{I}$, a random value is selected from X each time a test cases requires an X-input. A set of experiments has been performed and published in [4], showing that the test strength of the resulting suite is significantly higher for SUT behaviours outside $\mathcal{D}(m, \mathcal{I})$ than the strength of naive random testing, where inputs are just selected at random from the *complete* range of input data in each test step, instead of performing random selections from IECs and generating the test cases by means of a complete method.

4.7 Boundary Value Tests

When selecting representatives from input equivalence classes at random, we will apply a strategy ensuring that the selected values are evenly distributed over the inner part of an input equivalence class and its boundary. The experiments evaluated in Sect. 5 show that this further increases the test strength for implementations outside the fault domain. For the solution sets of propositions the boundaries of these sets can be calculated using the MC/DC coverage conditions; this is explained in detail in [7, Sect. 4.8].

4.8 Compositional Reasoning

A system S consisting of components $C_1, \ldots, C_n$ is called *compositional*, if the specification fulfilled by S can be derived from the specifications fulfilled by each of its components C_i and from the way these components interact (e.g. sequential or concurrent composition). Compositionality depends on the underlying communication and synchronisation mechanisms applied by the components, and on the condition that components will not interfere with each others' private data.

We observe that the route controllers in this paper are compositional, provided that the controller sub-components are scheduled either sequentially or concurrently with proper protection of their critical sections. As a consequence, we can test each controller sub-component separately and then conclude, that their composition operates correctly as well.[5] As a consequence, we can apply the testing methods described above locally to the controller sub-component of each route, verify the HAL, verify the synchronisation mechanism used to protect critical sections, and then conclude by compositional reasoning that these local verification activities yield certification credit for the integrated HW/SW system.

4.9 Resulting Test Strategies

In the following description of test strategies evaluated for testing route controller sub-components, S always denotes the SysML reference model of the controller sub-component, interpreted in RIOSTS semantics. $\mathcal{I}$ denotes the input equivalence class partitioning constructed for S as specified in Sect. 4.2. F denotes the minimal DFSM with input alphabet $\mathcal{I}$ created from S by means of the abstraction technique described in Sect. 4.3. It is assumed that F has n states. By $\mathcal{W}$ we denote the DFSM test suite created from F using the Wp-method

---

[5] The hardware abstraction layer would also have to be verified locally, but this is outside the scope of this paper.

with assumption $n = m$. This induces the fault domain $\mathcal{D}(n, \mathcal{I})$. A (possibly erroneous) implementation $\mathcal{S}'$ is part of the fault domain if and only if $\mathcal{I}$ applies also as IECP for $\mathcal{S}'$ and the DFSM abstraction F' of $\mathcal{S}'$ has at most n states.

As an alternative, we also use a refined IECP $\overline{\mathcal{I}}$ that partitions each $X \in \mathcal{I}$ into several boundary value segments and the "interior" part of X. The DFSM test suite created from $\overline{F}$ using the Wp-method is denoted by $\overline{\mathcal{W}}$. The induced fault domain is $\mathcal{D}(n, \overline{\mathcal{I}})$. Obviously $\mathcal{D}(n, \mathcal{I}) \subset \mathcal{D}(n, \overline{\mathcal{I}})$ holds.

With these prerequisites, the following test strategies have been applied and compared with respect to their test strength.

STRAT 1. Input equivalence class partitioning $\mathcal{I}$, fault domain $\mathcal{D}(n, \mathcal{I})$, $\mathcal{W}$ is translated to an RIOSTS test suite by using a *fixed representative* $c \in X \in \mathcal{I}$, whenever X occurs in an input sequence of $\mathcal{W}$.

STRAT 2. Input equivalence class partitioning $\mathcal{I}$, fault domain $\mathcal{D}(n, \mathcal{I})$, $\mathcal{W}$ is translated to an RIOSTS test suite by performing a *random selection* $c \in X \in \mathcal{I}$, whenever X occurs in an input sequence of $\mathcal{W}$.

STRAT 3. Input equivalence class partitioning $\mathcal{I}$, fault domain $\mathcal{D}(n, \mathcal{I})$, $\mathcal{W}$ is translated to an RIOSTS test suite by performing a *random selection* $c \in X \in \mathcal{I}$, whenever X occurs in an input sequence of $\mathcal{W}$. 50 % of these random selections are chosen from *inner points of X*, the other half is chosen from *boundary values of X*.

STRAT 4. Refined input equivalence class partitioning $\overline{\mathcal{I}}$, fault domain $\mathcal{D}(n, \overline{\mathcal{I}})$, $\overline{\mathcal{W}}$ is translated to an RIOSTS test suite by performing a *random selection* $c \in X \in \overline{\mathcal{I}}$, whenever X occurs in an input sequence of $\overline{\mathcal{W}}$.

STRAT-RND. For comparing the test strength of the other test strategies under investigation, a naive random test strategy is used which does not require a model, but only an interface specification: in each test step, the input vector to the route controller is changed at random.

5   Experiments and Evaluation

5.1   Experiment Setup

Reference Models. As reference models, the two route controller sub-components $C(7)$ and $C(\text{Lyngby})$ described in Sect. 3 were used.

Reference Implementations. For $C(7)$, two reference implementations in Java were programmed, using different programming paradigms: IMPL1 uses the state machine paradigm to create a code structure that is directly traceable to the reference model: for each control mode of the model, a separate Java method evaluates control decisions, handles actions in the respective mode and sets the new mode if state machine transitions are performed. As an alternative, implementation IMPL2 uses a generic interpreter programming paradigm, where the executable evaluates conditions and performs actions according to the interlocking table data specified for the route. IMPL2 is close to typical implementations of route controllers used in practise. For $C(\text{Lyngby})$, only IMPL2 was re-used with the Lyngby-interlocking table. Due to the considerable programming effort that would have been required for creating an implementation in the style of IMPL1, this has not been evaluated for C(Lyngby).

Mutations. From each reference implementation, mutations have been generated, using the *Major* mutation framework [5]. For IMPL1, 277 non-equivalent mutations were generated (non-equivalence has been verified by hand). For IMPL2, 246 non-equivalent mutations were generated for $C(7)$, and 269 non-equivalent mutations were generated for C(Lyngby). Note that the mutant generator is unaware of fault domains. It simply injects syntactical changes to the reference implementation in a systematic way. Thus, the resulting mutants are both from inside and outside the pre-defined fault domains. This facilitates a fair assessment of the test strength of different strategies, given that in realistic black-box scenarios the validity of the testing hypotheses cannot be checked either.

Test Suites. For both reference models $C(7)$ and C(Lyngby), test cases were automatically generated according to the strategies STRAT 1,2,3,4 as described above. Then for STRAT-RND test suites with the same number of test cases with the same length as generated for STRAT1,2,3,4 were produced at random.

Test Execution. Each test suite has been executed against every mutant, and the mutation score for each suite was recorded. Since strategies STRAT 2,3,4,RND depend on the utilisation of random numbers, each of their test suites has been executed 10 times against every mutant, and the standard deviation from the mean number of mutants killed has been recorded.

5.2 Experimental Results

Table Description. Table 2 below shows the evaluation results for tests against model $C(7)$, and Table 3 shows the evaluation results for tests against model C(Lyngby).

In each table, the second column shows the number of test cases that have been generated with the respective strategy; in each case, abstract tests on DFSM level were generated by means of the Wp-method. The results for STRAT 4 are not shown here, because the refined input equivalence class partitioning

Table 2. Evaluation results for $C(7)$ (route `mb20` → `mb11`), Wp-method.

Strategy	No. test cases	Mutation score (IMPL1) avg.	σ	M utation score (IMPL2) avg.	σ
STRAT 1	670	236/277 (85.2 %)	-	240/246 (97.6 %)	-
STRAT 2	670	264.2/277 (95.4 %)	3.3	245/246 (99.6 %)	0
STRAT 3	670	271.5/277 (98.0 %)	2.1	244.8/246 (99.5 %)	0.4
STRAT-RND	670	136.5/277 (49.3 %)	14.5	98.7/246 (40.1 %)	18.1

Table 3. Evaluation results for C(Lyngby) (route `mb30` $\rightarrow$ `mb21`), Wp-method.

Strategy	No. test cases	Mutation score (IMPL2)	
		avg.	σ
STRAT 1	2291	256/269 (95.2 %)	-
STRAT 2	2291	259.9/269 (96.6 %)	0.7
STRAT 3	2291	264.7/269 (98.4 %)	1.2
STRAT-RND	2291	46.4/269 (17.2 %)	1.3

resulted in significantly larger test suites, while the increase in test strength was negligible; again, details are shown in [7].

The double columns with heading 'mutation score' show the test strength achieved with the respective strategy. The first sub-column documents this in format k/m (p %), where m denotes the number of generated non-equivalent mutants, k the mean value of killed mutants, and p the mean percentage of killed mutants. Column σ records the standard deviation of k.

Interpretation of Results. Unsurprisingly, naive random testing (strategy STRAT-RND) is unacceptable as a candidate for testing route controllers, since it does not exhibit sufficient test strength: less than 50 % of the mutants are killed for the simpler C(7) controller; for C(Lyngby), where the detection of errors depends on passing longer sequences of guards, the test strength even drops to less than 20 %. Further results described in [7] also show that the test strength is only marginally improved for STRAT-RND when increasing the size of the test suite.

All verification results show that STRAT 3 exhibits the best test strength among strategies STRAT 1,2,3 and STRAT-RND. Therefore STRAT 3 in combination with the Wp-method is the preferred testing strategy.

In [7], an extensive discussion of threats to validity is performed. The utilisation of different reference models and implementations ensures that the excellent performance of strategy STRAT 3 is not an accidental result; furthermore, the result is confirmed by previous experiments with other types of control systems [4]. From our analysis, the only critical threat to be addressed in future experiments is the fact that the current evaluation does not consider typical HW/SW integration faults originating from mismatches of SW design and HW design.

6   Conclusion

In this paper, a novel testing strategy with guaranteed error detection capabilities has been presented for the purpose of HW/SW integration testing in route-based railway interlocking systems. This strategy is based on a complete input equivalence testing method, but performs random selections whenever a representative from an input equivalence class is needed. The selection is performed in such a way that an even distribution of input data selected from the boundary and from the interior of each class is achieved. It has been demonstrated that this strategy can be practically applied with fully automated model-based testing support. The strategy guarantees the detection of every possible error for implementations whose behaviours are captured by models inside a well-defined fault domain. Moreover, the experiments performed suggest that this strategy is superior to heuristic test case development approaches, because it exhibits significant test strength even for erroneous implementations outside the fault domain.

Our observation of the current state of practise in industrial V&V of safety-critical systems indicates that, while test execution and test evaluation is certainly automated, the elaboration of test cases is often done in a manual way, without utilising formal test models as advocated in this paper. It should be emphasised, however, that test case generation for the strategy described in this paper can only be performed with tool support, because the underlying test case and test data generation algorithms are quite complex. This suggests that a change of paradigm is still required in industry before the advantages of the approach presented here can be fully exploited.

Acknowledgements. The authors would like to express their gratitude to Anne E. Haxthausen and Linh Hong Vu for their contributions to the field of formal modelling and automated verification of railway interlocking systems, and for the excellent collaboration in this field, which was always most productive and very enjoyable.

The work presented in this paper has been elaborated within project *ITTCPS – Implementable Testing Theory for Cyber-physical Systems*(http://www.informatik.uni-bremen.de/agbs/projects/ittcps/index.html) which has been granted by the University of Bremen in the context of the German Universities Excellence Initiative (http://en.wikipedia.org/wiki/German_Universities_Excellence_Initiative).

References

1. Anand, S., Burke, E.K., Chen, T.Y., Clark, J.A., Cohen, M.B., Grieskamp, W., Harman, M., Harrold, M.J., McMinn, P.: An orchestrated survey of methodologies for automated software test case generation. J. Syst. Softw. **86**(8), 1978–2001 (2013)
2. Chow, T.S.: Testing software design modeled by finite-state machines. IEEE Trans. Softw. Eng. **SE–4**(3), 178–186 (1978)
3. Huang, W., Peleska, J.: Complete model-based equivalence class testing. Int. J. Softw. Tools Technol. Transf. pp. 1–19 (2014). http://dx.doi.org/10.1007/s10009-014-0356-8
4. Hübner, F., Huang, W., Peleska, J.: Experimental evaluation of a novel equivalence class partition testing strategy. In: Blanchette, J.C., Kosmatov, N. (eds.) TAP 2015. LNCS, vol. 9154, pp. 155–172. Springer, Heidelberg (2015). http://dx.doi.org/10.1007/978-3-319-21215-9_10
5. Just, R.: The Major mutation framework: efficient and scalable mutation analysis for Java. In: Proceedings of the International Symposium on Software Testing and Analysis (ISSTA), San Jose, pp. 433–436, 23–25 July 2014

6. Luo, G., von Bochmann, G., Petrenko, A.: Test selection based on communicating nondeterministic finite-state machines using a generalized wp-method. IEEE Trans. Softw. Eng. **20**(2), 149–162 (1994). http://doi.ieeecomputersociety.org/10.1109/32.265636

7. Peleska, J., Huang, W., Hübner, F.: A novel approach to hw/sw integration testing of route-based interlocking system controllers - technical report. Technical report, University of Bremen, 10 Mar 2016. http://www.cs.uni-bremen.de/agbs/jp/jp_papers_e.html

8. Petrenko, A., Yevtushenko, N., Bochmann, G.V.: Fault models for testing in context. In: Gotzhein, R., Bredereke, J. (eds.) Formal Description Techniques IX - Theory, Application and Tools, pp. 163–177. Chapman & Hall, London (1996)

9. Vu, L.H., Haxthausen, A.E.: Formal development and verification of railway control systems - in the context of ERTMS/ETCS level 2. Ph.D. thesis (2015)

10. Vu, L.H., Haxthausen, A.E., Peleska, J.: Formal modeling and verification of interlocking systems featuring sequential release. In: Artho, C., Ölveczky, P.C. (eds.) FTSCS 2014. CCIS, vol. 476, pp. 223–238. Springer, Heidelberg (2015). http://dx.doi.org/10.1007/978-3-319-17581-2_15

Security

A Formal Security Analysis of ERTMS Train to Trackside Protocols

Joeri de Ruiter, Richard J. Thomas$^{(\boxtimes)}$, and Tom Chothia

School of Computer Science, University of Birmingham, Birmingham, UK
r.j.thomas@cs.bham.ac.uk

Abstract. This paper presents a formal analysis of the train to trackside communication protocols used in the European Railway Traffic Management System (ERTMS) standard, and in particular the EuroRadio protocol. This protocol is used to secure important commands sent between train and trackside, such as movement authority and emergency stop messages. We perform our analysis using the applied pi-calculus and the ProVerif tool. This provides a powerful and expressive framework for protocol analysis and allows to check a wide range of security properties based on checking correspondence assertions. We show how it is possible to model the protocol's counter-style timestamps in this framework. We define ProVerif assertions that allow us to check for secrecy of long and short term keys, authenticity of entities, message insertion, deletion, replay and reordering. We find that the protocol provides most of these security features, however it allows undetectable message deletion and the forging of emergency messages. We discuss the relevance of these results and make recommendations to further enhance the security of ERTMS.

1 Introduction

The European Railway Traffic Management System (ERTMS) is a European standard for next-generation train management and signalling. It is intended to make it easier for trains to cross borders and optimise the running of the railway. Currently the system is being rolled out across Europe, and on high-speed lines across the world. By the end of 2014, over half of the 80,000 km of tracks that were equipped with ERTMS were located in Asia.[1]

Within this wholly-digitised system, a number of protocols are employed to provide functionality to the ERTMS platform. For example, the EuroRadio protocol is used to ensure that messages exchanged between entities are genuine and have not been forged by an attacker, or to handover trains from one system responsible for a stretch of track to another. Moving from a largely analogue, manual or semi-automatic system to a digital, fully supervised system may expose it to threats which were not previously possible. These threats require appropriate analysis to ensure that the replacement system protects the underlying infrastructure and vehicles from attacks. In such a safety-critical system,

---

[1] http://www.ertms.net.

© Springer International Publishing Switzerland 2016
T. Lecomte et al. (Eds.): RSSRail 2016, LNCS 9707, pp. 53–68, 2016.
DOI: 10.1007/978-3-319-33951-1_4

it is key that the train is never allowed to be influenced externally to enter an unsafe state or perform in a manner which is not expected.

In this paper we perform a formal analysis of the EuroRadio protocol and parts of the ERTMS application protocol using the applied pi-calculus [1] and the ProVerif analysis tool [4,5]. The applied pi-calculus provides an expressive, powerful framework to model protocols; functions can be used to define new cryptographic primitives. The ProVerif tool can automatically check a wide range of security properties including the secrecy of particular values, equivalence between processes and correspondence assertions between modeller-defined events. ProVerif uses a theorem proving method to establish if these queries hold, therefore it is able to establish if secrecy properties hold even in the face of an active attacker, for an unlimited number of protocol runs and arbitrary attacker behaviour. However, it may not always terminate and it makes the usual Dolev-Yao assumptions: i.e., the cryptography is unbreakable, the attacker cannot learn key material by other means than observing communication and interacting with the protocol participants, etc. The applied pi-calculus's expressiveness and the powerful checking methods of ProVerif have led to them being used to analyse a wide range of security properties for many important systems.[2]

We model the EuroRadio protocol in the applied pi-calculus, with one process representing the train side of the communication and another process representing the Radio Block Controller (RBC) which receives messages from the train. Our model allows for an arbitrary number of trains and RBCs running at the same time, and, using standard ProVerif methods, we can check if EuroRadio keeps its keys secret and successfully authenticates the trains and the RBC. After the EuroRadio protocol finishes, we model the application level sending three messages. These application level messages sent over EuroRadio use a counter-style timestamp to help ensure freshness and stop attacks, where we introduce new functions to model this. We tag our model with events indicating each party starting a run of EuroRadio, finishing a run of EuroRadio, sending messages and receiving messages. We then come up with novel correspondence assertions between these events which let us check if messages can be deleted, inserted, reordered or replayed.

Checking our correspondence assertions in ProVerif, we find that the protocol succeeds in most of its security goals, i.e., an attacker cannot learn the secret keys in use, or pretend to be a train or a RBC. Furthermore, after successfully completing a run of the EuroRadio protocol both sides will have securely established a secret session key. However, we also find that the attacker may delete/jam messages without this being detected, they can inject emergency stop messages into a communication between an train and an RBC, and that an attacker may change the "safety feature" in a communication, possibly downgrading security. These issues could be looked at as moderately security critical, we do not believe that they require immediate fixes but that designers and train operators should be aware of them.

---

[2] A collection of such studies can be found at http://prosecco.gforge.inria.fr/personal/ bblanche/proverif/proverif-users.html.

Related Work: Some past work has also looked at the EuroRadio protocol: Esposito et al. [10] and Franekova et al. [11] use UML, Zhang et al. [18] use the SPIN model checker and Hongjie et al. in [14] use Petrinets. However, all of these analyses only look at single runs of the protocol, they do not consider an active attacker, and they do not try to test the security properties we focus on in this paper, rather they look at general correctness issues such as deadlock detection. A generic analysis of ERTMS was performed by Bloomfield et al. [6], however the paper itself gives a high-level overview of the process involved, and does not specify exact issues and mitigations. Our methodology in this paper is similar to our previous work that has included looked at modelling EMV protocols [8] and e-passports [3] in the applied pi-calculus. Other work looks at complex models of time in the applied pi-calculus (e.g. [7,15]) - our novel modelling of counter-style timestamps provides an abstract model of time which is much similar than these, but still expressive enough to model ERTMS.

The contributions of this paper are:

– Formal analysis of the EuroRadio protocol using the ProVerif tool.
– Introduction of a light-weight notion of counter-style timestamps in ProVerif.
– Showing how it is possible to use ProVerif to check if the attacker can delete, insert and re-order messages.
– Identification of potential issues in the ERTMS protocols, with appropriate recommendations.

In Sect. 2, we describe ERTMS and the EuroRadio protocol. We describe our formal model in Sect. 3 and then analyse this model in Sect. 4. We discuss the implications of our results in Sect. 5, and then we conclude in Sect. 6.

2   ERTMS Communication

In this section, we present a high-level overview of the components within ERTMS that are used for communication between the train and trackside equipment.

During its journey, a train communicates with a *Radio Block Centre (RBC)*, which provides commands to the train. RBCs are responsible for a specific geographical area of approximately 70 kilometres [2]. They authorise trains to drive on particular parts of the track using Movement Authorities, which also include maximum speeds. Every RBC is connected to a fixed network in order to hand over trains to the next RBC when a train leaves its area of responsibility.

Within ERTMS, several layers are used for communications between the train and trackside (see Fig. 1), where each layer provides some services and security features to upper layers.

GSM-R is the lowest layer for the communication between trains and the back-end specified in ERTMS [12,13]. It is based on the original GSM specification, but provides additional rail-specific functionality and makes use of different

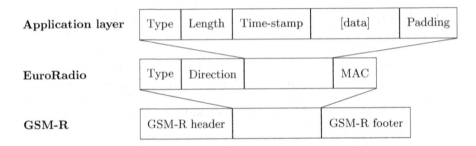

Fig. 1. Overview of the different communication layers in ERTMS.

frequencies. The additional functionality includes emergency calls and communications involving multiple drivers. Also, pre-defined short messages are included in the specification, which may be sent by driver and signaller, for example, 'standing at signal' [16], where the signaller may also send a message to the train at any time informing the driver that they must contact the signaller.

The EuroRadio Protocol is used on top of GSM-R and added to provide additional authentication and integrity protection to the communication [17]. EuroRadio uses the GSM-R communication layer to send messages between the base station and the train. When a connection is set up, an authentication protocol is used to provide mutual authentication for the train and back-end (see Fig. 2). The two parties exchange nonces and compute a shared symmetric session key based on this and a unique train key. This session key is then used to compute a MAC to prove knowledge of the session key to the other party. Once the authentication protocol has completed successfully, the application layer can use the communication channel and the EuroRadio layer will add a MAC to all messages that have a normal priority. Exactly which MAC algorithm is used is indicated in a data field called the *Safety Feature*.

The Application Layer builds on top of the EuroRadio layer and is described in [9]. As not all threats are taken care of by the lower layers, the application layer has to provide protection against replay and deletion attacks. A 32 bit timestamp is added to the messages. Every received message needs to contain a timestamp that is greater than that of the previous message, the exact value of the time stamp is not important, therefore it acts partly as a counter. If the timestamp is not greater than the last message received, the new message will be discarded. In order to synchronise the time between the train and the RBC, the RBC will maintain multiple clocks and sets them based on the time from the train.

3   Formal Modelling in ProVerif

We performed our formal analysis of the EuroRadio key establishment protocol and part of the application level protocol using the applied pi-calculus [1] and

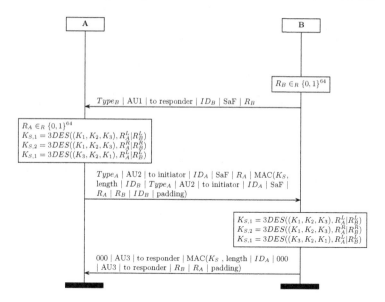

Fig. 2. Authentication protocol used by EuroRadio. A and B share a symmetric key K. R^L and R^R are used to indicate the leftmost and rightmost 32 bits respectively. A 3DES key K consists of three single DES keys: $K = (K_1, K_2, K_3)$.

the ProVerif automated verifier [4]. This protocol analysis framework can be used to identify potential leakage of information or other flaws in the protocols. The ProVerif syntax for the applied pi-calculus is given in Fig. 3.

This language allows us to specify processes that perform inputs and outputs, run in parallel and replicate. The calculus also allows processes to declare new, private names which can be used as private channels or nonces [5]. Functions in the applied pi-calculus can be used to model a range of cryptographic primitives, e.g. MACs, signing and key generation. These functions abstract any implementations, which are therefore considered to be cryptographically perfect. In our analysis, we focus only on the protocol, rather than any weaknesses and exposure as the result of cryptographic schemes used. The "let" statement can be used to check that two terms that used these equations are equal and branch on the result. This can be used to encode "if" statements, and conditional inputs $in\ (c, =a).P$ which inputs a value from channel c and proceeds only if the value received equals a (see e.g. [5]). For the verification, events can be added to a

$$
\begin{aligned}
M, N ::= &\quad \text{terms}\\
\quad x, y, z &\quad \text{variables}\\
\quad a, b, c, k, s &\quad \text{names}\\
\quad f(M_1, \ldots, M_n) &\quad \text{constructor application}\\[1em]
D ::= g(M_1, \ldots, M_n) &\quad \text{destructor application}\\[1em]
P, Q ::= &\quad \text{processes}\\
\quad 0 &\quad \text{nil}\\
\quad \text{out } (M, N).P &\quad \text{output } N \text{ on channel } M\\
\quad \text{in } (M, x).P &\quad \text{input } x \text{ from channel } M\\
\quad P \mid Q &\quad \text{parallel composition}\\
\quad !P &\quad \text{replication}\\
\quad \nu\, a.P &\quad \text{create new name}\\
\quad \text{let } x = D \text{ in } P \text{ else } Q &\quad \text{term evaluation}\\
\quad event(x) &\quad \text{execute event}
\end{aligned}
$$

Fig. 3. Syntax of the applied pi calculus

model. These events can be used to identify critical points of the protocol, and may be parameterised with variables from the model. Currently, the ProVerif tool is able to make guarantees for soundness, where if no attack is found, it is correct, however, it is not complete and might return false attacks [5].

ProVerif supports several types of queries to check security properties of protocols. The most basic type is to check for secrecy, i.e. whether the attacker is able to learn specific values. This can be used to verify whether cryptographic keys do not leak in a protocol. Another type of query is correspondence assertions, which can be used to check that if a particular event is executed, another event was executed before. Two types of correspondence assertions can be checked by ProVerif: non-injective and injective. An example of a non-injective query is `ev:event1(vars) ==> ev:event2(vars)`, which holds if `event2` was executed at some point before `event1`. For an injective assertion to hold, say `evinj:event1(vars) ==> evinj:event2(vars)`, for every execution of `event1` there must have been a *unique* execution of `event2`.

Our Model of EuroRadio. Our models of the two parties in the EuroRadio protocol are given in Figs. 4 and 5. For the analysis of normal priority messages, these processes are followed by the ones in Figs. 6 and 7 respectively. In these last processes three messages are sent and received, where MACs and timestamps are added and checked. Another model was constructed to check high-priority messages. This model is almost the same as for the normal priority messages, except no MACs are added to messages in the application layer and timestamps are not checked. All models are available online.[3]

The expressive language of ProVerif allows us to define processes which are run by the verifier in a number of ways. In our model, we instantiate both

---

[3] http://www.cs.bham.ac.uk/~rjt195/rssrail2016.

```
let Train =
    (* Set up a new session for the model *)
    (* Create a fresh session identifier used to link different events
        in the model *)
    new session;
    (* Get the identity of the RBC the train wants to communicate with *)
    in(id, rbc_etcs_id);
    (* Start of the actual authentication protocol *)
    (* T-CONN.request -- Au1 SaPDU *)
    new trainNonce;
    event trainStartSession(rbc_etcs_id, train_etcs_id, trainNonce, SAF);
    out(c, (TRAIN_ETCS_ID_TYPE, AU1, DF_SEND, train_etcs_id, SAF,
        trainNonce));
    (* T-CONN.confirmation -- Au2 SaPDU *)
    in(c, (=RBC_ETCS_ID_TYPE, =AU2, =DF_RESP, in_rbc_etcs_id, rbcSaF,
        rbcNonce, inMAC));
    (* Generate the session key *)
    let trainKS = genSessionKey(trainNonce, rbcNonce, getKey(
        in_rbc_etcs_id, train_etcs_id)) in
    (* Output encrypted secret to check secrecy of keys *)
    out(c, encrypt(SECRET, trainKS));
    out(c, encrypt(SECRET, getKey(in_rbc_etcs_id, train_etcs_id)));
    (* Verify whether the received MAC is correct *)
    if inMAC = mac(trainKS, ((PAYLOAD_LENGTH, train_etcs_id,
        RBC_ETCS_ID_TYPE, AU2, DF_RESP, in_rbc_etcs_id, rbcSaF), rbcNonce,
        trainNonce, train_etcs_id)) then
    (* T-DATA.request -- Au3 SaPDU *)
    event trainFinishSession(in_rbc_etcs_id, train_etcs_id, trainNonce,
        rbcSaF, rbcNonce, trainKS);
    out(c,(ZEROS, AU3, DF_SEND, mac(trainKS, (PAYLOAD_LENGTH,
        train_etcs_id, ZEROS, AU3, DF_SEND, trainNonce, rbcNonce))))
```

Fig. 4. The ProVerif model of the calling party in the EuroRadio protocol

models for the RBC and train as replicating processes using the '!' command, which may be nested, i.e. an arbitrary number of trains and RBCs can be run in parallel. This allows the verifier to provide a thorough examination of the protocol, giving the attacker in ProVerif the opportunity to reuse variables it has previously observed in previous protocol runs. ProVerif is then able to assess whether the properties defined hold, or it provides a trace if an attack is found.

Next we will discuss the models in Figs. 4 and 5. To represent the EuroRadio protocol, we must first introduce a session value which allows us to perform additional verification on the protocol for the reordering and replay of messages. Additionally, during the setup process, the train and RBC are sent the identity of the RBC. This allows us to assert that the train knows the identity of the RBC it is connecting to. The session, as specified by the EuroRadio specifications then starts, where the nonces and identities are exchanged, with the appropriate derivation of the session key to use. We generate and output some secret value encrypted with the negotiated session key. The confidentiality of this secret value is checked to verify that the attacker is not able to establish the session key. At each stage of messages being received, we verify the MAC prior to proceeding with protocol execution. This simulates the process that is in use within Euro-Radio. After this, the EuroRadio link is established. We then are able to use one of two different variants of the model - for normal or high-priority messages.

Figures 6 and 7 show the application messages sent through EuroRadio, including the use of timestamps. Once the session is established, we generate

```
let RBC =
    (* Set up a new session for the model *)
    (* Get an RBC identity *)
    in(id, rbc_etcs_id);
    (* Start of the actual authentication protocol *)
    (* T-CONN.indication -- Au1 SaPDU *)
    new rbcNonce;
    in(c, (sent_ETCS_ID_TYPE, =AU1, =DF_SEND, in_train_etcs_id, trainSaF,
        trainNonce));
    event rbcStartSession(rbc_etcs_id, in_train_etcs_id, rbcNonce,
        trainSaF, trainNonce);
    (* Generate the session key *)
    let rbcKS = genSessionKey(trainNonce, rbcNonce, getKey(rbc_etcs_id,
        in_train_etcs_id)) in
    (* Output encrypted secret to check secrecy of keys *)
    out(c, encrypt(SECRET, rbcKS));
    out(c, encrypt(SECRET, getKey(rbc_etcs_id, in_train_etcs_id)));
    (* T-CONN.response -- Au2 SaPDU *)
    out(c, (RBC_ETCS_ID_TYPE, AU2, DF_RESP, rbc_etcs_id, trainSaF,
        rbcNonce, mac(rbcKS, ((PAYLOAD_LENGTH, in_train_etcs_id,
        RBC_ETCS_ID_TYPE, AU2, DF_RESP, rbc_etcs_id, trainSaF), rbcNonce,
        trainNonce, in_train_etcs_id))));
    (* AU3 SaPDU *)
    in(c,(=ZEROS, =AU3, =DF_SEND, inMAC));
    (* Verify whether the received MAC is correct *)
    if inMAC = mac(rbcKS, (PAYLOAD_LENGTH, in_train_etcs_id, ZEROS, AU3,
        DF_SEND, trainNonce, rbcNonce)) then
    event rbcFinishSession(rbc_etcs_id, in_train_etcs_id, rbcNonce,
        trainSaF, trainNonce, rbcKS)
```

Fig. 5. The ProVerif model of the called party in the EuroRadio protocol

```
    (* Send three messages from the train to the RBC *)
    new time;
    let msg1 = (DT, time, MESSAGE_1) in
    event DataSent1(session, msg1);
    out(c, (msg1, mac(trainKS, msg1)));
    let msg2 = (DT, inc(time), MESSAGE_2) in
    event DataSent2(session, msg2);
    out(c, (msg2, mac(trainKS, msg2)));
    let msg3 = (DT, inc(inc(time)), MESSAGE_3) in
    event DataSent3(session, msg3);
    out(c, (msg3, mac(trainKS, msg3)))
```

Fig. 6. The ProVerif model of the application layer to send messages with normal priority

some value for a timestamp, and proceed to use it when sending messages. Each time, we use a light-weight notion of time which we discuss below. The RBC then verifies the timestamps were greater than that of the previous received message, and if it is, it will accept the message and execute the appropriate event to indicate that it was received in the context of that session. We include the session to verify that an attacker cannot combine messages from different sessions.

Modelling Counter-Style Timestamps. To support the checking of timestamps, we add a minimal notion of time to our model. In the application layer, it is checked whether the timestamp on a message is greater than on the previous message. For the time a counter on the train is used. In our model, we therefore only modelled relative time: time can increase and we can com-

```
(* Receive messages from the train *)
in(c, ((=DT, timeA, msgA), macA));
(* Check the MAC of the received message *)
if macA = mac(rbcKS, (DT, timeA, msgA)) then
event DataReceived1((DT, timeA, msgA));
in(c, ((=DT, timeB, msgB), macB));
(* Check the MAC and timestamp of the received message *)
if macB = mac(rbcKS, (DT, timeB, msgB)) then
if greater: timeB, timeA then
event DataReceived2((DT, timeB, msgB));
event MessagesReceived2((DT, timeA, msgA), (DT, timeB, msgB));
in(c, ((=DT, timeC, msgC), macC));
(* Check the MAC and timestamp of the received message *)
if macC = mac(rbcKS, (DT, timeC, msgC)) then
if greater: timeC, timeB then
event DataReceived3((DT, timeC, msgC));
event MessagesReceived3((DT, timeA, msgA), (DT, timeB, msgB), (DT,
    timeC, msgC))
```

Fig. 7. The ProVerif model of the application layer to receive messages with normal priority

```
data inc/1.
pred greater/2.
clauses
    greater: inc(x),x;
    greater: x,y -> greater: inc(x),y.
```

Fig. 8. The ProVerif model for counter-style timestamps

pare different timestamps that are based on the same initial timestamp. This mean we have no notion of how much time actions take, but our model proves to be sufficient for its purpose. In Fig. 8, our model of time can be found. A timestamp can be increased using *inc*, and two timestamps can be compared using the predicate *greater*.

4   Analysis of ERTMS Protocols

Using ProVerif, we can check that the protocol keeps the keys secret and that an attacker cannot disrupt the agreement process. These checks are standard ProVerif queries. Next, we wish to check if an attacker can insert, reorder, replay or delete messages without being noticed. Our methods of doing this are new, and a contribution of this paper. We perform these checks by making the train send three messages to the RBC and tagging each of these with a particular event. We also use events to tag the three messages send by the train, and their order, and the three messages received by the RBC and their order. We then check for insertion, reordering, replay and deletion using queries on these events.

Secrecy of Keys. We check if the EuroRadio protocol keeps the long term RBC/train key and session key secret from an active attacker. This check is performed by creating a new private value 'SECRET', encrypting this value using these keys and publicly broadcasting the encryption. If the attacker can then learn the value 'SECRET' it means the keys have been learnt. We checked this using the query `attacker:SECRET`. This verifies whether the attacker is able to establish the value 'SECRET'. Private values are not disclosed to the attacker and 'SECRET' is only output on the public communication encrypted using the long term and session key. Therefore, if the attacker is able to learn the value 'SECRET' this means at least one of the keys was compromised.

Running ProVerif, we find that the attacker cannot learn the value 'SECRET', this means that the EuroRadio protocol succeeds in its main goal of keeping the cryptographic keys secure from an active Delov-Yao attacker. The theorem proving method of ProVerif, further tells us that this holds for an unlimited number of runs of the protocol.

Agreement on Shared Session Key. Even if attackers cannot learn the session key, they may still be able to interfere with the key establishment process. To check if any such attacks are possible, we use the injective ProVerif correspondence assertions:

```
evinj:trainFinishWithKey(ks) ==> evinj:rbcUsing(ks)
evinj:RBCFinishWithKey(ks) ==> evinj:trainUsing(ks)
```

These queries will only hold if, whenever the train believes it has successfully completed the EuroRadio protocol having established the key ks, then there is a single RBC that has also run the protocol and believes the established key is ks, and vice versa. ProVerif tells us that these queries hold, therefore the EuroRadio protocol succeeds in its second major goal of security and successfully setting up a key between a train and a RBC.

Mutual Authentication: Agreement on All Shared Values. To check if it is possible for an attacker to interfere with any other parts of the protocol we extend our queries with all the key values used by the train and the RBC, i.e., the nonces, the trains and RBC identities and the safety feature (SaF):

```
evinj:trainFinishSession(rbc_id,train_id,train_nonce,saf,
   rbc_nonce,ks) ==>
evinj:rbcStartSession(rbc_id,train_id,rbc_nonce,saf,train_nonce)

evinj:rbcFinishSession(rbc_id,train_id,rbc_nonce,saf,train_nonce,
   ks) ==>
evinj:trainStartSession(rbc_id,train_id,train_nonce,saf)
```

While the first correspondence assertion holds, the second fails. Looking at the attack trace produced by ProVerif, we see that it is possible for the attacker to redirect the messages from the train to a second, different RBC as the train does not verify whether the returned ID is the same as the expected one. While implemented systems might add a check of the RBC ID, the protocol specification does not specify that the train explicitly checks it, or what to do if it is incorrect. Second, we see that it is possible for an attacker the change the SaF used in the communication as, again, this is not properly checked. We discuss the relevance of these findings in the section below.

Ability to Insert Attacker Messages. We use the event DataSent'i'(m) to mean that message m was the i-th message sent by the train, and the event DataSent'i'(m) to mean that message m was the i-th message received by the RBC. We can check if an attacker can insert a message into the communication phase of the protocol by checking that all message m received by the RBC where send by the train either as its first, second or third message:

```
ev:DataReceived1(m) ==>
 (ev:DataSent1(s2, m) | ev:DataSent2(s2, m) | ev:DataSent3(s2, m))
ev:DataReceived2(m) ==>
 (ev:DataSent1(s2, m) | ev:DataSent2(s2, m) | ev:DataSent3(s2, m))
ev:DataReceived3(m) ==>
 (ev:DataSent1(s2, m) | ev:DataSent2(s2, m) | ev:DataSent3(s2, m))
```

This holds, showing that the attacker cannot insert their own messages.

Ability to Replay Messages. The above correspondence assertions show that an attacker cannot insert their own messages, but they may still be able to replay an old message, tricking the receiver into thinking it is fresh. We test for replay attacks with a similar correspondence assertion, but this time we require the correspondence to be injective, i.e., for each receive event there must exist a *single, unique* send event:

```
evinj:DataReceived1(m) ==>
 (evinj:DataSent1(s,m)|evinj:DataSent2(s,m)|evinj:DataSent3(s,m))
evinj:DataReceived2(m) ==>
 (evinj:DataSent1(s,m)|evinj:DataSent2(s,m)|evinj:DataSent3(s,m))
evinj:DataReceived3(m) ==>
 (evinj:DataSent1(s,m)|evinj:DataSent2(s,m)|evinj:DataSent3(s,m))
```

These correspondence all hold showing that the attacker cannot replay messages.

Ability to Reorder Messages. Another way in which an attacker could interfere with the communication would be to reorder the message, for instance causing disruption by swapping the order of a go and stop message. As this would not require additional messages, or replaying a message, it would not be detected by the two correspondence assertions above.

The MessagesReceived3(m1, m2, m3) event indicates that the messages m1, m2, m3 were received in that order. We check reordering using this event, and an injective correspondence assertion on the order of the three messages sent by the train:

```
evinj:MessagesReceived3(m1, m2, m3) ==>
(evinj:DataSent1(s,m1)&evinj:DataSent2(s,m2)&evinj:DataSent3(s,m3))
```

We find that this correspondence assertion holds. In our model the attacker may also block messages, therefore even though this correspondence assertion holds it may still be possible for an attacker to block one message and reorder the other two (so meaning that the `MessagesReceived3(m1, m2, m3)` event is never reached. Therefore, we also check the possible reordering of two messages:

```
evinj:MessagesReceived2(m1, m2) ==>
  ((evinj:DataSent1(s, m1) & evinj:DataSent2(s, m2)) |
  (evinj:DataSent1(s, m1) & evinj:DataSent3(s, m2)) |
  (evinj:DataSent2(s, m1) & evinj:DataSent3(s, m2)))
```

This correspondence assertion also holds showing that reordering is not possible.

Ability to Delete Messages Without the Receiver Knowing. While the attacker can stop any message from being delivered we would like the protocol to allow this to be detected. For example, the receiver should not accept a message if the message sent before it did not arrive. We can check this with the following correspondence assertions:

```
evinj:DataReceived1(m) ==> evinj:DataSent1(s, m)
evinj:DataReceived2(m) ==> evinj:DataSent2(s, m)
evinj:DataReceived3(m) ==> evinj:DataSent3(s, m)
```

These correspondence assertions checks to see if deletion *or* reordering is possible, but as we have already shown that reordering is not possible this correspondence assertion will only hold if deletion is impossible and only fail if messages can be deleted.

We find that these correspondence assertions fail to hold, in particular, as the counter-style timestamp can be any value greater than the previous message. There is no simple method for the receiver to detect the absence of a message, however, this can be partly mitigated by acknowledgements messages and timeouts, as we discuss in the next section.

Analysis of Emergency Messages. As described earlier, the application level protocol does not use MACs to verify the emergency stop messages. To see what effect this has, we run each of the test described above on our second model, which includes the sending of messages with no accompanying MAC. We find that, as before, the secrecy of keys and authentication and agreement on the key hold. However, message insertion, deletion, reordering and replay fail to hold. This means that the attacker still cannot pretend to be a train or a RBC, and it is still only possible to set up a communication between a genuine train and RBC. However, once such a session has been set up it is possible for the attacker to insert a stop message, which will be accepted by the train. We discuss the relevance of this finding below.

5   Discussion and Recommendations

In this section, we present recommendations regarding the different issues that were discovered in our analysis.

5.1   Inserting High-Priority Messages

Our analysis showed it is possible to insert messages with high-priority as there is no protection provided over these messages. Therefore, anyone with access to the EuroRadio communication layer can insert emergency stop messages and trigger a train to brake. Though this might not directly lead to incidents with trains colliding, it can cause serious disruptions, for example, due to displaced crew and rolling stock. These disruptions can have a higher impact on the network if the emergency stop is carefully timed. For example, this happens when a train is in a GSM-R radio hole with no reception. In this case, the RBC will not know what has happened as it will not be able to communicate with the train and therefore will not be able to cancel the emergency stop. The driver of the train will need to follow special procedures until GSM-R coverage is available again. It would then take even longer than usual to recover from the emergency stop, which could seriously affect other traffic in the system as well.

To prevent unauthorised emergency stop messages from taking effect, high-priority messages should be authenticated using MACs as is the case with regular priority messages. They can still be given priority over the other messages when checking the MAC. A concern might be that keys could become corrupted, in which case it should still be possible to fall back to voice communication (as is used in most current systems). The application of a MAC to the high-priority message would prevent misuse by an external actor by stopping them from being able to successfully inject messages in the communication between a train and RBC. Although, of course, an attacker could still cause disruption by other means, such as jamming signals.

5.2   Deletion of Messages

The EuroRadio protocol does not protect against deletion of messages. This needs to be taken care of by the application layer. The timestamps that are added by the application layer do not protect against this. The sender of a message can request an acknowledgement for the message from the recipient. This is not the default though and needs to be done explicitly. Moreover, recipients have no way to determine whether it had not successfully received messages. In the worst case, an attacker could prevent reception (i.e. delete) emergency stop messages, after which a train might enter a danger point, a stretch of track, where the safety of the train may be compromised.

Though it is hard to prevent deletion of messages as an attacker could jam all communication between two parties, it is possible to detect the deletion of single messages. A simple way to do this is by adding a counter to all messages. If this counter skips between two messages, you know a message was missed. This would require changes to the current specifications to change both the message format and add procedures what to do in case a missed message is detected.

The specification already has a measure that can help in the case of a jamming attack. It is possible to let a train make an emergency stop if no messages are received within a specific timeout period. This timeout and the action to be taken if it expires are set using nationally set parameters, respectively T_NVCONTACT and M_NVCONTACT. The possible actions to take are to trigger the normal brakes, trip the onboard systems, including an immediate application of the emergency brakes or perform no action. The default value, as set out in SUBSET-026 of the ERTMS specifications are set to 'no reaction' with an infinite amount of time specified, i.e. there is no timeout, for safe messages to be received. Using this measure might result in problems with GSM-R black spots, i.e. if a train spends too much time within a black spot the brakes would be automatically triggered. However, the standard provides ways to inform the train of GSM-R black spots and therefore this should not be a problem.

5.3   Disagreement over RBC Identity and Safety Feature

One issue identified that is not specifically covered in the EuroRadio specifications is that of ensuring that when a train commences a EuroRadio session, the RBC that it establishes the session with is not only genuine, but also the correct one to handle the train. When a train tries to set up a session it doesn't always know the identity of the RBC it will be talking to. In this case the traffic could be redirected to another RBC. At the 'start of mission', the train may invalidate the RBC ID and phone number, for example, if it is recovered, in the case of the train breaking down, or it loses state following a system reboot. The specifications [9] allow the last RBC ID and number to be reused, however they allow the use of the EIRENE shortcode to use location-based addressing to contact the most appropriate RBC for the area the train is connected to via GSM-R. Finally, the driver may alternatively enter the number manually. The latter two options allow the connection to an RBC which is not directly in the area that the train should connect to.

When the train does know the identity of the RBC it wants to communicate with, the standard does not specify what needs to be done if the expected identity is different than the one received during the authentication protocol. It is not even specified whether this should be checked. To make things less ambiguous, we recommend to explicitly include in the protocol description that the RBC identity needs to be checked, if known, and the connection should be aborted if this check fails.

A similar issue involves the safety feature that is used to indicate which MAC algorithm is to be used. The initiator of the protocol chooses a safety feature and sends it to the recipient in the first message, after which the recipient returns it in the second message. The standard does not specify what to do if the safety features do not match. In the official specification, only one safety feature is currently supported, but for future versions, where different safety features might be supported, it is crucial to add this. It should be enforced that the selected safety feature is either equal to or more secure than what was sent by the initiator.

6   Conclusions

We have presented a security analysis of ERTMS's EuroRadio protocol and parts of the application layer protocol. To do this, we developed a novel representation of counter-style timestamps, and new correspondence assertions to test for message insertion, deletion, reordering and replay. We found that EuroRadio defends the security of its key and authenticates the parties involved against an active Dolev-Yao attacker. However, it failed in some of the additional properties we would liked to have seen, such as message deletion and insertion of emergency messages. We discussed the relevance of these findings in the previous section. Our results on messages are tested for the train sending three messages to the RBC, as future work we would like to find a way of testing these results for an arbitrary number of messages sent in either direction, and any interleaving of normal and high-priority messages. While our analyses finds that the protocols do not protect from the insertion of high-priority emergency messages, inserting packets into a GSM-R data stream may be difficult and merits further investigation. Our analysis also makes the assumption that the cryptographic primitives used in ERTMS are secure, as future work we would like to examine these primitives and test this belief.

Acknowledgements. We would like to thank Maria Vigliotti and Florent Pepin from the UK's Rail Safety and Standards Board (RSSB) for helpful discussion regarding the security of ERTMS. Funding for this paper was provided by the UK's Centre for the Protection of National Infrastructure (CPNI) and Engineering and Physical Sciences Research Council (EPSRC) via the SCEPTICS: A SystematiC Evaluation Process for Threats to Industrial Control Systems project.

References

1. Abadi, M., Fournet, C.: Mobile values, new names, and secure communication. In: Symposium on Principles of Programming Languages (POPL) (2001)
2. Ansaldo STS Group. Product portfolio and ERTMS/RTCS projects of Ansaldo Segnalamento Ferroviario (2008). http://old.fel.zcu.cz/Data/documents/sem_de_2008/AnsaldoSTS_08.pdf

3. Arapinis, M., Chothia, T., Ritter, E., Ryan, M.: Analysing unlinkability and anonymity using the applied pi calculus. In: Proceedings of the 23rd IEEE Computer Security Foundations Symposium, CSF 2010, pp. 107–121 (2010)
4. Blanchet, B.: An efficient cryptographic protocol verifier based on Prolog rules. In: Computer Security Foundations Workshop (CSFW), pp. 82–96. IEEE (2001)
5. Blanchet, B., Smyth, B., Cheval, V.: ProVerif 1.88: Automatic cryptographic protocol verifier, user manual and tutorial (2013)
6. Bloomfield, R., Bloomfield, R., Gashi, I., Stroud, R.: How secure Is ERTMS? In: Ortmeier, F., Daniel, P. (eds.) SAFECOMP Workshops 2012. LNCS, vol. 7613, pp. 247–258. Springer, Heidelberg (2012)
7. Cheval, V., Cortier, V.: Timing attacks in security protocols: symbolic framework and proof techniques. In: Focardi, R., Myers, A. (eds.) POST 2015. LNCS, vol. 9036, pp. 280–299. Springer, Heidelberg (2015)
8. Chothia, T., Garcia, F.D., de Ruiter, J., van den Breekel, J., Thompson, M.: Relay cost bounding for contactless EMV payments. In: Böhme, R., Okamoto, T. (eds.) FC 2015. LNCS, vol. 8975, pp. 189–206. Springer, Heidelberg (2015)
9. ERA: SUBSET-026: System requirements specification, version 3.5.0. Technical report (2015)
10. Esposito, R., Lazzaro, A., Marmo, P., Sanseviero, A.: Formal verification of ERTMS EuroRadio safety critical protocol. In: Proceedings 4th Symposium on Formal Methods for Railway Operation and Control Systems (FORMS 2003) (2003)
11. Franekova, M., Rastocny, K., Janota, A., Chrtiansky, P.: Safety analysis of cryptography mechanisms used in GSM for railway. Int. J. Eng. 11(1), 207–212 (2011). http://annals.fih.upt.ro/pdf-full/2011/ANNALS-2011-1-34.pdf
12. GSM-R Functional Group: EIRENE Functional Requirements Specification, version 7.4.0. Technical report (2014)
13. GSM-R Functional Group: EIRENE System Requirements Specification, version 15.4.0. Technical report (2014)
14. Hongjie, L., Lijie, C., Bin, N.: Petrinet based analysis of the safety communication protocol. TELKOMNIKA Indonesian J. Electr. Eng. 11(10), 6034–6041 (2013)
15. Li, L., Sun, J., Liu, Y., Sun, M., Dong, J.S.: A formal specification and verification framework for timed security protocols. TSE (2015, in submission)
16. RSSB: GSM-R User Procedures, issue 7.1. Technical report (2015)
17. UNISIG: SUBSET-037 - EuroRadio FIS, version 3.2.0. Technical report (2015)
18. Zhang, Y., Tang, T., Li, K., Mera, J.M., Zhu, L., Zhao, L., Xu, T.: Formal verification of safety protocol in train control system. Sci. China Technol. Sci. 54(11), 3078–3090 (2011)

Operational Security – A Coming Evolution of Railway Operational Procedures Under the IT Security Threat

Po-Chi Huang[✉] and Birgit Milius

Institute of Railway Systems Engineering and Traffic Safety (IfEV),
Technische Universität Braunschweig, Braunschweig, Germany
{po-chi.huang,b.milius}@tu-braunschweig.de

Abstract. The railway system has benefited from the rapid technology revolution since the 1990s. The mechanical and manpower intensive railway system has gradually evolved into a centralize- and digital-controlled, information- and communication-based system. IT security was not considered during the system (re)design. This paper begins with discussing the need and absence of procedures to sustain operations when an IT security breach has occurred or is suspected.

Then operational security is introduced. It is a new research field which focuses on operational procedures taking into account the effects of safety as well as security-related changes in the system e.g. due to failures or threats. The scope of operational security and general requirements on operational procedures will then be discussed. Lastly, we give an outline of a proposed project with its planned work packages.

Keywords: Operational security · Functional safety · IT security · Railway operation · Degraded operation · Operational procedures · Railway safety

1   IT Security – Evolutional Challenge to Railway Operation

The railway system has hugely benefited from the rapid development of Information and Communication Technology (ICT or commonly IT) since the 1990s and begins its own journey of evolution. The old-fashioned mechanical and manpower intensive railway system has gradually evolved into a centrally and digitally controlled, information- and communication-based system. Today, IT is widely used in railways. The achievements of technical systems and operation modes like European Train Control System (ETCS), Automatic Train Operation (ATO) and Operation Control Center (OCC) all took place with benefits of the IT development.

The issue of IT security is not a new topic in IT industry, it accompanies the development of IT since the beginning. But for the railway sector, IT security was not considered as a serious issue in the past as the railway system conventionally used proprietary, that are hard to hack, systems. The situation changed when the economic efficiency, privatization, modernization and the liberalization of railway systems became a requirement for the railway sector. The increasing use of commercial off-the-shelf (COTS) products makes the modern railway system affordable and flexible, but also more vulnerable.

© Springer International Publishing Switzerland 2016
T. Lecomte et al. (Eds.): RSSRail 2016, LNCS 9707, pp. 69–78, 2016.
DOI: 10.1007/978-3-319-33951-1_5

Considering the potential vulnerabilities and threats which come with using COTS products, the issue of IT security has received further attentions in the railway sector, especially for safety related technical systems. Railways is considered as a critical infrastructure, which means that it needs to retain its operation even in abnormal situations [1]. Safety is the core value of the railway system. However, shutting the railway system down when an IT security breach is suspected might be the safe option, but is not feasible and not acceptable. To fulfill the requirement of continued safe operations when facing IT security threats, a holistic view of the operational procedures taking into account safety- and security issues is necessary.

2   Operational Continuity – A Deficiency in Work of IT Security

As mentioned previously, the issue of IT security has received some attention in the railway sector during the last few years. Not only researchers, but also public authorities and standard committees have realized the possible severity of IT security threats on the railway system and the urgent need of countermeasures. For example, with the funding of European Union (EU) projects with international cooperation like SECRET[1], which focuses on the security of railways against electromagnetic attacks; SECUR-ED[2], a project to enhance the security of urban public transportation with work packages focused on IT security, have been carried out. Also the European Union Agency for Network and Information Security (ENISA) concentrates on developing IT security measures for the railway sector [2]. The International Union of Railways (UIC) has also started a project ARGUS with international cooperation on designing a security analysis approach for railway signaling system [3].

In Germany, the *Law of IT Security*[3] has come into effect in July 2015, which forces critical infrastructures like the railway system, whose unavailability or failure of the system could cause significant impact on the safety and living of the society, to implement adequate organizational and technical measures to avoid the complete failure or breakdown of the system. The law requires the critical infrastructure to use state of the art methods to protect the availability, integrity, authenticity and confidentiality of its IT systems [1]. Besides, in the German Commission for Electrical, Electronic & Information Technologies of DIN and VDE (DKE) two pre-standards were set up for considering the IT security threats in railway signaling: VDE V 0831-102 focuses on defining the protection profile for technical functions and VDE V 0831-104 offers an IT security guideline based on IEC 62443 for electric signaling systems in railway [4, 5].

However, all the current work in IT security, from researchers, railway undertakings, infrastructure managers to the public authorities and standard committees focusses mainly on the technical side of the railway system. The purpose of those current works is to find the vulnerabilities of today's technical system; to set up standards for technical system design; to integrate IT security management systems with the safety related

---

[1] *Security of Railways against Electromagnetic Attacks*, http://www.secret-project.eu.
[2] *Secured Urban Transportation – European Demonstration*, http://www.secur-ed.eu.
[3] Original in German: IT-Sicherheitsgesetz.

electronic systems, etc. However, even with all those technical measures in place, railways cannot be completely secure indefinitely. Therefore, concerns from the operational side should be considered when discussing how to deal with IT security threats, e.g.:

- What happens if the technical system fails to identify an attack?
- What happens if the technical system fails to defend against an attack?
- When and how should the operational personnel be informed about attacks?
- How can the operation be kept running safely and efficiently when the system state after a potential attack is not clear?
- How and when can operations go back to normal state, if the reasons and consequence of the attack are not completely understood?

Those questions can be summarized as: What happens when the technical measures against IT security breaches fail? Today's railway system has already shown that even technical systems with a high reliability do fail. Degraded operations are still part of operations in the daily praxis. Hence, those questions from the operational side are rational and should be seriously considered.

Network Rail has described in their IT security strategy: "We will operate in an assumed state of compromise, that is there will not be a presumption that our network boundaries, internal and external, are invulnerable" [6]. The French Network and information Security Agency (ANSSI) has considered the lack of Business Continuity Plan as a vulnerability of the industrial control system in IT security, and points out that the operation teams rarely know how to act in such IT security event [7]. In the urban transportation sector, the American Public Transportation Association (APTA) has also noticed this issue and introduces five kinds of plans that are needed for continuation of operation under the IT security threat. These plans are Incident Response Plan, Business Continuity Plan, Continuity of Operations Plan, Crisis Communications Plan and Disaster Recovery Plan [8].

3   Process of Operational Continuity

3.1   A Generic Bow-Tie Model of Operational Continuity

In Europe, the railway system has been recognized as the safest transportation mode in surface transport [9]. This achievement is built mainly on the high reliability of the system. This high reliability could not be reached without adequate operational procedures and qualified and reliable personnel. However, a system with very high reliability does not mean that no faults and no errors would occur during the system operation. As a critical infrastructure, measures and rules, both from technical and operational side, have been established in the past to achieve its high availability. Depending on the situations, measures and rules would be combined to set up procedure for the system to enable the continuation of operation.

As shown in Fig. 1, the procedures to continue railway operations can be displayed as a generic bow-tie process [10]. The process has been divided into technical and operational side, with technical on the upper side and operational on the lower side. The process begins in normal operation. With the monitoring program from one or both sides, it leads the system from normal into degraded operation. During the degraded operation, the operational side focuses on the degraded mode management to keep the operation running; the technical side supports the operational side with the failure mode management to identify and rectify the abnormal situation. After the abnormal situation has be rectified and controlled, the transition from degraded to normal operation begins within the restoration program.

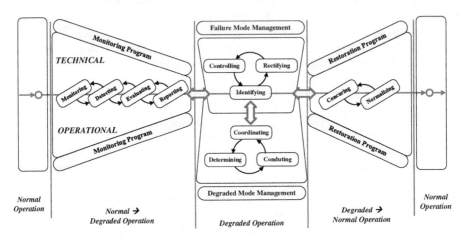

Fig. 1. General system procedure to continuation of operation in railway operation [10]

This generic bow-tie process was derived from the conventional railway procedures. The framework was set up before the issue of IT security had been considered. The question is therefore: Could this process be used when IT security has to be considered?

3.2   A Short Comparison of Safety Hazards and IT Security Threats

To decide if the model for safety can be used for IT security, a detailed analysis of the processes, relationships and dependabilities for both aspects needs to be done. As we will focus on operations, the criteria of comparison will be taken from the effects that hazards and threats might have on railway operations. The short comparison is done in Table 1. Due to page restrictions, only some chosen criteria are shown.

The comparison clearly shows that regarding its effect on operations, major differences between safety hazards and IT security threats exist. The characteristics and consequences of IT security threats are in general less well known. This means that procedures for operations in degraded mode after IT security attacks have to cover a wider set of scenarios. Therefore, we have to conclude that the procedures from today's operational rulebooks cannot be used directly to sustain operational continuity after security attack. However, we can still use them as a starting point for further research, aiming at adapting and further developing existing procedures. Based on the results shown in Table 1, we assume that today's procedures for degraded operation are a subset of the needed procedures for degraded operation in the future. Thus, the bow-tie process

Table 1. Comparison of safety hazard and IT security threats in railway operation

	Safety hazards	IT security threats
1. Frequency	• Controllable – System reliability – Preventive maintenance	• Might NOT be controllable – Willingness of attacker – Purpose of attacker
2. Cause	• Foreseeable – Operation conditions – Product lifespan	• Might NOT be foreseeable – System status – Capability of attacker
3. Effect	• Predictable – System failure behavior	• Might NOT be predictable – Unexpected behavior
4. Extent of effect	• Calculable – Controlled multiple-faults – Reliable system	• Might NOT be calculable – Network-wide attack
5. Duration of effect	• Could be estimated – Failure cause foreseeable – Long-time experience	• Might NOT be estimated – System behavior unknown – Merely no experience
6. Involved persons	• Could be estimated	• Might NOT be estimated – Extent, consequence and duration unknown
7. Detection measures	• Well developed and integrated – Reliable system monitoring – Operational procedures	• Less known – Huge technical deficiency – No operational procedures
8. Time to detection	• Foreseeable – Reliable system reactions – Routine maintenance	• Might NOT be foreseeable – Unknown system behavior – Manipulation

today will still be the core framework of future degraded operation and can be adapted and developed further when IT security has to be considered (Fig. 2).

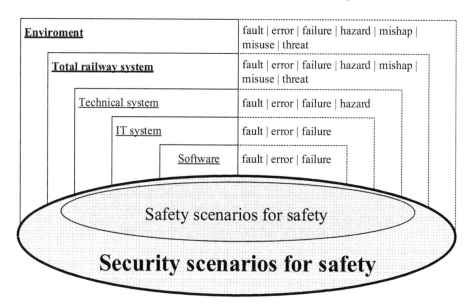

Fig. 2. Wider scenario considerations of security, adapted [11]

4   Introducing Operational Security

4.1   Scope

As previously mentioned, a modern railway system needs IT security to ensure its functional safety. This statement is correct indeed, but all the current work is only concentrated on the technical side in the railway sector. However, even though railway automation has been in process for several decades, the role of human stays indispensable in the railway operation. Therefore, a holistic view of railway operations needs to take the human into account and the effects of safety and security issues on them need to be addressed. For example, the operational personnel needs to know:

- how to identify and get aware of an attack, which was not detected with the technical measures,
- how to act during or after a successful attack,
- how the communication between operational personnel will work, e.g. regarding priorities and responsibilities and
- how to keep the operation running safely and efficiently when the status of the system is not clear.

Those requirements above are merely part of the complex set of requirements to be applied to the future railway operational procedures. Owing to the complexity and diversity of the railway operation, new approaches need to be developed to enable a systematic process to solve the problems. A new research field, which will be known as Operational Security [12], is now researching this topic intensively.

As discussed before, we assume that safety issues can be dealt with more easily because of a limited set of expected scenarios. We will include the assessment of today's rules for degraded mode in our research. Our aim is to develop a complete set of procedures to deal with safety and IT security issues. This is also necessary as we have to assume that often when an operational problem arises it cannot be decided quickly and surely if the reason for it lies in safety or security.

4.2   Essential Requirements

Before developing or adapting operational procedures, strict requirements need to be set against which the new procedures have to be proven. Identifying all requirements is still part of research, but four essential ones can already be presented as examples:

- **Operational procedures need to be safe**
  As safety is the core value of the railway system, all operational procedures need to be safe. Showing how safe is safe enough is a difficult topic.
- **Operational procedures need to be efficient**
  The operational procedures today were developed for a system with superior reliability and availability. The frequency and the duration of failures and therefore the necessity of operating in degraded mode was on a low and acceptable level. Thus, the efficiency of the procedures and the service level of the system in degraded operation was adequate to the status quo. However, the situation is changing as the

frequency, duration and also the consequences of attacks on IT can hardly be foreseen. Efficiency becomes a primary requirements for the degraded operation to keep the service level of the system acceptable as it is expected that e.g. degraded operation due to security breaches is longer in place than after typical technical failures.

- **Operational procedures need to be secure**
  The operational procedures should be secured against IT attacks. Operational procedures must not become vulnerabilities in the system. Otherwise, the attacker could force the technical system into failure mode. Since the operational side needs to take over, less secure operational procedures in the degraded operation could be exploited by the attacker. Today's operational procedures (for degraded operation) are safe but not necessarily secure, since its framework and core concept were developed in a time without the issue IT security.

- **Operational procedures need to be modular**
  Since efficiency is an essential requirement for the procedures, a modularity of procedures could be the essential point to achieve it. The operational procedures should be divided into secure procedure modules with more flexibility for interchange so that depending on the system state the modules can be chosen so that always the highest level of efficiency is possible.

4.3 Work Packages

The work of operational security can be divided into four main work packages according to the process shown in Fig. 3: Monitoring Program (WP-1), Degraded Mode Management (WP-2), Restoration Program (WP-3) and Interface Management (WP-4). Additionally, two further work packages are need. One will look at the state of the art in degraded operation and will derive a full set of requirements (WP-5). Another one will deal with the basic ontology to represent the intended meaning and relations of terms which to be used in operational security. (WP-6). The work packages are described below to give a first overview about the expected research efforts.

- **WP-1: Monitoring Program**
  The operational monitoring program begins with defining specific events which the operational personnel should be aware of in the running operation. Measures of how to detect and reveal those events will be integrated into procedures of normal operation. Criteria to evaluate the threat level of the detected events will then be set up to help the operational personnel to make decisions and to assess the potential consequences swiftly in the running operation. Regardless of whether the detected events could be instantly classified as threat or not, the events should be reported to the responsible person or unit in a defined process for further assessment. It will be defined which information of the given operational situation will be used as benchmarks for choosing the appropriate degraded mode operation and where to get those information from.

- **WP-2: Degraded Mode Management**
  The degraded mode management can be considered as a set of systematically defined procedures, which should be put into action immediately to ensure the operational

continuity after the detected event has been reported. Responsible persons for coordinating, determining and conducting the degraded mode operations will be defined. The communication process between operational personnel, criteria for determining proper countermeasures and priority of procedures will be established.

- **WP-3: Restoration Program**
  The restoration program focuses on procedures to bring the system from degraded operation back to the normal operation. After the detected event has been rectified and controlled from the technical side, the system status need to be concurred between technical and operational personnel before return to the normal operational procedures. Detailed processes and responsibilities are needed.

- **WP-4: Interface Management**
  There are interfaces between the phases of operations as well as between operational personnel and technical management. These interfaces will be clearly defined and the necessary information at interfaces are identified. It will furthermore be discussed how inaccuracies or missing information will invalidate the processes. It must be the aim of the whole setup to be stable and not lead to wrong conclusions when minor inaccuracies exist.

- **WP-5: Requirements**
  New operational rules have to take into account the requirements put on them by legal documents. Further requirements come from operations itself. Additionally, as

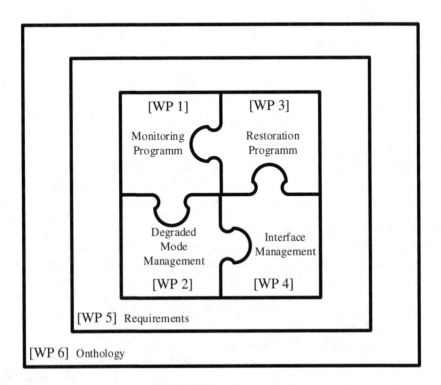

Fig. 3. Work package set-up

railways are very complex and difficult to change, they should be based on today's rules as these are known and accepted. The aim of this work package is to derive a complete set of requirements which the new rules have to adhere to. This will allow to check if and which existing rules will still work, but it can also be used as a benchmark to check if a new set of rules is feasible.

- **WP-6: Definitions**
  As security is a rather new topic, today's definitions are not completely usable in the context of operational security. An ontology is needed to merge, define and connect definitions and relationships which were established for safety with the ones used for security.

5   Conclusions and Further Works

This paper has shown the importance of operational continuity in railway operations under IT security threats. It was revealed that in the current work regarding IT security in the railway sector this aspect is not taken care of. A new research field named Operational Security has been introduced. Operational security aims at systematically developing a closed set of operational rules for dealing with suspected or actual IT security breaches. It was argued using some examples that today's rules for operations in degraded operation are not completely suitable as they were developed mainly for safety issues. On the other hand, we have to take into account that distinguishing between safety and security irregularities will not always be possible. It is an aim for operational security that the developed rules are applicable to safety as well as security issues. In the paper, we suggest a plan for researching operational security and discuss the main work packages and give an overview of what to focus on in each.

References

1. Gesetz zur Erhöhung der Sicherheit informationstechnischer Systeme (IT-Sicherheitsgesetz). Bundesgesetzblatt Jahrgang 2015 Teil I Nr. 31, Bonn (2015)
2. Lèvy, C.-B.: Cyber security for railway signalling (presentation). In: Workshop on "How to Protect Signalling System Against Cybercrime," Paris (2015)
3. Antoni, M.: ARGUS – Security & safety analysis for electric and computerized signalling systems (presentation). In: DKE Meeting 2014, Frankfurt (2014)
4. DIN VDE V 0831-102 Electric signalling systems for railways - part 102: protection profile for technical functions in railway signalling (2013)
5. DIN VDE V 0831-104 Electric signalling systems for railways - part 104: IT Security Guideline based on IEC 62443. (2015)
6. Cyber Security Strategy. Network Rail, London (2013)
7. Cybersecurity for Industrial Control Systems – Detailed Measures. The French Network and Security Agency (ANSSI), Paris (2014)
8. APTA: Cybersecurity Considerations for Public Transit. APTA (American Public Transportation Association), USA (2014)
9. Railway safety performance in the European Union 2014. European Railway Agency, Valenciennes (2014)

10. Huang, P.-C., Milius, B.: IT-Security für einen sicheren Bahnbetrieb. Deine Bahn. 2/2016, 13–16 (2016)
11. Raspotnig, C., Opdahl, A.: Comparing risk identification techniques for safety and security requirements. J. Syst. Softw. **86**, 1124–1151 (2013)
12. Huang, P.-C., Milius, B.: Why do we need operational security? (presentation). In: 8th Workshop on "Safety in Transportation," Braunschweig (2015)

Risk Assessment of the 3Des in ERTMS

Florent Pépin and Maria Grazia Vigliotti[✉]

RSSB, 1 South Place, London EC2M, UK
{Florent.Pepin,Maria.Vigliotti}@RSSB.CO.UK
http://www.rssb.co.uk

Abstract. The three-key Triple Data Encryption Algorithm (Triple Data Encryption Algorithm is also known in the literature as Triple-Des, or Triple DEA or TDEA) (3Des) is a symmetric encryption algorithm currently used in the European Traffic Management System (ERTMS) for integrity and authentication purposes. In a recent publication [1], 3Des has been withdrawn in favour of Advanced Encryption Standard (AES) [2] (The National Institute for Science and Technology (NIST) standard [1] allows to both algorithms can be used for specific purposes until 2030 with the intention of gradually phasing out 3Des towards AES). In this paper, we have investigated, from a practical point of view, known attacks to 3Des and proved that, in order to carry out such attacks, a disproportionate amount of hardware and money would be necessary. In practical terms this means that these attacks do not represent a realistic risk.

In our work we assume that basic security measures have been taken in the implementation such as: 3Des does not leak any information and a cryptographically secure random number generator for production of the keys is used.

Keywords: 3Des · ERTMS · Railway systems · Performance analysis · Key management · Key distribution

1 Introduction

European Rail Traffic Management System (ERTMS) is a major industrial project that aims at improving cross-border interoperability, replacing national rail infrastructure by a standardised system at European level. ERTMS comprises of the European Train Control System and GSM-R. The ETCS specification targets the signalling equipment, which will be replaced through centralisation of information and data transfer; movement authorities will be automatically transmitted from trackside equipment, Radio Block Centre (RBC) to the train via radio communication[1].

To guarantee the integrity and the authenticity of the data transmitted between the onboard equipment on the train and the RBC, 3Des encryption

---

[1] Movement authorities are automatically negotiated at ETCS Level 2 and ETCS Level 3.

© Springer International Publishing Switzerland 2016
T. Lecomte et al. (Eds.): RSSRail 2016, LNCS 9707, pp. 79–92, 2016.
DOI: 10.1007/978-3-319-33951-1_6

algorithm is used. 3Des is a symmetric-block-cypher encryption algorithm. The
adjective "symmetric" indicates that the same key is used for both encryption
and decryption. 3Des extends by three-folds the key size of the original Data
Encryption Algorithm (Des) [3], which was known to be subject to the brute-
force attack [4]. Des' key length is 64-bit long, but eight of these bits are used
to check parity, hence the effective key length is 56 bits. Therefore, 3Des' key
length is 192-bit long, and effective length is 168 bits.

3Des was designed with two main goals:

1. Keep the algorithm compatible with single Des.
2. Increase the key length of the Des to protect against brute force attacks without redesigning a new block cypher.

To encrypt data, 3Des requires three keys, which should ideally be independently
generated. The algorithm will use the three keys to encrypt the data. An attacker
who would want to recover the key to decrypt data, could use a divide and
conquer technique: learn each key individually.

In 1999 the American National Institute for Standards and Technology
(NIST) accepted 3Des as a standard cryptographic algorithm [3]. Since then,
it has been subject to security analysis with the goal of finding flows in the
design that would allow an attacker to recover the secret key(s). In the academic
literature two main key-recovery attacks can be found:

1. *The Related-Key Attack* [5]. This attack aims at recovering the first key,
   followed by a Meet-in-The-Middle attack (MTM) attack against 2Des [6] to
   recover the two other keys. For consistency with previous works, this sequence
   of attacks will be simply called Related-Key Attack (RKA). We have focussed
   our work on this attack.
2. *The Meet-in-The-Middle attack (MTM) against* 3Des. This attack is unrealistic due to the required computational power. Therefore, the rest of this
   paper will not cover this type of attack.

The RKA uses a dependency between two keys (introduced during key distribution or key generation) to make the first of the three Des encryption independent from the two other ones. After recovering the first key, an MTM attack
against 2Des follows: the last two encryption functions are treated separately,
and every possible key is tested until the result of the first function is equal to
the result of the inverse of the second function.

To the best of the authors' knowledge, there has been no attempt to implement the two attacks described above, and the feasibility of these attacks in
practice remains an open question in both the academic and the railway community. In 2005, 3Des was withdrawn from the NIST making the open question
on the feasibility of these attacks in practice even more important given the
current advances in hardware technology.

The work presented in this paper carried out in conjunction with the UK
railway industry addresses the question of the feasibility of the RKA attack.
Our work shows that the RKA remains confined to the theoretical domain, and
at this point in time, it does not represent an imminent risk.

Pioneering security analysis on ERTMS can be found in [7–9]. These three pieces of research consider, in a general setting, possible attacks and risks associated to the design of the ERTMS. Bloomfield et al. have assessed the safety and security of ERTMS in [7]. They have emphasised that it would be difficult for an attacker to cause damage as the general philosophy is to stop the train if any anomaly is detected. However, they have mentioned that attackers can cause passengers discomfort or panic by forcing the train to stop in strategic places (e.g. a tunnel). Baldoni et al. [9] have stated that communication is left unencrypted and that an attacker could learn sensitive information by doing a Man-In-The-Middle attack (MITM).

None of them performs an in-depth cryptographic analysis as we do in this work.

1.1 Research Contributions

The main research question that this paper addresses is: Is there a feasible attack to the 3Des that would allow an attacker to recover a key? To answer this question we make the following contributions:

1. We introduce a new theoretical Related-Key Attack against 3Des.
2. We compare the performance of a full attack, that would recover all three keys, on desktop computers and custom hardware Field-Programmable Gate Array (FPGAs).
3. We quantify the proposed attack in terms of costs and hardware resources and we show that the full attacks for the recovery of the three keys is not feasible in practice as the costs are exceptionally high. The assumption for this scenario is that basic security measures have been taken such that 3Des does not leak any information, and a cryptographically secure random number generator for production of the keys is used, and the keys are independently generated.
4. We quantify the cost of a possible attack in case of the basic measures on the generation of keys is violated and a dependency between two keys is introduced.

The rest of the paper is organised as follows: in Sect. 2 ERTMS architecture is described; Sect. 3 introduces our variation of the RKA; in Sect. 4, possible angle of attacks against ERTMS are shown; in Sect. 5 a cost analysis of implementing an attack is provided; and Sect. 6 concludes.

2 ERTMS

ERTMS specification includes the European Train Control System (ETCS), which incorporates an Automatic Train Protection system, and GSM-R, a radio system based on GSM using rail specific frequencies and functionality. The initiative includes four different levels functionality: Level 0, Level 1, Level 2, and Level 3. The attack presented in this paper could refer to the functionality at Level 2 or at Level 3.

In ERTMS, integrity and authenticity of messages exchanged between the train and the RBC are ensured with a Message Authentication Code (MAC). Specifically, the European specification requires a CBC-MAC with a post-processing phase [10], computed with a 192-bit session key $\mathbf{K_s}$. This session key is the *same* for both the RBC and the train, and to compute it, a 3Des key, called KMAC, had been previously *securely* distributed to both the train and the RBC. To ensure the freshness of the session, nonces, in this case two random numbers, are generated by both the train and the RBC. We use the notation $\mathbf{R_{train}}$ and $\mathbf{R_{rbc}}$ for the two random numbers generated by the train and the RBC, and the notation $\mathbf{R_X}$ as a variable to indicate either the nonce generated by the train or the one generated by the RBC.

To compute the 192-bit session key $\mathbf{K_s} = (\mathbf{K_{s_1}} \mid \mathbf{K_{s_2}} \mid \mathbf{K_{s_3}})$ 3Des is applied as described below:

$$
\begin{aligned}
\mathbf{K_{s_1}} &= \mathrm{DES}_{K_3}(\mathrm{DES}_{K_2}^{-1}(\mathrm{DES}_{K_1}(\mathbf{R_{train}^L} \mid \mathbf{R_{rbc}^L}))) \\
\mathbf{K_{s_2}} &= \mathrm{DES}_{K_3}(\mathrm{DES}_{K_2}^{-1}(\mathrm{DES}_{K_1}(\mathbf{R_{train}^R} \mid \mathbf{R_{rbc}^R}))) \\
\mathbf{K_{s_3}} &= \mathrm{DES}_{K1}(\mathrm{DES}_{K2}^{-1}(\mathrm{DES}_{K3}(\mathbf{R_{train}^L} \mid \mathbf{R_{rbc}^L})))
\end{aligned}
\tag{1}
$$

where $\mathbf{R_X^R}, \mathbf{R_X^L}$ are the right-half and the left-half of the random number $\mathbf{R_X}$. KMAC is created by the Key Management Centre, and each country in the EU is free to implement the Key Management Centre as they see it fit [11]. The Key Management Centre distributes to all entities (trains and RBCs) the KMAC. For security reasons the KMAC is encrypted with 3Des algorithm (in ECB mode [12]) with 192-bit key Ktrans$_2$. To ensure the authenticity of the key KMAC, CBC-MAC is applied using another 192-bit key called Ktrans$_1$ [13]. The same process is applied for distributing KMAC between two Key Management Centres though a special key K-KMC is used instead of Ktrans.

The keys Ktrans and K-KMC can be considered *master keys*. They are distributed to every entity unencrypted, and off-line with a physical device. Operational procedures ensures the security of this distribution.

Figure 1 summarises in a graphical way how keys are used and exchanged.

3   Presentation of a New RKA

The RKA first takes advantage of the inverted function used in 3Des, as well as a dependency between two keys introduced during key distribution or key generation, to recover one out of the three keys. The problem is then reduced to 2Des, and an MTM attack can be mounted. The two encryption functions are treated separately, and every possible key is tested until the result of the first function is equal to the result of the inverse of the second function.

Kelsey et al. [5] describe the first known RKA, where the adversary needs to know one pair $(P, C)_k$, and to be able to mount a Related-Key Adaptive Chosen Ciphertext query (RK-ACC) to get another pair $(P', C)_{k'}$, with k and k' two related keys whose relation Δ is known to him.

We consider our variation of this attack, where the adversary needs to know one pair $(P, C)_k$, and to be able to mount a Related-Key Adaptive Chosen

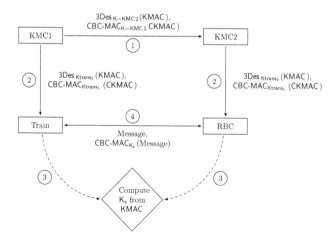

Fig. 1. Key distribution steps

Plaintext query (RK-ACP) to get another pair $(P, C')_{k'}$, with k and k' two related keys whose relation Δ is known to him. The relation between the keys is:

$$k = (k_1, k_2, k_3)$$
$$k' = (k_1, k_2, k_3 \oplus \Delta)$$

The specific relation allows the adversary to compute:

$$
\begin{aligned}
C' &= \mathsf{DES}_{k_3 \oplus \Delta}(\mathsf{DES}_{k_2}^{-1}(\mathsf{DES}_{k_1}(P))) \\
&= \mathsf{DES}_{k_3 \oplus \Delta}(\mathsf{DES}_{k_2}^{-1}(\mathsf{DES}_{k_1}(\mathsf{DES}_{k_1}^{-1}(\mathsf{DES}_{k_2}(\mathsf{DES}_{k_3}^{-1}(C)))))) \\
&\qquad\qquad\qquad \text{since } P = \mathsf{DES}_{k_1}^{-1}(\mathsf{DES}_{k_2}(\mathsf{DES}_{k_3}^{-1}(C))) \\
&= \mathsf{DES}_{k_3 \oplus \Delta}(\mathsf{DES}_{k_3}^{-1}(C))
\end{aligned}
$$

Because the adversary knows C', C and Δ, this equation allows him/her to recover k_3 by exhaustive search, i.e. trying all 2^{56} possible values. The problem can therefore be reduced to 2Des, by computing

$$
\begin{aligned}
C'' &= \mathsf{DES}_{k_3}^{-1}(C) \\
&= \mathsf{DES}_{k_3}^{-1}(\mathsf{DES}_{k_3}(\mathsf{DES}_{k_2}^{-1}(\mathsf{DES}_{k_1}(P)))) \\
&= \mathsf{DES}_{k_2}^{-1}(\mathsf{DES}_{k_1}(P))
\end{aligned}
$$

Finally, the adversary can recover k_1 and k_2 by doing a Meet-in-The-Middle attack on 2DES [6]. Rather than trying all possible keys for both encryptions, which would result in a time complexity of 2^{112}, the attacker proceeds as follows:

1. Computes the subcipher $\mathsf{DES}_{k_2}(C'')$ under every possible keys k_2 (2^{56} possibilities), and stores it in a lookup table.
2. Computes $\mathsf{DES}_{k1}(P)$ for every possible k_1, until an entry in the table such that $\mathsf{DES}_{k_2}(C'') = \mathsf{DES}_{k_1}(P)$ is found. This match implies that k_1 and k_2 are candidate keys.
3. The attacker only needs another pair to verify that these are the actual keys [14].

The complexity to recover the first part of the key k_3 requires 2^{57} single Des encryptions, but only 2^{56} on average. A basic MTM attack on double Des requires 2^{57} encryptions, hence the total time complexity is $O(2^{57})$. The MTM attack also requires to store 2^{56} pairs of (ciphertext, key), so the memory complexity is $O(2^{56})$. Finally, the attack requires one known-plaintext pair, and one related-key adaptive chosen plaintext.

However, this complexity in memory makes this attack very unrealistic. Therefore, a trade-off emerged in order to decrease memory complexity to the detriment of computational complexity. The time and memory product is constant though, and stays 2^{113}.

The key difference between these two RKA lies in the adversary's knowledge. Instead of being able to mount an RK-ACC, the attacker has to mount an RK-ACP. The next section shows that the former is not implementable whereas the latter is.

4   ERTMS Security Analysis

In this section we perform a security analysis of ERTMS infrastructure to identify how the attacks described earlier can be mounted. We clarify the attacker's capabilities that are assumed.

If the goal of an attacker is to interfere with the running of the train, or to let it go faster to derail it, one way to achieve this would be to impersonate the Radio Block Centre. The role of the MAC as described in Sect. 2 is to prevent this from happening by ensuring integrity and authenticity of the communication between the train and the RBC. However, if the attacker recovers the session key used to compute the MAC, then it would be possible to impersonate the RBC. The architecture described in Fig. 1 indicates that KMAC can be attacked at two points:

Case 1. During the transportation of KMAC to the ETCS entities or between two KMCs – see points 1, 2 in Fig. 1. However, we show later that this setting is not vulnerable to Related-Key Attacks.

Case 2. When deriving $\mathbf{K_s}$ – see Eq. 1 and point 3 in Fig. 1.

To mount the RKA discussed in Sect. 3 the attacker needs to intercept only two 192-bit long pairs in both Case 1 and 2.

Case 1: The attacker's goal is to recover the transport key Ktrans. As explained in Sect. 3, the attacker has to know two 64-bit pairs of plaintext-ciphertext encrypted under the same key, in addition to one 64-bit pair under a related key.

As 3Des is applied in ECB mode to a 192-bit plaintext (KMAC), if the attacker gets one pair (KMAC, CKMAC)$_{\text{Ktrans}_2}$ (i.e. one authentication key KMAC $= (K_1, K_2, K_3)$ and its encryption) and possesses three pairs of 64-bit plaintext-ciphertext. Indeed, if we have Ktrans$_2 = (Kt2_1 \mid Kt2_2 \mid Kt2_3)$, KMAC $= (K_1 \mid K_2 \mid K_3)$, and its encryption CKMAC $= (CK_1 \mid CK_2 \mid CK_3)$, the relation between these is:

$$CK_1 = \mathsf{DES}_{Kt2_3}(\mathsf{DES}_{Kt2_2}^{-1}(\mathsf{DES}_{Kt2_1}(K_1)))$$
$$CK_2 = \mathsf{DES}_{Kt2_3}(\mathsf{DES}_{Kt2_2}^{-1}(\mathsf{DES}_{Kt2_1}(K_2)))$$
$$CK_3 = \mathsf{DES}_{Kt2_3}(\mathsf{DES}_{Kt2_2}^{-1}(\mathsf{DES}_{Kt2_1}(K_3)))$$

This clearly gives the attacker three pairs of plaintext-ciphertext encrypted under the same key. The attacker needs only pairs of plaintext-ciphertext under the same key, and another pair encrypted under a related key.

Therefore, the attacker's goal is to obtain two pairs $(\mathsf{KMAC}, \mathsf{CKMAC})_{\mathsf{Ktrans}_2}$ to recover Ktrans_2 by mounting a RKA.

Case 2: The attacker's goal of is to recover KMAC. Because of $\mathbf{K_s}$'s derivation procedure (see Eq. 1), one 192-bit pair of plaintext-ciphertext gives the attacker two 64-bit pairs under the same key.

KMAC is used twice in the same setting to compute $\mathbf{K_{s1}}$ and $\mathbf{K_{s2}}$. Hence, if the attacker knows the two random numbers $\mathbf{R}_{\mathrm{train}}$ and $\mathbf{R}_{\mathrm{rbc}}$ (the plaintext) – which can be intercepted – and one session key $\mathbf{K_s} = (\mathbf{K_{s1}} \mid \mathbf{K_{s2}} \mid \mathbf{K_{s3}})$ (the ciphertext), the attacker knows two 64-bit pairs of plaintext-ciphertext encrypted under the same key.

Thus, his goal is to obtain two pairs $(\mathbf{R_x}, \mathbf{K_s})_{\mathsf{KMAC}}$ to get two 64-bit pairs encrypted under the same key, in addition to one 64-bit pair under a related key. Note that it is the same requirement as in Case 1.

4.1   Attacker's Capabilities and Knowledge

In this section we make different assumptions to allow an attacker to achieve the requirement described in the previous paragraphs in order to mount a RKA.

One known related-key plaintext (Case 2 dismissed). This assumption is not reasonable in Case 2, hence the possibility of a RKA in this setting is dismissed, and we will only cover Case 1 in the rest of the paper.

In order to perform a RKA, the two pairs the attacker needs to obtain should be related under two related keys whose relation is also known to him/her. Specifically, if he has a pair (P, C) under $k_a = (k_1 \mid k_2 \mid k_3)$, he needs another pair (P, C') under $k_b = (k_1 \mid k_2 \mid k_3 \oplus \Delta)$, or a pair (P', C) under $k_c = (k_1 \oplus \Delta \mid k_2 \mid k_3)$.

The latter possibility is discarded for both cases. In Case 1, making this assumption would imply the attacker sees twice the same ciphertext resulting from the encryption of two different KMAC under two different but related key Ktrans. The probability of this happening is $\frac{1}{2^{64}}$, which is very small. In Case 2, the same analysis apply. This implies ERTMS is not vulnerable to Kelsey's RKA.

The former possibility might happen in Case 1, if the plaintext (KMAC) does not change, but the transportation key does, being related to the previous one. Another way to have the required relation is if K-KMC is related to Ktrans, and KMAC is sent encrypted under the former to a KMC, then under the latter to ETCS entities, the attacker can obtain two different ciphertexts derived from the same plaintext (KMAC) under two related keys.

In Case 2, the attacker would need to send twice the same random number at communication establishment. Assuming the random number generator is correct, the probability of this event is $\frac{1}{2^{32}} \simeq 10^{-10}$. Even if the attacker manages to force the train to choose a random number every second, e.g. by aborting the connection set-up every time a number different from the one sought is generated, it would still take about 136 years to obtain the same number. This implies that 3Des encryption in Case 2 is not vulnerable to any Related-Key Attack.

Two Known Expired Keys. The attacker is able to obtain two expired keys that were encrypted under two different but related keys.

In Case 1, knowing two expired authentication keys (KMAC) that were encrypted under two related K-KMC or Ktrans, the attacker can use the corresponding encryption CKMAC, which gives him all the required knowledge to mount a RKA.

He can obtain these two keys if the KMC, onboard system or RBC archive old keys in a non-secure manner and he finds a way to break into one of them. He could also use social engineering; it might be easy to convince a careless employee to give away a file of expired key, by bribing and arguing it is not useful any more, or by pretending a security analysis of the system.

It should be noted that with this assumption, every attack requiring more than two pairs is dismissed, which includes all RKA tradeoffs requiring 2^{32} such pairs. It seems very unlikely the attacker can gather 2^{32} pairs (about 4 billions). To give an order of idea, even if KMAC is changed every minute, it would still take around 8000 years to get this number of pairs.

At Most 2^{50} bytes of memory available. This assumption forces the adversary to use a tradeoff for the MTM attack part of the RKA. Attacks requiring more than 2^{50} bytes, which represents 1.13 Petabytes, are not considered. To give an order of idea, according to Facebook engineers, the company has a 300 PB computer system [15], and the Utah Data Centre is believed to have a storage capacity greater than one Exabyte [16].

4.2 Assumptions on Keys

We assume the keys are strong. However, the key generation is assumed to introduce a relation between two keys, i.e. the random number generator is weak.

Moreover, the attacker only needs to break one valid Ktrans to corrupt the system's integrity. However, it takes much time to perform the attack and if Ktrans changes, the attacker would need to start over the key search. Hence, the time allowed to perform the attack is actually bounded by Ktrans's validity time.

As written in Offline Key Management FIS [11], specific key management solutions are left to national implementation. This implies there is no standard validity time for the authentication key. It will be assumed for the remaining of this paper that the attacker disposes of 5 years to perform the attack, before Ktrans is updated, which is the maximum cryptoperiod the NIST recommends in SP 800-57 [17] for Data Encryption Keys and Symmetric Authentication Keys.

5 Cost Analysis

In this section, we estimate the cost of implementing the attack described in the previous section. As explained in Sect. 3, the computational complexity is a function of the number of Des encryptions to perform. As this complexity is very high, any small improvement on the time to execute a single Des encryption can result in a substantial time saving. We are therefore seeking the most efficient implementation, hence we ran a performance analysis of Des encryptions on custom hardware as well as desktop computers, and we tried different cryptographic libraries.

Based on the results, it is possible to provide an estimate of the attack's cost. However, it should be noted that we did not implement the attack as it is too expensive given the hardware we had access to.

There are two ways to perform Des encryptions. The first one is using desktop computers, which is quite fast to implement, and the second one is using custom hardware (FPGAs). The latter requires to spend more time on implementation, but is more efficient when executed.

5.1 Performance Analysis of Des Encryptions on Desktop Computers

Method. The experiments have been driven on an HP elite Desk 800 G1 Tower running Ubuntu 14.04 with Linux kernel v3.13. The machine contains eight processors Intel i7-4770 @ 3.40 GHz, each of them possessing four cores. The computer has 15 GB of RAM, and a 4 GB swap partition.

In order to monitor hardware utilisation, Linux perf software is used, and allows to retrieve useful information such as the number of CPU cycles required to finish the program, or the average clock frequency during the program run.

Three different cryptographic libraries of three different programming languages are compared: javax.crypto (Java), PyCrypto (Python), and OpenSSL (C). A parallel program with eight threads handling its share of encryptions is written.

The maximum number of encryptions considered is 2^{28}. Beyond that point, the program fills all the available memory, including the swap, resulting in an intervention from the Linux Out-Of-Memory (OOM) killer, which killed the process. Nevertheless, it has been verified that the programs continue to run if there is more RAM available.

Results. The execution of the C program is found to be the fastest, which can be explained by the fact that C code is directly compiled into machine code. Moreover, the Java Virtual Machine (JVM) ensures that a Java program can be run on every architecture, but adds some complexity; this is why it is slower. Python is even slower due to its interpreted characteristic. Therefore, the cost analysis will only be based on the results found with the C program.

The average clock frequency found is around 3.74 GHz, whereas the clock speed in the vendor specification is said to be 3.4 GHz. This is because Intel processors enter in turbo mode when computations are heavy, which allows them to run slightly faster. In fact, the processor's specification shows that a maximum of 3.90 GHz can be achieved.

These results cannot be used to estimate the performance on another processor model. Even if clock frequency is a good point of comparison, it does not take into account the memory management or other improvements that vendors made on different versions of processors. However, it is possible to compare with processors from the same family. An Intel i7-4770 with a maximum speed of 3.90 GHz has been used for this experiment. It can be compared to the i7-4790K, which is from the family i7-47xx as well. The i7-4790K can run at 4.40 GHz in turbo mode. With a simple rule of three, the average frequency can be approximated to 4.13 GHz. Moreover, the number of CPU cycles found to encrypt 2^{28} 64-bit plaintexts is 6.01×10^{11}, and 7.77 CPUs appear to be used. We can now calculate the encryption rate and find 9.19×10^8 bits/sec.

Distributed Program. In order to parallelise even more the key search, it is desirable to distribute the programs across multiple computers. Doing this will inflate the attack's cost, but also make it more realistic.

5.2   Performance Analysis of Des Encryptions on FPGAs

An FPGA is an integrated circuit to be customised by the user. It consists of programmable logic cells organised in rows and columns that can be interconnected at will, and perform simple operations such as logic gates (e.g. XOR and AND gates) or more complex functions.

One way to make the most of the iterative nature of Des with FPGAs is to build a pipeline. Several works have implemented this sort of version of Des [18–20]. Pipelining is a technique that allows one to overlap the processing of atomic tasks. In the case of Des , as it consists of 16 identical encryption rounds, a 16-stage pipeline is suited for this purpose. Therefore, the 16 blocks can be handled simultaneously, resulting in a throughput increase.

We further consider that the Des algorithm cannot be processed at a clock frequency greater than 300 MHz because even though pipelining increases throughput, it also increases the delay.

Therefore, producing one 64-bit encryption per clock cycle at a clock frequency of 300 MHz gives an encryption rate of 1.92×10^{10} bits/sec, which represents a considerably better efficiency compared to desktop computers.

It is also possible to use several programmable cards in parallel to try more keys per clock cycles. With this technique, the execution time is divided by the number of devices.

5.3   Memory Bandwidth Evaluation

As the memory complexity is also very high, it is necessary to explore which hardware has the greatest transfer rate, i.e. the number of bits that can be read from or written into memory per second.

Today, the most efficient bus that connects host bus adapters to mass storage devices is Serial ATA 3.2 (SATA 3.2), which can achieve a bit rate of 1,969 MB/s, when used with Solid State Drives.

Nevertheless, when implementing the attack on FPGAs, one should think about memory management exhaustively. Due to the massive amount of data being transferred between external drive and programmable card, the attack could trash the computing units, i.e. overwhelmed them by making them process more data transfer than actual computations, resulting in a poor computational efficiency.

5.4   Cost Analysis

The cost is a function of the number of machines n owned by the attacker used to parallelise the key search. The cost analysis is realised on desktop computers and FPGAs, having respectively an encryption rate of 9.19×10^8 bits/sec and 1.92×10^{10} bits/sec according to Sects. 5.2 and 5.1. The amount of time to perform the attack is assumed to be 2 years. Finally, the cost analysis done for 56-bit keys, but also 7-bit ASCII keys, in order to appreciate how important it is to generate random sequences of bits to make the keys rather than choosing it within a given restricted set.

Based on [21], it can be shown that for an attacker running in 2 years, having 2^{50} bytes of memory available and n machines, the probability to recover 3Des keys is the solution of the following optimisation problem, where ER denotes the encryption rate, c_t and c_m the time and the memory complexity:

$$
\begin{cases}
-\min_{c_t, c_m} \left(-\dfrac{2 \times 365 \times 24 \times 3600}{64 \times \frac{2^{c_t}}{n \times ER} + 256 \times \frac{2^{c_m}}{1.97 \times 10^9}} \times \left(\dfrac{1}{1 + 2^{-16}} \right) \right) \\
c_t + c_m = 113 \\
\qquad c_t \geq 57 \\
\qquad c_m \geq 0 \\
\qquad c_m \leq 46 \\
\qquad c_t \leq 113
\end{cases}
\tag{2}
$$

Cost Analysis on Desktop Computers. With desktop computers, the encryption rate is $ER = 9.19 \times 10^8$. Figure 2 shows the evolution of the probability to recover 3Des keys depending on the value of n. For 56-bit keys, the adversary has average luck to recover 3Des keys when $n = 88,000$. When $n = 200,000$, the attacker has full probability of recovering the key (Fig. 3).

The price of one desktop computer capable of this encryption rate is estimated at $525, which raises the cost of this attack to $46,200,000 in terms of computing power. Finally, one 1TB SSD disk is available at the price of $500, hence the total cost for 2^{50} bytes capacity is around $500,000, raising the total cost of the attack at around 47 million dollars.

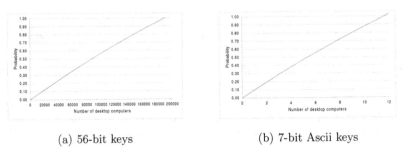

(a) 56-bit keys   (b) 7-bit Ascii keys

Fig. 2. Advantage depending on n desktop computers

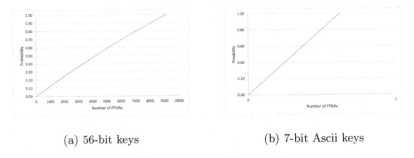

(a) 56-bit keys   (b) 7-bit Ascii keys

Fig. 3. Advantage depending on n FPGAs

For 7-bit ASCII keys, probability of 0.5 is reached for $n = 6$. Hence, computing power cost is \$3,150. Adding the memory cost raises the total cost to \$503,150.

Cost Analysis on FPGAs. In the case of FPGAs, the same reasoning applies, but the encryption rate is $ER = 1.92 \times 10^{10}$. For 56-bit keys, the adversary has average luck to recover the keys when $n = 4,200$. When $n = 9,200$, the attacker has full probability of recovering the key.

The price of one FPGA with this type of requirements (e.g. a Xilinx Virtex-6) is around \$1500. Hence, the total cost of the attack, adding the \$500,000 of memory cost, is 7 million dollars.

For 7-bit ASCII keys, only 1 FPGAs is needed to break the algorithm in 2 years, which implies a total cost of \$501,500.

5.5 Summary of the Costs to Break 3Des

A summary of the costs is provided in Table 1.

This table allows us to conclude that if keys are chosen from a given restricted set (such as 7-bit ASCII), the security of the system is weakened substantially. However, if the keys are really chosen at random with a Cryptographically Secure Pseudo-Random Number Generator, there is not any RKA possible.

Table 1. Cost of breaking 3Des in dollars

	RKA	
	56-bit keys	ASCII-128 keys
FPGAs	$7 m	$501,500
Desktop computers	$47 m	$503,150

6 Conclusion

We have presented an in-depth security assessment of ERTMS from a crypto-graphic point of view, and we have proved that the system is secure as long as basic security measures are implemented, such that the secrecy and dependency of the cryptographic keys are maintained.

We also have introduced a new Related-Key Attack that could be carried out against the system if such security measures are not taken. Albeit ERTMS is not susceptible to cryptographic attacks known in the literature, the railway should consider new generations of cryptographic algorithms such as AES to secure ERTMS and future signalling systems, as computing power is increasing exponentially.

References

1. National Institute of Standards and Technology (NIST): Recommendation for the triple data encryption algorithm (TDEA) block cipher. Technical report (2012)
2. National Institute of Standards and Technology (NIST): Announcing the advanced encryption standard (AES) (2001)
3. National Institute of Standards and Technology (NIST): Data encryption standard (des) (1999)
4. SciEngines: Break Des in less than a single day (2009). http://www.sciengines.com/company/news-a-events/74-des-in-1-day.html
5. Kelsey, J., Schneier, B., Wagner, D.: Key-schedule cryptanalysis of IDEA, G-DES, GOST, SAFER, and triple-DES. In: Koblitz, N. (ed.) CRYPTO 1996. LNCS, vol. 1109, pp. 237–251. Springer, Heidelberg (1996)
6. Merkle, R.C., Hellman, M.E.: On the security of multiple encryption. Commun. ACM **24**(7), 465–467 (1981)
7. Bloomfield, R., Bloomfield, R., Gashi, I., Stroud, R.: How secure is ERTMS? In: Ortmeier, F., Daniel, P. (eds.) SAFECOMP Workshops 2012. LNCS, vol. 7613, pp. 247–258. Springer, Heidelberg (2012)
8. Capra, G.S.: Protecting critical rail infrastructure. Technical report (2006)
9. Baldoni, R. et al.: Critical infrastructure protection: threats, attacks, and counter-measures. Technical report (2014)
10. European Railway Agency: Unisig subset-037, euroradio fis. Technical report (2014)
11. European Railway Agency: Unisig subset-038, offline key management fis. Technical report (2015)

12. National Institute of Standards and Technology (NIST): Recommendation for block cipher modes of operation (2001)
13. European Railway Agency: Subset-114, kmc-etcs entity off-line km fis. Technical report (2015)
14. Menezes, A., Van Oorschot, P.C., Vanstone, S.: Handbook of Applied Cryptography. CRC Press, Boca Raton (1996)
15. Traverso, M.: Presto: interacting with petabytes of data at facebook (2013)
16. Hill, K.: Blueprints of nsa's ridiculously expensive data center in utah suggest it holds less info than thought. Forbes (2013)
17. National Institute of Standards and Technology (NIST): Recommendation for key management - part 1: general (revision 3) (2012)
18. Taherkhani, S., Ever, E., Gemikonakli, O.: Implementation of non-pipelined and pipelined data encryption standard (des) using xilinx virtex-6 fpga technology. In: IEEE 10th International Conference on Computer and Information Technology (CIT 2010), pp. 1257–62, Los Alamitos, CA, USA, Engineering Information Science, Middlesex University, London, United Kingdom. IEEE Computer Society (2010)
19. McLoone, M., McCanny, J.V.: A high performance fpga implementation of des. In: IEEE Workshop on Signal Processing Systems Design and Implementation, SiPS 2000, pp. 374–83, Piscataway, NJ, USA, School of Electrical and Electronics Engineering, Queen's University Belfast, Belfast, UK. IEEE (2000)
20. Teo, P.C., Yusoff, Z.M., Sha'ameri, A.Z.: Implementation of pipelined data encryption standard (des) using altera cpld. In: Intelligent Systems and Technologies for the New Millennium, TENCON Proceedings, vol. 3, pp. 17–21, Piscataway, NJ, USA, Faculty of Electrical Engineering, University of Teknologi Malaysia, Johor Bahru, Malaysia. IEEE (2000)
21. Pépin, F.: A probabilistic framework for 3des to assess railway systems cyber threats (2015)

Systems

Failure Analysis of Chinese Train Control System Level 3 Based on Model Checking

Xiao Han[1(✉)], Tao Tang[1], Jidong Lv[2], and Haifeng Wang[2]

[1] State Key Laboratory of Rail Traffic Control and Safety,
Beijing Jiaotong University, Beijing 100044, China
{hanxiao,ttang,jdlv,hfwang}@bjtu.edu.cn
[2] National Engineering Research Centre of Rail Transportation Operation
and Control System, Beijing Jiaotong University, Beijing 100044, China

Abstract. The complexity of railway control system makes some requirement deficiencies hard to find, which results in system failures. It is essential to locate those deficiencies using logs recorded during failure events. In this paper, a model checking based failure analysis approach was proposed and applied to a case of abnormal emergency brake. First, a system model describing the system requirement and an event model depicting the logs were constructed. Next the compositional model was verified through model checking in UPPAAL which then produced a counterexample trace that describes the system behaviour in the failure event. By analysing this trace, an inadequacy was found in the requirement and a modification strategy was brought up which was formally verified to be effective.

1 Introduction

Chinese Train Control System level 3 (CTCS-3) is a safety-critical distributed computer control system, the failure of which may cause catastrophic accidents. Lots of reasons can lead a CTCS-3 to fail, including hardware faults, software errors, interface malfunctions, or environment factors like EMI etc. Software errors can originate from flawed designs, wrong implementations, improper deployments, or what were concerned in this paper, deficient requirements. Errors or inadequacies in requirements are normally unfolded through V&V process. Validation approaches like review, simulation, or testing is widely adopted in industrial practice for their simplicity and are proved to be effective in some degree. The problem with those validation approaches roots in the complexity of systems where human mind is overwhelmed and completeness is unable to achieve. Verification is mainly about formal verification. Applying formal verification into railway has been studied in [11,13]. The problem with formal verification is a conflict between model size and computational complexity. With the modelling and verification techniques available for now, it is very hard to verify a whole CTCS-3 for its huge scale and complexity. So implemented from a requirement with deficiencies, CTCS-3 may encounter system failures, or worse, contribute to an accident which can't be prevented through reliability measures.

© Springer International Publishing Switzerland 2016
T. Lecomte et al. (Eds.): RSSRail 2016, LNCS 9707, pp. 95–105, 2016.
DOI: 10.1007/978-3-319-33951-1_7

It is then vital to find the requirement deficiencies of CTCS-3 through failure analysis, before a same failure would cause an accident.

There are generally two approaches applicable to software failure analysis, one is software hazard analysis, and another is model checking. Software hazard analysis techniques can be categorized into 3 types. One is structural hazard analysis techniques, such as Software Fault Tree Analysis [9]. One is failure logic modelling methods, such as FPTN [8]. One is fault-injection techniques, such as FSAP/NuSMV-SA platform in [4]. Model checking is a formal verification technique which verifies whether a formal model satisfies certain properties such as safety or liveness. When the property is unsatisfied, a counterexample trace that indicates how the property is violated can be generated automatically. Let *system will not fail* be the property to be verified, then the counterexample trace generated, if any, would indicate how the system can fail. Thus model checking can be used to analyse failure causal reasons or locate faults in software as in [10].

In model checking, a refutation means there are modelling and formulation mistakes or the undesired sequence of events could indeed happen in reality [6]. Furthermore, several traces that lead to a same property violation could exist at the same time, yet only one of them is generated. Thus a counterexample trace generated by model checking could represent (1) an impossible story in reality, (2) a possible sequence of events that didn't happen, or (3) the process of system failure that we want to understand. So failure analysis by checking the system model alone may not necessarily produce the trace that represents the actual sequence of events leading to the failure. The reason behind this, we believe, is neglect of information collected during failure process such as system logs. In this paper, we propose a novel failure analysis method based on model checking which utilizes both system model and system logs.

The rest of the paper is organized as follows: Sect. 2 gives a simple introduction to CTCS-3 and a short review of how CTCS-3 can fail. Section 3 presents the rationale of the method. Section 4 gives a case study of applying this method to a real CTCS-3 failure case. Section 5 concludes this paper with a discussion about this method and a plan for our future work.

2   CTCS-3 and Failure Causes

CTCS-3 is a safety-critical control system dedicated to ensure safe operation of trains in most operation scenarios. In the requirement specification of CTCS-3, 14 operation scenarios in total are given. Equipments in CTCS-3 can be categorized into on-board subsystem and track-side subsystem. The on-board subsystem includes equipments that are installed on a train, like Vital Computer, Track Circuit Receiver, Driver Machine Interface, Juridical Record Unit, etc. It provides a driver necessary information for safe operation while carrying out speed/distance supervision. The safe running of a train in CTCS-3 is controlled by a MA that describes how far and how fast the train can go safely. The on-board subsystem on that train can decide if a MA is violated or not, and if so, some intervention measures, such as an emergency brake, may be initiated. The generation of MA is the main function of track-side subsystem which includes Radio Block Centre (RBC), Balise, Train Control Centre (TCC), Track Circuit (TC) etc.[1] The on-board subsystem and track-side subsystem communicates with each other through a dedicated wireless network called GSM-R.

For the safety-critical nature, failures of CTCS-3 could lead to catastrophic accidents. While CTCS-3 is a very complex system with multiple kinds of equipments and various communications, the complexity extends the scope of failure sources. Many reasons could lead a CTCS-3 to fail, including functional failures of each equipment, and dysfunctional interactions between them. According to [7], faults leading to failures can be categorized into systematic faults and random faults. Systematic faults are caused by human errors in various stages of the system life-cycle, while random faults, particularly random hardware faults, are the results of finite reliability of hardware components. In the perspective of where faults are located, faults can be divided into software errors and hardware faults. Software errors are systematic faults, which are caused by human errors in requirements elicitation and specification, software design, implementation, or deployment. This paper is dedicated to analyse software errors originated from requirement deficiencies.

3   Failure Analysis Based on Model Checking

3.1   System Failure Analysis

When a system fails, it is essential to find the reason for this failure besides bringing system back into normal operation, so the same software error or hardware fault won't result in another system failure, which in certain circumstances will bring about a catastrophic accident. Same system failure may be caused by various reasons, as shown in the fault tree in Fig. 1. Yet there is always only one of those reasons that happened in the real system failure. The objective of system failure analysis is to find this particular reason that happened in deed, in other words, to identify the real propagation path from root reason to system failure (such as the path denoted by solid line in the fault tree in Fig. 1) out of all possible paths. Several intermediate events my exist in the path from root event(s) to top event. Different paths may go through different intermediate events. Thus it is possible to distinguish each root event by intermediate events.[2] In computer systems, logs give clues of which intermediate events happened. So it is possible to identify the real reason by extracting information from logs. Figure 1 describes this methodology. The problems with this methodology are twofold. First, a complete fault tree for a complex system, especially for software is hard to construct. Second, drawing useful information from a mass of raw log files is not easy. Researches are focused on the second problem, as in [5,12], to extract failure-related information from a big load of log files automatically.

---

[1] Interlocking (IL) is a widely used signalling system which works together with CTCS-3 to ensure safety, while not included in it.

[2] It is only possible when each root event has different intermediate event directly connected to it. We will make it an assumption in this paper.

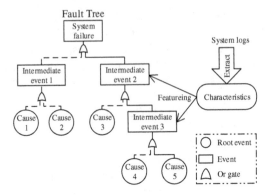

Fig. 1. Failure analysis using FTA.

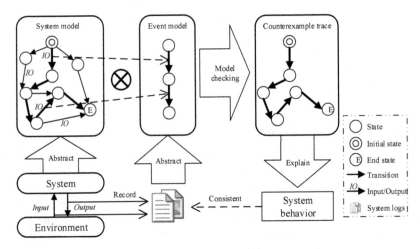

Fig. 2. Failure analysis using model checking.

In this paper, a different methodology was adopted in which we focused on how the behaviour of system evolves into a failure rather than event chains, so log extracting is no more necessary. This methodology is presented in Fig. 2: The system model which is an abstraction of the real system depicts system behaviours, including normal behaviours and abnormal behaviours. The event model is constructed based on logs which record system input/output information. Model checking the product of system model and event model will give a counterexample trace, which indicates how the system can fail while reserves what was recorded in the logs. By explaining this trace, we can obtain the behaviour of the system and understand why the system failed.

CTCS-3 is a real-time system, which means the correctness of the system behaviour depends not only on the logical results of its outputs, but also on the physical time when these results are produced. It is then imperative to describe temporal properties of CTCS-3 in the model. We chose timed automata as the modelling language, definition of which can be found in [1]. The model checking tool used in this paper to verify timed automata is UPPAAL [2] released by Aalborg University and Uppsala University in 1995. Definitions and theorems related to model checking of timed automata can be found in [3], and with no further citations in the rest of this paper.

3.2   Problem Definition and Solution

In this section, we will explain the problem of failure analysis in terms of timed automata, and give a solution to the problem.

Definition 1. *For a timed trace* $\Delta = \delta_1\delta_2...\delta_i... \in L$, *where* $\delta_i = (t_i, a_i)$ *is a timed action meaning event* a_i *takes place at time* t_i, *and* L *is timed language, if there is a function* $S \in L \mapsto L, S(\Delta) = \Delta'$, $\Delta' = \delta_{s_1}\delta_{s_2}...\delta_{s_n}$, *satisfying* $\forall \delta_{s_j}, \exists \delta_i \in \Delta$, *s.t.* $\delta_{s_j} = \delta_i$, *and* $\forall \delta_{s_j} \in \Delta' \wedge j \neq n \to s_j < s_{j+1}$, *then we call this function* S *a **timed trace sampling function** over* Δ.

The purpose of failure analysis then can be described as identifying a timed trace Δ^f, which satisfies:

Property 1. Let $\mathcal{A}$ denotes the timed automata model of system, and ψ the system property indicating the system won't fail, then $\Delta^f \in L(\mathcal{A}) \cap L(\neg\psi)$, and

Property 2. There exists a timed trace sampling function S, that $S(\Delta^f) = \Delta'$, where Δ' represents failure records.

Property 1 indicates that Δ^f should be a behaviour of what system model describes while violating the system property, that is, leading to failure. Timed traces satisfying Property 1 can easily be generated by model checking $\mathcal{A}$ against ψ. Property 2 indicates that Δ^f should describe what actually happened in the system failure. To get a timed trace complying with Property 2, we define a special timed automaton:

Definition 2. *For a timed trace* Δ, *and a timed automaton* $\mathcal{A}$, *if* $\forall\Delta' \in L(\mathcal{A})$, *there exists a timed trace sampling function* S *over* Δ' *that* $S(\Delta') = \Delta$, *then we call* $\mathcal{A}$ *the **event model** of* Δ, *denoted as* $\mathcal{A}_\Delta$.

Theorem 1. *Denote the system model as* $\mathcal{A}_s$, *system property as* ψ, *the timed trace describing failure records as* Δ', *then timed trace* $\Delta \in L(\mathcal{A}_s) \cap L(\neg\psi) \cap L(\mathcal{A}_{\Delta'})$ *satisfies Properties 1 and 2.*

Proof. As $\Delta \in L(\mathcal{A}_s) \cap L(\neg\psi) \cap L(\mathcal{A}_{\Delta'})$, we can easily get $\Delta \in L(\mathcal{A}_s) \cap L(\neg\psi)$, which indicates the satisfaction of Property 1. According to Definition 2, $\Delta \in L(\mathcal{A}_{\Delta'})$ indicates that there exists a timed trace sampling function S, that $S(\Delta) = \Delta'$, then Property 2 is satisfied.   □

Theorem 1 gives us a solution to the problem of identifying a timed trace satisfying Properties 1 and 2, by model checking the compositional model $\mathcal{A} \times \mathcal{A}_{\Delta'}$ against ψ, and the counterexample trace generated, if exists, is the result.

3.3 Failure Event Model

One key problem in failure analysis according to the approach proposed above is the construction of event model defined in Definition 2. In this section ,we will present a template of event model, based on which one can construct an event model given a timed trace Δ' representing the failure records.

If $\Delta' = \delta_1'\delta_2'...\delta_i'...\delta_n'$, where $\delta_i' = (t_i, a_i)$, then we construct a timed automaton $\mathcal{A}$ as:

$$l_0 \xrightarrow{x=x_1,a_1,x:=0} l_1... \xrightarrow{x=t_i-t_{i-1},a_i,x:=0} l_i... \xrightarrow{x=t_n-t_{n-1},a_n,x:=0} l_n$$

where only l_n is accepted by $\mathcal{A}$, then $\mathcal{A}$ is the event model of $\mathcal{A}$.

Proof. From the construction of $\mathcal{A}$, we can see that once $\mathcal{A}$ is in l_n, only time elapse is possible. That is, $\forall \Delta \in L(\mathcal{A}), \Delta = \delta_1\delta_2..., \exists m$, s.t. $\forall j \geq m, \delta_j = \langle l_n, u \rangle$, where u is any clock assignment. Any run of $\mathcal{A}$ can be expressed as follows:

$$\langle l_0, 0 \rangle \xrightarrow{d_1^0} \langle l_0, d_1^0 \rangle \xrightarrow{d_2^0} \langle l_0, d_1^0 + d_2^0 \rangle... \xrightarrow{a_1}$$

$$\langle l_1, 0 \rangle \xrightarrow{d_1^1} \langle l_1, d_1^1 \rangle \xrightarrow{d_2^1} \langle l_1, d_1^1 + d_2^1 \rangle... \xrightarrow{a_2}$$

$$...$$

$$\langle l_n, 0 \rangle \xrightarrow{d_1^n} \langle l_n, d_1^n \rangle \xrightarrow{d_2^n} \langle l_n, d_1^n + d_2^n \rangle...$$

where $\sum d_i^j = t_{t+1} - t_i, i < n, t_0 = 0$.

It is obvious that the state before transition $\xrightarrow{a_k}$, where $k \leq n$, in the run of $\mathcal{A}$ is $\langle l_{k-1}, t_k - t_{k-1} \rangle$. Then we can infer that $\forall \Delta \in L(\mathcal{A}), \forall k \leq n$, there is a timed action $(\sum_{j=1}^{k} t_j - t_{j-1}, a_k)$ in Δ. Then we can define a timed trace sampling function S over Δ, that:

$$S(\Delta) = (\sum_{j=1}^{1} t_j - t_{j-1}, a_1)...(\sum_{j=1}^{n} t_j - t_{j-1}, a_n)$$

As $\sum_{j=1}^{k} t_j - t_{j-1} = t_k - t_0 = t_k$, then we get:

$$S(\Delta) = (t_1, a_1)(t_2, a_2)...(t_n, a_n) = \Delta'$$

which means $\mathcal{A}$ is the event model of Δ'.   □

With log files exported from failure-involved equipments, we can translate each selected record $(t, msg, args)$, where t is the time when communication took place, msg stands for the message transferred during the communication, and $args$ includes arguments for this message, into a timed action (t', a'), where t' is the relative time in model corresponding to t, and a' is the action composed of a synchronization representing msg and several guarding conditions made according to $args$. Concatenating those timed actions translated from selected records in time order, a timed trace Δ' representing the failure records is then obtained. Then the failure event model can be constructed according to the proposed template as depicted above.

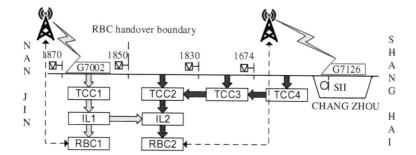

Fig. 3. A Snapshot before failure.

4   Case Study

4.1   Failure Event Description

In 2012, a high-speed passenger-rail train G7126 on a trip from Shanghai to Nan-jin initiated an emergency brake which should never happened. Figure 3 shows a snapshot of G7126, its preceding G7002, and other related equipments before this failure happened. Several equipments including RBCs, TCCs, ILs, and on-board subsystems were involved, and scenarios like RBC handover, moving authority were covered in this failure. The flow of track information is shown in Fig. 3 as arrows. The state of a track that whether there is a train occupying it is detected by a TC installed along this track. A TCC connected with the TC receives track state and passes it to IL directly or through other TCCs. The TC is informed with the states of all the tracks in its area, and sends Signal Authority (SA) which is the state variation of certain track in essence to the RBC connected to it. The RBC then calculates a MA based the SA received from IL. The RBC inside a RBC handover boundary like RBC2 in Fig. 3 must know the states of some tracks that are outside of the boundary, to determine if it is possible to extend the MA to certain point outside of the boundary, so that the train can pass the boundary without a stop or deceleration. The state of tracks outside of the boundary are transferred from the IL outside to the IL inside[3]. Communications between RBCs and trains are also shown in Fig. 3, where a RBC sends MA it calculates to the train in its region and the train sends MA acknowledgement and its position detected by on-board sensors back to the RBC.

4.2   Modelling

To understand why G7126 initiated an emergency brake, system model should be constructed first. Objects or equipments considered in our system model include two trains G7126 and G7002, IL1 inside of the boundary, IL2 and RBC2 outside of the boundary, tracks, and TCCs modelled as communication components.

---

[3] Other solutions are possible, like the one suggested in CTCS-3 technical scheme that track state information is transferred though RBCs.

Table 1. Failure records and its mappings to system model

Time	Message	Arguments	Synchronization	Assignments	Duration
07:55:43	SA-TR	1850	receive-SA?	received-SA.Type=TR and received-SA.section=3	1
07:55:44	SA-USED	1870	receive-SA?	received-SA.Type=USED and received-SA.section=4	13
07:55:57	SMA	1850	send-MA!	sent-MA.Type=SMA and sent-MA.End=3	2
07:55:59	SA-USED	1674	receive-SA?	received-SA.Type=USED and received-SA.section=1	1
07:56:00	UEM	-	send-MA!	sent-MA.Type=UEM	-

We defined 6 sections in our model numbered from 0 to 5. The RBC handover boundary is located between Sects. 3 and 4. G7002 is in Sect. 3 and G7126 is in section 0 initially.

Interlocking models: Two ILs are included in our model, namely IL1 and IL2. IL1 is modelled as an automaton receiving variations in state of tracks outside of RBC handover boundary and sending them to IL2. IL2 is modelled as 3 automata which are similar with IL1 in that they receive track state variations and send SA. The differences are that they send SA to RBC2 and two of them receive variations in state of tracks that are inside of handover boundary caused by G7002 and G7126 respectively, while the last one communicates with IL1 and receives information from it.

Train models: Two trains are modelled: the failed train G7126 and its preceding G7002. G7126 is modelled by two automata. One describes the moving of G7126 and sends track state variations to ILs, and the other describes the communication between the on-board subsystem on G7126 with RBC2. For 7002, only the moving part is modelled.

RBC model: From the information flow in Fig. 3, we can see that RBC1 couldn't influence the behaviour of G7126 in any sense, so only RBC2 needs to be modelled. RBC2 is modelled as an automaton which has functions as follows: receiving and updating the position of trains, receiving SA and calculating MA based on the position of trains and SA, and then sending MA to trains, and receiving MA acknowledgement.

Communication models: All the communications involved are modelled as communication components automata as implementations of a communication template. The main purpose of communication models are to capture communication delays which may have big influences on the behaviour of CTCS-3.

Event model: For simplicity, we selected several crucial records from the raw log files from RBC2 manually and mapped those records to the system model as shown in Table 1. An event model P, as shown in Fig. 4 was constructed based on mappings of those records.

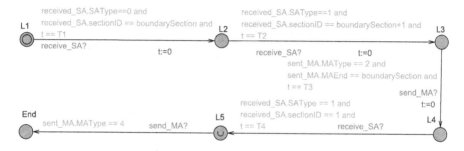

Fig. 4. Event model.

4.3 Failure Cause Analysis

Model checking the compositional model against property *A[] not P.End* in UPPAAL gave us a counterexample trace displayed in the simulator. By analysing this timed trace, we managed to understand what happened that caused G7126 to initiate an abnormal emergency brake:

- At 07:55:38, the rear end of G7002 passed RBC handover boundary.
- At 07:55:43, clearance of section 1830→1850 was received by RBC2. At that moment, RBC2 had not received occupation of section 1850→1870 by G7002 as the long communication delay, so it thought section 1830→1850 was clear and sent to G7126 an EMA extending MA to some place after 1870.
- 07:55:44, RBC2 finally received the occupation of 1850→1870. In the MA generation algorithm, RBC2 was supposed to wait for 13 seconds before calculating MA as section 1850→1870 was the first section outside of boundary.
- 07:55:57, RBC2 sent a SMA which commanded G7126 to stop before 1850 after expiration of 13 s.
- 07:55:59, RBC2 received the occupation of section SII→1674 by G7126. Because of communication delay, the latest position of G7126 that RBC2 received was still before SII, so RBC2 was supposed to send a CEM[4] to G7126, and G7126 was supposed to ignore it. But instead, RBC2 sent an UEM to G7126 because the acknowledgement of the last SMA it sent had not been received and together with a possible CEM to send made RBC2 thought there could be some problems.

4.4 Modification

From the scenario analysed above, we can see that the reason for this failure event is that, RBC2 thought the section 1850→1870 was clear which was not the case during 07:55:43 and 07:55:44 and extended MA. False cognition of state of tracks by RBC2 is caused by communication delays, which were not considered in the requirement of CTCS-3 in detail. To prevent this requirement inadequacy from

---

[4] When a train receives a CEM, it will first check if it has already passed the end of this CEM, then initiate an emergency brake if not, or ignore this CEM otherwise.

resulting in another system failure, a modification was brought up. The RBC was added a function called delayed clearance, that is, after a RBC receives a section-clear message, it should wait for some time before it calculates a new MA according to it. The modified model was verified against the property *A[] not Train2.EMBrake* which means G7126 should never initiate an emergency brake in UPPAAL, and passed.

5   Conclusion

In this paper, a failure analysis approach using failure records based on model checking was proposed and applied to a case study of CTCS-3. We found that with a well constructed system model and carefully selected failure records, it is possible to reproduce the system behaviour leading the analysed failure which can then be used to find requirement deficiencies. Furthermore, compared with conventional model checking, our method focused our modelling effort on certain part of the system instead of the whole system, leading to a relatively smaller and more verifiable model. Yet a distance between the scalability of this method and industrial practice still remains. Another problem we realized with this method concerns the selection of failure records. The records selected actually represents what would be considered in failure analysis, so the more records selected, the more accurate analysis result would be. But more records means more modelling effort and computation burden. The trade-off between accuracy and cost is more art than accurate science.

Our next job is to explore the depth and scope of this approach that can be applied. As the assumption we made in the fault tree based approach that all root events have different intermediate events connected to them is not always the case, some failure causes may not be distinguishable based solely on failure records. Then a formal description of the characteristics that the system model has as far as identifying failure is concerned should be defined, as the basis of our further discussion. Still, a more realistic and complex case study should be carried out to explore the limitations of this approach.

Acknowledgement. The work has been supported mainly by the Nation Natural Science Foundation of China (Grant No. 61304185, U1434209), and the National Program on Key Basic Research Project (973 Program) (Grant No. 2014CB340700).

References

1. Alur, R., Dill, D.: Automata for modeling real-time systems. In: Paterson, M. (ed.) ICALP 1990. LNCS, vol. 443, pp. 322–335. Springer, Heidelberg (1990)
2. Bengtsson, J., Larsen, K., Larsson, F., Pettersson, P., Yi, W.: UPPAAL a tool suite for automatic verification of real-time systems. In: Alur, R., Sontag, E.D., Henzinger, T.A. (eds.) HS 1995. LNCS, vol. 1066, pp. 232–243. Springer, Heidelberg (1996)

3. Bengtsson, J.E., Yi, W.: Timed automata: semantics, algorithms and tools. In: Desel, J., Reisig, W., Rozenberg, G. (eds.) Lectures on Concurrency and Petri Nets. LNCS, vol. 3098, pp. 87–124. Springer, Heidelberg (2004)
4. Bozzano, M., Villafiorita, A.: The fsap/nusmv-sa safety analysis platform. Int. J. Softw. Tools Technol. Transf. **9**(1), 5–24 (2007)
5. Chuah, E., Kuo, S.h., Hiew, P., Tjhi, W.C., Lee, G., Hammond, J., Michalewicz, M.T., Hung, T., Browne, J.C.: Diagnosing the root-causes of failures from cluster log files. In: 2010 International Conference on High Performance Computing (HiPC), pp. 1–10. IEEE (2010)
6. Clarke, E.M., Grumberg, O., Peled, D.: Model Checking. MIT Press, Cambridge (1999)
7. En, N.C.: 50129: Railway application-communications, signaling and processing systems-safety related electronic systems for signaling. British Standards (2003)
8. Fenelon, P., McDermid, J.A.: New directions in software safety: Causal modelling as an aid to integration. In: Workshop on Safety Case Construction, York, March 1994. Citeseer (1992)
9. Leveson, N.G., Harvey, P.R.: Software fault tree analysis. J. Syst. Softw. **3**(2), 173–181 (1983)
10. Ming, L.: Fault Location Research Based on Model Checking. Master's thesis, Central China Normal University (2010)
11. Platzer, A., Quesel, J.-D.: European train control system: a case study in formal verification. In: Breitman, K., Cavalcanti, A. (eds.) ICFEM 2009. LNCS, vol. 5885, pp. 246–265. Springer, Heidelberg (2009)
12. Stearley, J.: Towards informatic analysis of syslogs. In: 2004 IEEE International Conference on Cluster Computing, pp. 309–318. IEEE (2004)
13. Zou, L., Lv, J., Wang, S., Zhan, N., Tang, T., Yuan, L., Liu, Y.: Verifying chinese train control system under a combined scenario by theorem proving. In: Cohen, E., Rybalchenko, A. (eds.) VSTTE 2013. LNCS, vol. 8164, pp. 262–280. Springer, Heidelberg (2014)

Correct Formalization of Requirement Specifications: A V-Model for Building Formal Models

Marco Filax[✉], Tim Gonschorek, and Frank Ortmeier

Chair of Software Engineering, Otto-von-Guericke Universität Magdeburg, Magdeburg, Germany
{marco.filax,tim.gonschorek,frank.ortmeier}@ovgu.de

Abstract. In recent years, formal methods have become an important approach to ensure the correct function of complex hardware and software systems. Many standards for safety critical systems recommend or even require the use of formal methods. However, building a formal model for a given specification is challenging. This is, because verification results must be considered with respect to the validity of the model.

This leads to the question: "Did I build the right model?". For system development the analogous question "Did I build the right system?". This is often answered with requirements traceability through the whole development cycle. For formal verification this question often remains unanswered.

The standard model, which is used in development of safety critical applications is the V-model. The core idea is to define tests for each phase during system development. In this paper, we propose an approach - analogously to the V-model for development - which ensures correctness of the formal model with respect to requirements. We will illustrate the approach on a small example from the railways domain.

Keywords: Formal modelling process · Requirements traceability · System verification · Railway system verification

1 Introduction

Reliability, Availability, Maintainability and Safety are important aspects of the development of railway transportation systems. But, the more complex the system gets the harder it becomes to verify, often by hand, whether a system meets its given specification. Since modern systems are too complex to get verified and validated by hand, especially for the safety critical parts, formal verification comes into the focus. Moreover, formal verification techniques are highly recommended in standards, like the EN 50129 [7]. However, developing a formal model which is a sufficient representation of the real system, is a quite challenging task. It is not only to build the model, but to ensure that the formal models meets all requirements, i.e., is a representative projection of the system-to-build – especially in front of some governmental certification authority.

© Springer International Publishing Switzerland 2016
T. Lecomte et al. (Eds.): RSSRail 2016, LNCS 9707, pp. 106–122, 2016.
DOI: 10.1007/978-3-319-33951-1_8

The goal of this paper is to propose a development approach that simplifies the application of formal methods in the development of safety critical systems in general, but in special in the development of railway systems. The whole process had been determined in cooperation with the German Federal Railway Authority[1] and an independent and certified appraiser for the rail domain.

To overcome the difficulty of building the correct formal model, we focus on the traceability of all requirements to their formal realization, i.e., as for the real system, it shall be possible to trace each formal model element to its original requirement. Moreover, we derive additional acceptance and system tests from the different development phases and present how they can be verified with the help of model checking [11] techniques. In the scope of this paper, we concentrate on the verification of system safety requirements. However, with the help of the formal model, other reliability and availability measures, e.g., Fault Tree Analysis or Failure Mode Effects Analysis, can be executed.

Unfortunately, domain experts are often unfamiliar with formal verification languages and techniques. Therefore, we use our Verification Environment for Critical Systems (VECS[2]) [17], aiming to simplify the application of formal methods, which implements an import interface to the more popular Unified Modeling Language (UML). For the life-cycle pattern, we propose a process inspired by the established V-model. Project specific variations of the V-model have already been applied successfully in a range of different software projects and they all share the prominent V-shape. In 1984 Boehm introduced the characteristic V-shape [1]. However, it still symbolizes a linear project progression. It is divided into two branches: the left branch symbolizes exploratory and design tasks whereas the right branch represents verification and validation tasks. The methodology does not require a specific (formal) implementation language. It rather specifies what a product describes and recommends methods for the production [3] and thus can be used to develop a formal model. Further, it helps to ensure the traceability throughout the whole process.

The paper is structured as follows: Sect. 2 gives a short overview of related works from other authors. In Sect. 3 we present the proposed approach ensuring the correct formalization of large requirement sets while preserving traceability. Section 4 reports our experiences made with the proposed process while verifying a real world spot transmission based train breaking system. In the end, we conclude our paper in Sect. 5.

2   Related Work

A lot of work has been done for formalizing a set of requirements using UML as an intermediate language. Typically, these approaches cover the extraction and formalization of a semi-formal given architecture [2,4,16,19]. Some approaches consider the extraction of behavior, denoted as state machines, in order to generate a formal model from UML [12,20–22,24,27]. However, the execution semantics of state machines in UML is ambiguous [14]. Snook and Butler proposed an

---

[1] http://www.eba.bund.de.
[2] http://cse.cs.ovgu.de/vecs.

approach to translate architectural and behavioral UML entities into B [24]. The authors propose to develop a formal model from classes and their relation. Further, they require a complete behavioral description in UML. Utilizing classes requires the definition of a detailed architecture derived only from the set of requirements. Defining a system in this degree of detail requires a lot of insight in the developed system inappropriate for requirement analysis. The authors also propose to translate contents of a package into a single formal component, which we think is unsuitable for larger requirement specifications.

Brill et al. use the V-model in order to generate a formal model, but developed as state charts, in particular statemate [3]. In contrast to our approach, they propose to use live sequence charts derived in earlier and refined in later phases in order to "aid in debugging" the formal model. Although not proposed, their approach can be extended to be similar to ours. This is, because the methodology to use commonly known behavior descriptions in order to proof the feasibility of the formal model is shared. In contrast to our approach they utilize send and receive events in order to express interfaces between components. Thus, their approach does not feature parameters for operations - vital in almost every state-of-the-art programming language. This means, that their approach cannot be used to validate whether the architecture of the model is feasible.

Other approaches verify the feasibility of scenarios described in a SRS [25]. The authors propose to refine scenarios, manually extracted from the requirements, with sequences. Every sequence shall then be translated into a temporal logic formula. A model checker can compute whether the specification holds for a specific model. The authors do not convincingly demonstrate how architecture and behavior of the formal model are developed nor emphasize the traceability between model and requirements in their approach. Further, the computation of witnesses in order to support reviews through domain experts is not covered. However, we think such witnesses are important for the proposed approach as the formal model can be erroneous and witnesses can serve as provable example paths in the models state space, emphasizing the requirement coherence.

Carnevali et al. proposed a methodology to integrate preemptive time petri nets into a given software development cycle [5]. They utilized a V-model issued by the German Federal Administration for software development, maintenance and modification. However, they did not describe the integration in a semi-formal description language, such that the traceability of requirements through the hole process life cycle is not emphasized. As a result, a reviewing process of domain experts which are typically not familiar with timed petri nets is required.

3   A Process for Building Formal Models "right"

Building a formal model is a challenging task. It typically takes numerous iterations until one is satisfied with the model. In each iteration some unwanted behavior is removed, extra functionality is added and/or inconsistencies are eliminated. In contrast to unstructured modeling, we propose a structured process, inspired by the V-model, which ensures the coherence of the formal model and

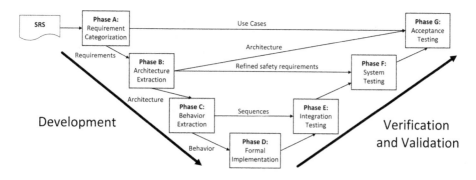

Fig. 1. The adapted V-model for developing a traceable, complete, consistent and correct formal model.

its informal SRS by preserving the traceability between elements in the formal model and their origin. The core idea is – like in the system development model – to define different phases of the modeling process and use state as well as sequence acceptance criteria, test properties or hierarchically analysis questions for validating the model (cf. Sects. 3.5, 3.6 and 3.7).

Figure 1 illustrates the proposed process. All in all, the proposed process consists of seven consecutive phases (Phase A - Phase G). As starting point, we assume some informal specifications to be given, mainly written system requirements or additional documents, e.g., some sketched system architecture, specifications of subcomponents, failure mode specifications or other safety relevant documents.

In the following, we give a more detailed description of the different phases. For a better understanding, we illustrate each phase with a small example from a real world case study, issued by the Federal Railway Authority of Germany. This is a standard protection system in German railroads: the *"Punktförmige Zugbeeinflussung" (PZB[3])* – a spot transmission based train braking system. The informal specification consists of a 46 paged document, containing text, graphics and tables. Altogether, this results in 777 requirements and a formal model with a state space of approx. $5,8 * 10^{24}$ states[4].

3.1 Phase A: Requirement Categorization

The goal of this phase is to prepare the informal text such that it can be better processed by the following phases. Therefore, the SRS is divided into a set of atomic and indexable text fragments. Further, the atomic fragments are categorized to determine their semantics for the following process phases. For example, a requirement categorized as architecture fragment is proposed to be used in connection with the architecture modeling (cf. Sect. 3.2). According to the projects

---

[3] https://cse.cs.ovgu.de/vecs/index.php/techniques/examples/17-casestudies/25-pzb-achievements.

[4] Worst case approximation by multiplying all possible state variable values.

needs one can choose different requirement patterns. In our developed case studies, we found an adoption of the pattern [15] originally defined by Cimatti et al. [8] most applicable for our process. This pattern defines eight different categories for functional requirement fragments. Every category is defined by a condition rule (shown in Table 1) supporting the mapping of fragment and category. Unfortunately, this categorization has to be done manually. This is the case, because processing informal requirements, written without given rules, is, even for humans, a challenging task. Especially, since the mapping of the fragments is not unique. Of course, it is possible that one fragment can be responsible for the architecture (e.g. defining a required method) as well as for some system state behavior (the method sets a specific value). However, the benefit of having ordered requirements, that can be mapped to the different design stages, make it easier to get an overview of the set of requirements. This preponderates the effort of categorizing each requirement fragment by hand.

Table 1. Functional requirement categories adopted from Cimatti et al. [8].

Category	Condition
Glossary requirement	Does the text fragment define a specific concept of the domain?
Architecture requirement	Does the requirement introduce some system's modules and describe how they interact?
State requirement	Does the requirement describe the steps a particular module performs or the states where a module might be in?
Communication requirement	Does the requirement describe messages modules exchange?
Property requirement	Does the requirement describe expected properties of the domain or constraints of the system-to-be?
User requirement	Does the requirement describe actions or constraints which have to be considered, satisfied or performed by the user?
Safety requirement	Does the requirement describe necessary safety constraints?
Annotation	Is the text fragment a note that does not add any information about the ontology or the behavior of the specified system?

We illustrate this phase with a subset of requirements taken from the PZB (Table 2). Requirement PZB1 does not provide any new information and thus is an annotation. PZB2 and PZB3 introduce two different modules, thus they are architecture fragments. PZB4 defines a message being issued by the system's modules and is a communication requirement. PZB5 gives further information on the methods issued in PZB4. PZB6 describes interaction with a surrounding

Table 2. Excerpt of requirements taken from the case study.

ID	Requirement	Category
PZB1	The PZB is a train protection system developed in Germany.	Annotation
PZB2	The system relies on onboard transmitter coils with different frequiencies.	Architecture requirement
PZB3	On the *trackside* different passive tuned *inductors* are installed.	Architecture requirement
PZB4	If a trackside inductor is passed the active *onboard transmitter coil* induces a voltage.	Communication requirement
PZB5	Three frequencies, which can be induced by the *magnets*, have to be distinguished: 1000 Hz, 500 Hz, 2000 Hz.	Property requirement
PZB6	Trackside inductors can be deactivated or activated depending on the signal.	User requirement
PZB7	If the frequencies match, an oscillation is generated in the trackside inductor resulting in an onboard voltage drop indicating an overrun.	State requirement
PZB8	Depending on the transited inductor's frequency different actions have to be issued.	Safety requirement
PZB9	2. The Indusi	Glossary requirement

system: the signal. Here, we consider the signal as an external actor and thus consider it as an user interaction. PZB7 describes the steps a trackside inductor has to perform and thus is a state requirement. PZB8 states that specific actions have to be triggered – relevant for the overall systems safety – meaning an overrun should not be missed and thus, is a safety requirement. PZB9, a section heading, introduces a concept of the domain and therefore is categorized as a glossary fragment.

3.2   Phase B: Architecture Extraction

Typically, functional requirements contain information about system modules and surrounding systems. Their direct formalization, however, is error-prone, as natural language is ambiguous. Thus, we propose to translate informal text into an intermediate language: UML [23]. This is, because UML, as a de facto standard, has a broad audience ensuring that domain experts not familiar with formal verification methods are able to understand basic architecture and in later phases intended behavior (cf. Sect. 3.3) of the formal model. Further, it offers the possibility to derive the architecture of the actual implementation.

In order to represent an architecture, UML offers a variety of elements. We restrict ourselves to components, ports and interfaces in order to define the high-level architecture. This is, because elaborate elements like classes are designed to reflect implementational aspects. Formal models typically behave differently. Hence, to be able to define a proper transformation from UML into a more formal representation, we need to define the used subset of UML elements.

Definition 1 (Component). *Components in UML describe hierarchically ordered units within a system or subsystem [23]. C is the set of a all components defined by the given requirements. A single component $c_i \in C$ is a tuple $c_i = \langle n_i, P_i, C_{Sub_i} \rangle$ with an identifier n_i, a set of ports P_i and a set of subcomponents C_{Sub_i}.*

Further, we define that $c_i \notin C_{Sub_i}$. In order support the interaction of different components, we need to define interfaces. I is the set of all interfaces defined by the requirement specification in specific: also derived from architectural requirements.

Definition 2 (Interface). *An interface $i_j \in I$ is a declaration of a set of coherent public features and obligations [23]. It is a tuple $i_j = \langle n_j, A_j, O_j \rangle$ with an identifier n_j, a set of attributes $A_j \in A$ where an attribute $a_k = \langle n_k, t_k \rangle$ is a tuple with an identifier n_k, a type t_k and a set of operations $O_j \in O$. An operation is a tuple $o_l = \langle n_l, t_l, PAR_l \rangle$ with an identifier n_l, a type t_l and a set of parameters PAR_l where every parameter par_l is a tuple $par_m = \langle n_m, t_m \rangle$ with an identifier n_m and a type t_m.*

Components can either provide or require an interfaces, which is exposed through a port.

Definition 3 (Port). *A port $p_l \in P$ is a tuple $p = \langle n, i, type \rangle$ with an identifier n, an interface i and the type $\in \{provides, requires\}$.*

Further, we define a function **provides** : $P \to (I \cup \bot)$ mapping a port to exactly one interface:

$$\langle n, i, type \rangle \mapsto \begin{cases} i & \text{iff } type = provides \\ \bot & \text{iff } type = requires \end{cases}. \tag{1}$$

Analogously, **requires** : $P \to (I \cup \bot)$ is defined as

$$\langle n, i, type \rangle \mapsto \begin{cases} i & \text{iff } type = requires \\ \bot & \text{iff } type = provides \end{cases}. \tag{2}$$

Multiple components shall be assembled using their shared boundary: the interface exposed through a port.

Definition 4 (Assembly). *An assembly is a tuple assembly $= \langle P, P \rangle$ where*

$$(p_1, p_2) \in assembly \implies requires(p_1) = provides(p_2) \wedge \\ provides(p_1) = requires(p_2) = \bot. \tag{3}$$

All UML elements must be manually derived from the requirements. The categorization of requirements (cf. Phase A) allows to define components much more systematically. Components are typically derived from architecture or glossary requirements. Interfaces and methods shall be extracted from property requirements. We illustrate the proposed approach with the running example. The architecture in Fig. 2 has been derived from the requirements in Table 2. The three different components are derived from the glossary and architecture requirements PZB2, PZB3 and PZB9 namely *trackside inductors* (ti), *onboard transmitter coils* (otc) and *indusi*. PZB5 was used to derive the interfaces *magnet* and *transit*. Further, ports needed to be specified, i.e. *inductors* requiring *magnet* and *coils* providing *magnet*. Both components *ti* and *otc* interchange information, thus an assembly connector is denoted to visualize this information. Analogously, the information has been modeled for *otc* and *indusi*. In order to ensure traceability all requirements had been linked to their UML element as shown in Fig. 2.

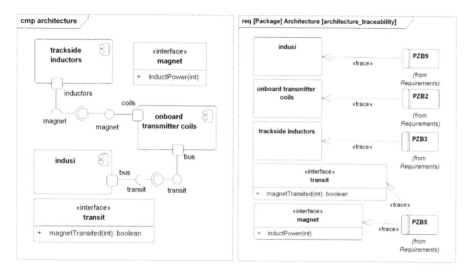

Fig. 2. Example architecture derived from the requirements of the real world case study defined in Table 2.

During this phase, we also refine the requirements that are important for the system testing phase. Safety requirements shall be used in context with the architecture. In order to refine the requirements we propose to use a formal specification language, e.g. linear temporal logic [13]. But the actual formalization depends on the used model checker. An example from the running example, namely for requirement PZB8, is given in Sect. 3.6.

3.3 Phase C: Behavior Extraction

In this step, the intended system behavior is modeled. This is, of course, done with respect to the architecture modeled in the previous step. Often the behavior in the SRS is not specified completely, i.e., some parts are free to be designed by the modeler in the way that no requirements are not violated. We propose to translate communication requirements into sequences, as a sequence is intended to represent some excerpt of the complete behavior.

Definition 5 (Sequence). *A sequence is a tuple $seq_m = \langle n_m, C_m, M_m \rangle$ where n_m is its identifier, $C_m \in C$ a finite set of components and a finite set of messages $M_m \in M$.*

Each sequence describes some communication between different modules specified as messages [23].

Definition 6 (Message). *A message $m = \langle source, target, o, val, v, index \rangle$ is a tuple with a source $\in C_m$ and a target $\in C_m$ representing the origin and destination component of the message m. Further, the tuple consists of a operation o. Each operation o must be discrete, meaning each parameter $par_o \in o$ shall be valued. This is expressed through the function $val : PAR_o \to V$, which labels every parameter with a concrete value with respect to its type. v is the return value of the operation and index sorts all messages of a sequence seq.*

An example sequence is given in Fig. 3, it depicts the behavior described in PZB4. Three actors are imported from the architecture: *ti, otc* and *indusi. indusi* checks whether a 2000 Hz magnet has been overrun (cf. *magnetTransited(2000)*)

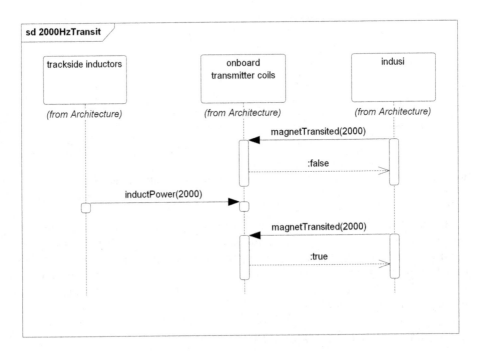

Fig. 3. An example sequence derived from the requirement PZB4: If a trackside inductor is passed the active onboard transmitter coil induces a voltage.

or not. Every time a voltage is inducted from *ti* into *otc* an overrun shall be symbolized. The exchanged messages utilize operation defined in the architecture shown in Fig. 2.

3.4   Phase D: Formal Implementation

During this phase the formal model is implemented. In order to ensure traceability, we propose to generate a formal skeleton from the UML model which had been build from the requirements. Thereby, we retain the option to later use specifications, automatically generated from the corresponding UML sequences, to build integration tests (see Sect. 3.5). Further, it is possible to provide traceability links from the formal implementation tool to the corresponding requirement. However, the modeler has to complete the formal model manually by defining the complete behavior, i.e., modeling all necessary state variables and transition rules.

Definition 7 (Formal Model). *We define a formal model fm as a tuple $fm = \langle FC, SPEC \rangle$ of a finite set of formal components FC and a finite set of formal specifications $SPEC$.*

Definition 8 (Formal Component). *A formal component $fc \in FC$ is tuple $fc = \langle n, V, T, F, FC_{Sub} \rangle$ where n is the name, V is a finite set of state variables and a set of transition rules T. FC_{Sub_p} is the set of subcomponents in fc_p where $\forall fc_p \in FC : fc_p \notin FC_{Sub_p}$. F is a set of formulae, whereas a formula $f = \langle n, t, prop \rangle$ is a tuple with an identifier n, a type t and a proposition $prop$. Thus, a formula is a stateless, parameter-free, typed and named expression that commonly is an abbreviation for conditions.*

Using formal components and formulae, we are able to define a translation from the previous defined UML subset (cf. Sect. 3.2) into a formal model fm. In order to translate the architecture, every component $c \in C$ has to be transformed into a formal component fc. We define a translation function $transComp : C \to FC$ with

$$\langle n, P, C_{Sub} \rangle \mapsto \langle n, \bot, \bot, \bot, \{transC(C_{Sub}) \cup transP(P)\} \rangle. \tag{4}$$

It generates for every component $c \in C$ a formal component fc with the same identifier. Further, it recursively invokes the translation of every subcomponent in C_{Sub}. Note that state variables and transition cannot be generated as the architecture does not contain a behavioral definition.

Every port in c has to be translated using $transP : P \to FC$ with

$$\langle n, i, t \rangle \mapsto \langle n, \bot, \bot, transI(i), \bot \rangle. \tag{5}$$

This generates a new formal component for each port with the same identifier. Further, it invokes the translation $transI$ (cf. Eq. 6) for the interface. It returns the formalization of an interface provided or required by the port. The function $transI : I \mapsto F$ translates an interface into a set of formulae where

$$\langle n, A, O \rangle \mapsto \{transA(A) \cup transO(O)\}. \tag{6}$$

The formalization of an attribute is specified by $transA : A \rightarrow F$, whereas

$$\langle n, t \rangle \mapsto \langle n, t, \bot \rangle. \tag{7}$$

It transforms an attribute with name and type into a formula with the same name and type. The proposition is empty, because its value is not defined by the attribute.

A given operation is translated into a set of formulae with $transO : O \rightarrow F$. With the '.' operator, we access an attribute of the object, e.g., $par_i.type$ access the $type$ of parameter par_i.

$$\langle n, t, PAR \rangle \mapsto \{\langle n_{call}, bool, \bot \rangle, \langle n_{par_i}, par_i.type, \bot \rangle, ..., \\ \langle n_{par_j}, par_j.type, \bot \rangle, \langle n_{return}, t, \bot \rangle\}. \tag{8}$$

Every operation is translated into a formula representing the method call, a formulae for every parameter and a formula representing the return. Note that the propositions cannot be generated as the complete intended behavior is not defined in UML. Thus, the propositions have to be denoted manually.

Applying these translation rules to the UML model generates a formal model with multiple components and formulae. Until now, assemblies have not been considered. It can be done automatically by linking the call, parameter and return formulae in the code of the formal model. An interface provided by a port exposes methods to other components. Its methods must react on external input and provide feasible return values, determined through the formal implementation of the modeler. Hence, call and parameter formulae are determined through the requiring port. Methods not defined by an interface can not be "invoked". This increases the quality of the formal model as the modeler has to use provided interfaces to "invoke" necessary behavior. In the formal model return values have to be computed with respect to the method call and parameter formulae.

An example is given in Listing 1.1. The example is denoted in the System Analysis Modeling Language (SAML) [18]. A SAML model describes a set of finite state automata. These are executed in a synchronous parallel fashion. An automaton is described as a component that can contain state variables which are updated according to a set of transition rules. An example is shown in line 1. As we described before, the formal skeleton does not contain any states or transition rules, thus they are not shown here. Only formulae can be generated. An example formulae is shown in line 4, typically it is used as an abbreviation for typed expressions. Valid types are bool, integer, floats, and previously specified enumerations. In addition to components and formulae, traceability links are generated. These links are added as structured comments (cf. lines 1, 2 and 8). They are used by the VECS-IDE, to provide one-click tool support, for tracing formal elements to their original requirement (in the requirement specification IDE). Note that we use the abbreviations ti and otc for the components $trackside$ $inductors$ and $onboard$ $transmitter$ $coils$. Further, we abbreviate $inductPower$ and $magnetTransited$ with iP and mT.

Listing 1.1. Formal skeleton generated from the architecture given in Fig. 2.

```
1  component ti //<<trace>> PZB3
2     //<<trace>> PZB5
3     component inductors
4        formula bool iP_call := null;
5        formula int iP_freq := null;
6     endcomponent
7  endcomponent
8  component indusi //<<trace>> PZB9
9     //<<trace>> PZB5
10    component bus
11       formula bool mT_call := null;
12       formula int mT_freq := null;
13       formula bool mT_return := otc.bus.mT_return;
14    endcomponent
15 endcomponent
16 component otc //<<trace>> PZB2
17    //<<trace>> PZB5
18    component bus
19       formula bool mT_call := indusi.bus.mT_call;
20       formula int mT_freq := indusi.bus.mT_freq;
21       formula bool mT_return := null;
22    endcomponent
23    //<<trace>> PZB5
24    component coils
25       formula bool iP_call := ti.inductors.iP_call;
26       formula int iP_freq := ti.inductors.iP_freq;
27    endcomponent
28 endcomponent
```

Having the formal skeleton generated, the model needs to be manually completed by the modeler. The modeler has to systematically formalize all state requirements manually. If completed, the correct formal implementation shall be validated. Utilizing control data, a formal modeler is able to test single formal components through its behavioral triggers. Depending on overall project structure, the specification of the control data is either indirectly defined through requirements (e.g. it can be inherited from state requirements) or it can be generated through state-of-the-art algorithms (e.g. [3]). The corresponding assertions, representing the test checks, have to be formalized as temporal logic specifications and executed using a model checker.

3.5   Phase E: Integration Testing

The correct integration of every single formal unit is validated during this phase. Having the correct behavioral integration formally validated can help finding requirement specification errors by proving mathematically that the given behavior is underspecified or inconsistent. The modeler can identify erroneous behavior and trace the corresponding transitions rules through the UML to their origin in the SRS with counterexamples calculated by the model checker.

In order to efficiently ensure the correct behavioral requirement formalization, we utilize the UML behavior descriptions. We defined sequences to rely on the architecture, thus, every message of a sequence is well-defined and invoked from one component to another. This is, because a message symbolizes a method call and/or return with a parameter configuration and a return value.

Under these assumptions, we can automatically formalize every sequence. We propose to generate a specification for every sequence such that it evaluates to true if the correct method call/return with the specific parameters is invoked in the correct order. Applying these semantics to the running example we can generate the branching-time logic specification shown in Listing 1.2.

Listing 1.2. Formal specification generated from Fig. 3.

```
1 SPEC EF( indusi . bus . mT_call  = true & indusi . bus . mT_freq = 2000
       ↪ & EF( otc . bus . mT_return = false & EF( ti . inductors . iP_call
       ↪ = true & ti . inductors . iP_freq = 2000 & EF( indusi . bus .
       ↪ mT_call  = true & indusi . bus . mT_freq = 2000 & EF ( otc . bus
       ↪ . mT_return = true )))));
```

However, this specification does not generate a witness – a proof that the specified path exists in the state space. Thus, we propose to translate every specification into an acceptor automaton [26]. A witness can then be calculated by constructing a specification such that it evaluates to true if there is globally no path to the final valuation of the acceptor. The model checker then computes a counterexample providing a path such that the sequence is fulfilled which can be used during a safety assessment in order to argue about the feasibility of the formal model.

3.6   Phase F: System Testing

The goal of the system testing phase is to ensure that the formal implementation is tested for compliance. To do so, we utilize the safety requirements defined in the SRS. Safety requirements typically state unwanted hazardous behavior or states of system components or the whole system. With the help of the described architecture these requirements can be translated into temporal logic specifications. Further, state-of-the-art model checkers can be used to evaluate these specifications and objectify the assessment.

We use PZB8 to demonstrate the manual extraction of a safety specification from the running example. PZB8 states that a magnet transit triggers different safety relevant action, e.g. an emergency stop of the train. Thus, an overrun shall not be missed. Utilizing the architecture defined in phase B the following linear time logic formula was developed:

$$G((iP_{call} = true \wedge iP_{freq} = 2000) \Rightarrow$$
$$(mT_{call} = true \wedge mT_{freq} = 2000 \wedge mT_{return} = true)) \ . \tag{9}$$

With respect to the formal architecture depicted in Listing 1.1 the formula can be translated into the specific formal language as follows:

Afterwards, a state-of-the-art model checker computes whether the specification holds or not. If so, the formalization of the requirements is correct. If not, the model checker generates a counterexample indicating where an error is stated. Then, the modeler has to manually locate the error and conclude different solutions. The manual translation of state requirements can be erroneous which has to be resolved. If the formal behavior is correct, the UML model can be faulty. Further, the SRS can be under specified or erroneous. Thus, the proposed approach can either be used to validate if a formal model violates the SRS, the UML model is not consistent or if the SRS is erroneous.

Listing 1.3. Final formal specification generated from Eq. 9.

```
1  //<<trace>> PZB8
2  SPEC G(( ti . inductors . iP_call = true & ti . inductors . iP_freq =
       ↪ 2000)  =>  ( indusi . bus . mT_call = true & indusi . bus . mT_freq
       ↪ = 2000 & otc . bus . mT_return = true ))
```

3.7 Phase G: Acceptance Testing

Acceptance testing aims to validate if the system meets its user requirements. Cimperman defines user acceptance tests as the validation if the system works for the user [10].

In phase A user requirements have been identified and have been modeled in UML as use cases. In order to objectify the test a use case is refined with multiple sequences. This is necessary, because a use case does not specify behavior in terms of the architecture. Using sequences refines a use case with the underlying architecture. Thus, we can use the same mechanism as described phase E (cf. Sect. 3.5) to verify the validity: acceptor automata. This eliminates a manual review of use cases.

4 Using the V-Model to Formalize the PZB

We demonstrate the proposed approach on a real world example from the railways domain: the *"Punktförmige Zugbeeinflussung"*. The PZB is a train protection system which uses three different kind of trackside and onboard magnets to detect speed limitations and signals in order to ensure the safety of the train with automatically breaking actions if speed limits or signals are ignored. The German Federal Railway Authority issued a SRS with over 770 text fragments. These fragments were indexed, inter-linked and categorized resulting in over 500 functional requirements. A domain expert identified 18 use cases from four user requirements refined through 13 sequence diagrams.

An UML model with ten components, 19 ports and eleven interfaces has been derived from 45 glossary and 35 architecture requirements. Further, we identified 62 methods with 17 parameters where 32 were non-void from 129 property requirements. 23 sequences have been exemplary derived from 38 communication requirements.

We developed elaborate tool support integrated in the verification environment VECS [17]. We generated a formal skeleton in SAML [18] with 29 formal components with 226 different formulae. 73 state requirements have been formalized into 76 state variables and 164 transition rules. Further we added 129 components, 228 formulae for readability purposes. In order to test the behavior of single formal units, a variety of individual tests have been developed.

Further, 23 acceptor automata have been generated with 23 state variables and 1037 update rules. Using the IC3 approach [28] of NuXMV [6] a variety of errors have been found. Typical errors found were incorrect value assignments across different components. With the proposed approach these mistakes have been found systematically. At the end of the integration testing phase, each acceptor automaton provided a witness for its corresponding sequence. These witnesses were used to demonstrate feasibility of the formal model and as a proof for the correctness of the process method.

Further, 30 safety specifications have been checked with the k-liveness approach [9] of NuXMV. Especially underspecified behavior in the SRS has been found during this phase. For example, stopping the train directly on an trackside inductor has not been mentioned in the SRS. Using the proposed approach, a counterexample has been generated describing the unintended behavior in detail. With the help of the requirement links the intended behavior was traced to the SRS, where the requirements had been extended to cover this behavior. Afterwards, the faulty behavior definition has been fixed in the formal model.

In order to validate if the developed formal model does fulfill all user stories, the refined use cases have been formalized into additional acceptor automata. Through their formalization and executing using the IC3 approach, we proved the correct implementation of all required use cases.

Following the proposed approach for building a "correct" formal model improved the quality and feasibility of the PZB model. Architecture and behavior for the model had been specified more systematically. Further, traceability of requirements had be achieved by automatically adding structured comments as requirements links. These links helped identifying faulty behavior and getting deeper insight the formal model. Generating automated tests cases also improves the quality of the model. This is, because erroneous behavior had be found much more systematically.

5   Conclusion and Further Work

In this paper, we proposed a process in order to formalize even large system requirement specifications while preserving traceability through all stages. We apply the well known V-model to ensure the correct transformation of requirements. Doing so, we ensure that a formal model is developed which is mathematically proven consistent to a set of requirements.

This was done by categorizing requirement fragments and transforming them into UML. It ensures that domain experts, not familiar with formal verification techniques but with a set of UML artifacts, can review the generated formal verification results and trace them to their origins. Further, we proposed a method to transform an architecture into a formal representation without the need of generating state variables. We showed how to transform partial UML behavior to ensure a correct a formal model. By utilizing state-of-the-art model checkers manual reviewing of correct formal behavior specification was eliminated. Further, we have shown how to validate mathematically that the formal model fulfills every use case specified in the requirements.

Finally, we successfully applied the proposed process on a real world system requirement specification from the railway domain. We were capable of finding and correcting specification errors in all three formalization stages: we found inconsistencies in the informal requirements, manual transformation errors in UML artifacts and faulty behavior in the formal model.

We plan to apply and extend the proposed methodology in an even larger case study: In cooperation with the German Federal Railway Authority, we will formalize a subset of the European Train Control System requirement specification in order to prove its functional safety. We will develop new mechanisms to support a broader subset of UML artifacts like combined fragments, activity diagrams and state charts. Further, we will extend the process in order to work in cooperation with state-of-the-art code generators and develop new methodologies to ensure the consistency of the generated code and the developed formal model.

Acknowledgment. The work presented in this paper is funded by the German Ministry of Education and Science (BMBF) in the VIP-MoBaSA project (project-Nr. 16V0360).

References

1. Boehm, B.W.: Verifying and validating software requirements and design specifications. IEEE Softw. **1**, 75–88 (1984)
2. Bose, P.: Automated translation of UML models of architectures for verification and simulation using spin. In: ASE, pp. 102–109. IEEE (1999)
3. Brill, M., Buschermöhle, R., Damm, W., Klose, J., Westphal, B., Wittke, H.: Formal verification of LSCs in the development process. In: Ehrig, H., Damm, W., Desel, J., Große-Rhode, M., Reif, W., Schnieder, E., Westkämper, E. (eds.) INT 2004. LNCS, vol. 3147, pp. 494–516. Springer, Heidelberg (2004)
4. Burmester, S., Giese, H., Hirsch, M., Schilling, D.: Incremental design and formal verification with UML/RT in the FUJABA real-time tool suite. In: SVERTS, pp. 1–20. Citeseer (2004)
5. Carnevali, L., Grassi, L., Vicario, E.: A tailored V-model exploiting the theory of preemptive time petri nets. In: Kordon, F., Vardanega, T. (eds.) Ada-Europe 2008. LNCS, vol. 5026, pp. 87–100. Springer, Heidelberg (2008)
6. Cavada, R., et al.: The nuXmv symbolic model checker. In: Biere, A., Bloem, R. (eds.) CAV 2014. LNCS, vol. 8559, pp. 334–342. Springer, Heidelberg (2014)
7. CENELEC: 50129. Railway Applications: Safety Related Electronic Systems for Signalling (1998)
8. Cimatti, A., Roveri, M., Susi, A., Tonetta, S.: From informal requirements to property-driven formal validation. In: Cofer, D., Fantechi, A. (eds.) FMICS 2008. LNCS, vol. 5596, pp. 166–181. Springer, Heidelberg (2009)

9. Cimatti, A., Griggio, A.: Software model checking via IC3. In: Madhusudan, P., Seshia, S.A. (eds.) CAV 2012. LNCS, vol. 7358, pp. 277–293. Springer, Heidelberg (2012)

10. Cimperman, R.: UAT Defined: A Guide to Practical User Acceptance Testing. Addison-Wesley Professional, Upper Saddle River (2006)

11. Clarke, E.M., Grumberg, O., Peled, D.: Model Checking. MIT Press, Cambridge (1999)

12. David, A., Möller, M.O., Yi, W.: Formal verification of UML statecharts with real-time extensions. In: Kutsche, R.-D., Weber, H. (eds.) FASE 2002. LNCS, vol. 2306, pp. 218–232. Springer, Heidelberg (2002)

13. Emerson, E.A., Halpern, J.Y.: Sometimes and not never revisited: on branching versus linear time temporal logic. J. ACM **33**, 151–178 (1986)

14. Fecher, H., Schönborn, J., Kyas, M., de Roever, W.-P.: 29 new unclarities in the semantics of UML 2.0 state machines. In: Lau, K.-K., Banach, R. (eds.) ICFEM 2005. LNCS, vol. 3785, pp. 52–65. Springer, Heidelberg (2005)

15. Filax, M., Gonschorek, T., Lipaczewski, M., Ortmeier, F.: On traceability of informal specifications for model-based verification. In: IMBSA 2014: Short & Tutorial Proceedings, pp. 11–18 (2014)

16. Giese, H., Tichy, M., Burmester, S., Schäfer, W., Flake, S.: Towards the compositional verification of real-time UML designs. In: ESEC/FSE, pp. 38–47 (2003)

17. Gonschorek, T., Filax, M., Lipaczewski, M., Ortmeier, F.: VECS - verification enviroment for critical systems - tool supported formal modeling an verification. In: IMBSA 2014: Short & Tutorial Proceedings, pp. 63–64 (2014)

18. Güdemann, M.: Qualitative and quantitative formal model-based safety analysis. Ph.D. thesis, Otto-von-Guericke-Universität Magdeburg (2011)

19. Lano, K., Clark, D., Androutsopoulos, K.: UML to B: formal verification of object-oriented models. In: Boiten, E.A., Derrick, J., Smith, G.P. (eds.) IFM 2004. LNCS, vol. 2999, pp. 187–206. Springer, Heidelberg (2004)

20. Latella, D., Majzik, I., Massink, M.: Automatic verification of a behavioural subset of UML statechart diagrams using the spin model-checker. FAC **11**, 637–664 (1999)

21. Lilius, J., Paltor, I.P.: Formalising UML state machines for model checking. In: France, R.B. (ed.) UML 1999. LNCS, vol. 1723, pp. 430–444. Springer, Heidelberg (1999)

22. Lilius, J., Paltor, I.P.: vUML: A tool for verifying UML models. In: ASE, pp. 255–258. IEEE (1999)

23. OMG: OMG Unified Modeling Language (OMG UML), Superstructure. Object Management Group (2011)

24. Snook, C., Butler, M.: UML-B: Formal modeling and design aided by UML. TOSEM **15**, 92–122 (2006)

25. Tang, W., Ning, B., Xu, T., Zhao, L.H.: Scenario-based modeling and verification of system requirement specification for the european train control system. In: Computers in Railways XII, pp. 759–770 (2010)

26. Vardi, M., Wolper, P.: An automata-theoretic approach to automatic program verification. In: LICS, pp. 322–331. IEEE (1986)

27. Varró, A.: A formal semantics of UML statecharts by model transition systems. In: Corradini, A., Ehrig, H., Kreowski, H.-J., Rozenberg, G. (eds.) ICGT 2002. LNCS, vol. 2505, pp. 378–392. Springer, Heidelberg (2002)

28. Vizel, Y., Grumberg, O., Shoham, S.: Lazy abstraction and sat-based reachability in hardware model checking. In: FMCAD, pp. 173–181. IEEE (2012)

Static Verification of Railway Schema and Interlocking Design Data

Alexei Iliasov$^{(\boxtimes)}$, Paulius Stankaitis, and David Adjepon-Yamoah

Newcastle University, Newcastle upon Tyne, UK
`alexei.iliasov@ncl.ac.uk`

Abstract. The paper presents an experience of verifying a large scale, real-life dataset describing various aspects of railway station design. We discuss how a number of assorted digital artefacts were pooled together and converted into a set-theoretic model over which a type inference procedure is run. The typed model is then used to confirm or contradict logical conjectures over data elements. We employ a number of state-of-the-art SMT solvers as a verification back-end. The project is ongoing but has already identified a number of issues in topology definition and signalling data that were missed by other automated tests and not revealed by simulation tools.

1 Introduction

The SafeCap project has been working on railway modelling and formal verification for nearly five years. The original view consisted in fitting a railway description into a formal setting through the means of a formal domain specific language [4]. Such a language enables formal and automatic verification of integrity of a schema and its signalling as well as operational safety. True to the well respected practice in computing science, a strict top-down approach was used where a formal model spanning abstraction levels of increasing fidelity covered concepts of safety (e.g., something bad should not happen), principles of safety (e.g., route-based signalling) and implementation of safety principles (ladder logic diagrams for interlocking) [1]. However, the reality turned out to be far more fragmented and fluid to insist on a strict top-down view.

Collaboration with Siemens Rail Automation UK led to the realisation that railway models, i.e., a description of a station, are rarely available in their entirety while the scale of a project and the pace of changes make it unrealistic to undertake an unhurried top-down validation. The variety of ways employed in the industry to capture the same artefact both at conceptual and syntactic levels (say a schema rendered as a track topology or node/edge model and persisted in XML or LDL format) makes it much harder to come up with a universal verification pipeline. And at the signalling implementation level one finds a medley of proprietary technology, notations and tools.

It is increasingly evident that safe and efficient exploitation of a railway network depends on detailed and up to date knowledge of network characteristic

© Springer International Publishing Switzerland 2016
T. Lecomte et al. (Eds.): RSSRail 2016, LNCS 9707, pp. 123–133, 2016.
DOI: 10.1007/978-3-319-33951-1_9

spanning from macroscopic details of station and line capacity to precise characterisation of track side equipment positioning, capabilities and state. Given the scale and importance of such data, a modern railway operation critically depends on data acquisition and storage that are suitably supported by higher level activities of modelling, analysis and planning.

At the purely technological level, storage and distribution of large amount of data is no longer a challenging problem. The issues of scaling, querying, replication and persistence are well researched by the data science community.

A far harder problem, however, is to make sure that collected and stored data makes sense, especially in the presence of incremental updates and nontrivial semantic overlaps in data originating from differing companies. A data collection exercise carried out as merely a dutiful recording and redistribution of incoming data is bound to result in a situation where same information is duplicated and triplicated with slight changes and ever accumulating number of inconsistencies making data interpretation increasingly difficult and the data less valuable overall. What we endeavour to achieve in SafeCap is a way to 'interpret' data without human involvement and through this validate and normalise it to deter 'data rot' while enabling much more semantically involved data querying and processing.

One solution is defining a set of mechanisable validation rules that apply automatically every time a new piece of data is added to a storage. At the simplest level a rule is a piece of code (say, a stored routine for a database engine) which role is to go through entries and check for known signs of mismatch. This will undeniably save a great amount of time. However, given the scale of the challenge - real-life examples contain hundreds of distinct concepts - a new challenge arises almost immediately. Since the responsibility is now delegated to validation code, such code has to be developed, verified and maintained to the highest standard. This is a difficult task and, to start with, the formal verification of a piece of code requires a formal model of its intended behaviour to check against. What SafeCap offers is having just a formal model of data semantics and a technique to match it, automatically, against a piece of data.

The technique comprises two stages: container agnostic extraction of a formal model describing source data and model validation. To avoid a dependency on certain syntax and container, the information necessary for validation comes in the form of typed relations. We use a certain mathematical framework for representing and classifying relations and their typing constraints. Any structured data may be rendered as a collection of relations and, if it meets minimal consistency requirements, relation types may be inferred. This process is completely automatic and does not require any knowledge about structure or purpose of data source. It applies equally to structured textual formats and relational databases.

2   Formal Model

We build a simple conceptual model of a railway operation. The basic premise is that railway track is a contended resource and there is a number of actors that affect each other by consuming and freeing track resources. The basic unit of consumption is a block. We do not define how small or large a block is in terms of physical track; the block concept may be used for route-based and moving block (ERTMS) signalling.

A pre-existing model of data semantics would speak about mathematical relations as well; specifically the kind of relations that are permitted and considered well-formed. But these would generally be different from extracted relations and with differing types. However, in such a formal setting it is not necessary to translate source data into a new format: a potentially dangerous exercise that may alter source data semantics. In its stead, one defines a formal link model that semantically links extracted data model with the verification model. The link does not need to be total: some elements of source may be uninterpreted while some concepts of semantics might have no direct counterpart. Unlike a software translator tool, such link model is generally not executable as we don't need actual translation of data to perform verification. At the same time it is terse and white-box and can be easily evolved with the changes in source data formats.

Once these three models - source data, link and semantics - are put together we have a model that is consistent, when all model parts are in an agreement, or not. The check is performed via automated theorem proving using a range of state-of-the-art automatic verification tools. If the check fails, the reason can often be narrowed down to a specific source data structure and semantic model constraint.

Railway Track Topology. The first step is to define constraints on track topology, that is a graph of blocks. For instance, track graph must have nodes of only degree one (boundary), two (normal), three (point) and four (diamond crossing). There should be no cycles, self-loops and disjointed sections. Points and diamond crossings should not appear as boundary nodes.

Definition 1 (Track topology assumptions).

$$finite(BLOCK) \tag{1}$$
$$next \subseteq BLOCK \times BLOCK \tag{2}$$
$$BLOCK = ran(next) \cup dom(next) \tag{3}$$
$$next \cap (BLOCK \lhd id) = \varnothing \tag{4}$$
$$next\_closure \subseteq BLOCK \times BLOCK \tag{5}$$
$$next\_closure; next = next\_closure \tag{6}$$
$$next\_closure; (BLOCK \lhd id) = next\_closure \tag{7}$$
$$first = dom(next) \setminus ran(next) \tag{8}$$
$$last = ran(next) \setminus dom(next) \tag{9}$$
$$points \subseteq BLOCK \tag{10}$$
$$\dots \tag{11}$$

Signalling Model. At the most abstract level we observe blocks being consumed and freed. This is a high-level metaphor for train movement and point/route locking. The following diagram shows three blocks consumed at some point of time.

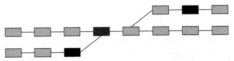

The model of behavior is given in a formal notation called Event-B. The first model is extremely simple and defines one variable *consumed* $\subseteq$ BLOCK (the set of consumed blocks) and two events (actions) to consume and free blocks.

Definition 2 (Abstract model).

consume $\triangleq$
any b **where**
    $b \in$ BLOCK $\setminus$ *consumed*
then
    consumed $:=$ *consumed* $\cup \{b\}$
end
free $\triangleq$ **any** b **where** $b \in$ *consumed* **then** *consumed* $:=$ *consumed* $\setminus \{b\}$ **end**

Refinements. The abstract consume/free model is gradually refined to capture route-based signalling based on a control table. We introduce the notion of actors and keep track of which actor consumes which block. There are two main actor kinds: the control actor that consumes only points and diamond crossing; and a train actor that may consume any block kind. The following depicts a situation where three blocks are consumed by three different actors (red, green and black - colours differentiate into block reservation and train occupation).

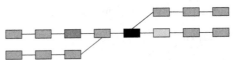

We make model realistic by requiring that train actors consume contiguous blocks and also keep track of train orientation. A train actor may only appear and disappear (that is, consume its first block) on a boundary block; it may also reverse its direction when its head is on a buffer stop block. At this stage, trains travel through a point or crossing in any direction (even when point topology would not allow this). The following diagram shows occupation and reservation for directed trains (a triangle in block depicts train head):

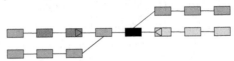

The subsequent refinements introduce the notion of train path through a schema; point and diamond crossing states, and the concept of block locking. Now a block may only be consumed once it is locked for a given actor (a slanted stripe in the diagram below). For a control, the consumed state corresponds to the switching time of points and crossings. A train may only lock a point or crossing block if the block is in the right state for the train path. Hence, we might observe the following sequence of actions of train B to travel through some point block X after train A travelling over a conflicting route.

- free block X for train A
- lock block X for control
- consume block X for control
- free block X for control
- lock block X for train B
- consume block X for train B

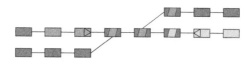

The final stage is to introduce the notion of a route as a sequence of blocks. Once the individual blocks of a route are locked, an actor may lock the route made of the locked blocks. Train head movement has a dedicated action for switching between two routes.

While a train actor is forced to inspect a route locking state, it is also directly inspecting the state of blocks in front. To make the behaviour localised we introduce conditions defining when a locked route may show one of proceed aspects. It is then formally proven that inspecting route state alone is sufficient to ensure train safety.

Definition 3 (Move train head onto a next route). *Localised version.*

$move\_head\_new\_route \triangleq$

any h, i, j, nr, t **where**

   $t \in \text{dom}\,(train\_seq)$

   $h = train\_seq\,(t)\,(train\_seq\_head\,(t))$

   $j = \text{line}\,(train\_line\,(t))^{-1}\,(h)$

   $i = \text{line\_routes}\,(train\_line\,(t))^{-1}\,(train\_head\_route\,(t))$

   $i + 1 \in \text{dom}\,(\text{line\_routes}\,(train\_line\,(t)))$

   $nr = \text{line\_routes}\,(train\_line\,(t))\,(i + 1)$

   $route\_aspect\,(nr) \geq \text{PROCEED}$

then

   $train\_seq\_head\,(t) := train\_seq\_head\,(t) + 1$

   $train\_seq\,(t) := train\_seq\,(t) \cup \{(train\_seq\_head\,(t) + 1) \mapsto \text{line}\,(train\_line\,(t))\,(j + 1)\}$

   $locking := \{\text{line}\,(train\_line\,(t))\,(j)\} \lhd locking$

   $train\_head\_route\,(t) := nr$

   $route\_locking := \{train\_head\_route\,(t)\} \lhd route\_locking$

   $route\_aspect\,(nr) := \text{STOP}$

end

The diagram below shows blocks numbered with route indices. In reality, the same block may be attributed to several routes.

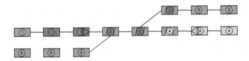

The model is still fairly abstract but covers all the essential aspects of safety principles: we prove freedom of collision and derailment. We have not considered many advanced properties such as absence of deadlocks, provision and treatment of overlaps, flank protection and etc. These may be introduced in next refinements of increasing fidelity.

3   Reading Station Dataset

The testing ground for the technique is a simulation data set provided by Siemens Rail Automation UK. The data is made of roughly 12MB of XML and structured text files describing topology and signalling of Reading station with signalling split into three overlapping interlocking areas. The diagram in Fig. 1 provides an indication of the scale of the studied data. The diagram was rendered directly from a subset of the data which include the visual layout for tracks.

One immediate issue was that a part of the data is not XML but a proprietary text-based format called LDL (originating at Invensys Rail). The SafeCap Platform has an import facility for LDL files but this silently ignores unknown data fields. We thus developed a new, more basic import tool that treats XML-based and LDL-based data on the same footing of an abstract relation-based data representation.

There is a considerable overlap between various parts of this data set. Many of them are not trivial to spot and for historic reason same elements are sometimes known under differing names. In addition, no provision for distinguishing between sets of elements and a sequence of elements. A strict interpretation would require regarding any multiplicity as a sequence or a tuple rather than a set. This is inefficient from the verification viewpoint. To counter this, we allow a user to manually demote sequence and tuples types into set types. For the case of tuples, a unified type (which might not exist for incompatible types) is used.

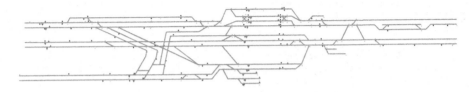

Fig. 1. Rendering of Reading Station *track layout data* as a track schema from a subset of the dataset (produced by SafeCap Platform). Black and orange (light gray) circles are signal and fixed speed limit positions; triangles denote train stopping points.

3.1   Reading Station Verification

The formal model presented above is used to validate Reading St. data. There is no simple correspondence between the data structures used in our formal abstraction and the real-life data characterizing Reading St. Yet some correspondence is bound to exist since both define, in their own way, a railway schema and route-based signalling.

Our verification technique consists in matching a data set against the assumptions of formal behaviour model (such as, for instance, given in Definition 1. This means there is no danger of state explosion and verification is comprehensive and conclusion, when it can be reached, is definite.

In the source dataset, there is a significant amount of duplication. Some cases are not trivial to spot and for various reasons same elements may, at times, be known under differing names. At the structural level there is no indication whether a collection of elements is a sequence or a set. A strict interpretation necessitates sequences at all times but this make it harder to write and check verification conditions. When data is imported, all such cases are treated as sequences and user can do one of two things: manually demote type to set, or request that there should be a separate, set based view of the same data. Thus, for instance, relation $r \in A \rightarrow \text{seq}(B)$ can be replaced by some $r' \in A \rightarrow \text{pow}(B)$ or r and r' may be present at the same time together with an axiom statement $r' = r; (\lambda t. \text{ran}(t))$.

The process of verification consists in positing a conjecture and checking it by combing with the data model to see if a contradiction arises. For instance, to check no two train detection circuits overlap we can state the following:

$$P_1 := [\forall\, t, s, a, x, y, b, i, j\ .$$
$$t : \text{TrackSection and } s : \text{TrackSection and } t \neq s \text{ and}$$
$$a \mapsto x \mapsto y : \text{ran}(\text{``TRACK\_CIRCUIT.M\_SECTION''}(t)) \text{ and}$$
$$b \mapsto i \mapsto j : \text{ran}(\text{``TRACK\_CIRCUIT.M\_SECTION''}(s)) \text{ and}$$
$$a = b$$
$$\Rightarrow x > j \text{ or } y < i]$$

Here "INTERLOCKING.M_SECTION" is a function name defined in a data source (detailed station topology). It is taken into quotes to escape characters clashing with operator syntax. Expression ran("TRACK_CIRCUIT.M_SECTION"(t)) defines all pieces of a graph defining the sub-graph of a train detection circuit. This gives a set of track names. The condition checks that any two distinct train detection circuit t and s do not physically overlap.

The statement is conjoined with the mathematical model of source data **H** to form conjecture $\mathbf{H} \vdash P_1$. The conjecture undergoes a conservative filtering to remove parts of data model **H** irrelevant to P_1 and form a less constrained model $\mathbf{H}_f$ where $\mathbf{H} \subseteq \mathbf{H}_f$. The typing information is removed and all the literal values are encoded as integers. The un-typing and coding process has fairly modest impact on proof success per se but without it some tools cannot ingest and parse otherwise typically a very large input file. Every condition is checked twice - once in the positive (i.e., as given) form and once in the negative form.

Both cases must have a definite answer (that is, *unknown* result for either case renders the whole condition *false*) so that a conjecture is assumed to hold only when its positive is truth and the negative is false. The double check addresses potential well-definedness problems such as applying a relation outside of its domain or having self-contradictory data model.

When a conjecture of the form $\forall x.P(x)$ is found to be false it is, at times, possible to obtain a witness for $\exists x.\neg P(x)$ from the verification back-end. And for certain types of expressions (sequences and sets and single elements of signals, routes, tracks, points, etc.) a counter-example may be visualised on a track diagram.

3.2   Verification Results

We went through all the conditions (47 total) of track topology assumptions from Definition 1. In the process we have found that one condition does not hold:

Condition (18) of Definition 1 states that edge (sink) blocks may not be points or diamond crossings. However, we found a counter-example: track *UpReaWestC*.

The majority of verification load is concerned with routes and signalling rules. The data set does not define possible train paths but defines routes. The analysis revealed a fair number of broken conditions but nearly all of these turned out to be due to cutting of signalling data across interlocking area boundaries. A simple aggregation of data leads to basic well-formedness problems, i.e., same entity is defined twice. But throwing out overlapping data seems to produce a number of validation errors. For instance

Mappings between track circuit and a sub-route must agree in both directions:

$$\forall r.r \in \text{``ILTrackSectionControlTables.SubRoutes''} \Rightarrow$$
$$r \in \text{``ILSubRouteControlTables.TrackSection''}^{-1}$$

There is a number of counter-examples.

and also

In a control table, track circuits locked that must be locked for a point must be among the required track sections of a route. It is an essential safety conditions and is rendered as the following property.

$$\text{id(dom(``ILRouteControlTables.NormalPoints''))} \subseteq$$
$$(\text{``ILRouteControlTables.NormalPoints''};$$
$$\text{``ILPointsControlTables.NormalLockingTrackSections''};$$
$$\text{``ILRouteControlTables.TrackSections''}^{-1})$$

It does not hold for a number of cases when a route goes across interlocking boundary.

There are six more issues that seems to arise due to basic data completeness and consistency issues. This will need further investigation.

All in all, we have checked the data against 72 verification conditions and the vast majority of the conditions were discharged. All the conditions were handled completely automatically by a collection of theorem provers and constraint solvers. It takes less than 2 min to go through all the conditions for the whole station.

The majority of unsatisfied conditions exhibit the same pattern of incomplete definitions and seem to be stemming from the issue of splitting and then reassembling signalling data for the three interlocking areas.

4   Discussion

Perhaps the most prevalent validation technique in the railway industry is simulation. Simulation engines range from coarse-grained time stepping of a national railway network to a detailed model of various aspects of mechanical performance of specific rolling stock over certain track. Validation concerns span from the analysis of digital communication protocols connecting trains and regional control to stressing of tunnels and bridges by passing trains. Simulation is widely applied for time table optimisation and interactive 3D simulation is sometimes used for driver training. RailSys [12] and OpenTrack [10] are two of the more well-known simulation suites applied in time table optimisation and general analysis of signalling performance.

The main attraction of simulation is that it does not require deep understanding of railway functioning. Simulation tools present many aspects of railway performance in an intuitive, visual manner helping to quickly obtain the big picture of overall layout and signalling performance. There is, however, no guarantee of safety as simulation can only ever consider a tiny proportion of all scenarios.

The safety challenge of railways and the fact that collision and derailment properties may be dealt with within the setting of discrete, inertia-less train movement makes railway safety verification especially appealing for formal method practitioners. The principal idea of railway model checking is quite simple: a model of train movement laws is combined with the definitions of track topology and signalling rules. A model checking tool attempts to go through all or many execution scenarios to confirm that unsafe scenarios are ruled out. The list of modelling notations used in this setting is practically endless. Notable examples include Coloured Petri nets [2], process algebra CSP [5], a continuation work based on the model-based notation ASM [6], an algebraic language Maude [3] and the B Method together with ProB model checking tool [9]. The latter can also be used in the capacity of a property verifier for assertions written against B or Event-B contexts. In this form ProB has been used for the validation of railway datasets [8] and this led to the development of a commercial toolset [11]. Our approach differs by the kind of properties we try to prove (safety principles of signalling) and the provenance of verification constraints (an Event-B model of signalling).

Model checking imposes limitations on the model size and performs best with a relatively limited logical language. Theorem proving overcomes these limitations and offers potentially unlimited opportunities for verifying safety with the utmost level of rigour. Theorem proving is not necessarily an all-manual process: there is a large and successful community developing automated theorem provers [13]. At the moment, automated prove support is best in the domain of first order logic and set theory; an attempt at reasoning about continuous train dynamics is likely to require an intervention by a highly skilled verification expert - the kind of people mostly found in academia.

Theorem proving, even with excellent tool support, requires a high level of expertise in formal verification and mathematical modelling. The semantic gap between logic and railway concepts is formidable. This leads to generally low productivity (but we should notice efforts like the BART tool for automatic refinement of B models [7]), difficulties in interpreting tool feedback, and posing verification statements in a manner convincing to a non-expert reviewer.

References

1. Iliasov, A., Lopatkin, I., Romanovsky, A.: Practical formal methods in railways - the SafeCap approach. In: George, L., Vardanega, T. (eds.) Ada-Europe 2014. LNCS, vol. 8454, pp. 177–192. Springer, Heidelberg (2014)
2. Janczura, C.W.: Modelling and Analysis of Railway Network Control Logic using Coloured Petri Nets. PhD thesis, School of Mathematics and Institute for Telecommunications Research, University of South Australia (1998)
3. Hagalisletto, A.M., Bjørk, J., Chieh Yu, I., Enger, P.: Constructing and refining large-scale railway models represented by Petri Nets. IEEE Trans. Syst. Man Cybern. Part C **37**, 444–460 (2007)
4. Iliasov, A., Romanovsky, A.: SafeCap domain language for reasoning about safety and capacity. In: Pacific-Rim Dependable Computing Conference (PRDC 2012), Niigata, Japan. IEEE CS, November 2012
5. Winter, K.: Model checking railway interlocking systems. In: Proceeding of the 25th Australian Computer Science Conference (ACSC 2002) (2002)
6. Winter, K., Robinson, N.: Modelling large railway interlockings and model checking small ones. In: Proceeding of the Australian Cumputer Science Conference (ACSC 2003) (2003)
7. Burdy, L.: Automatic refinement. In: Proceedings of BUGM at FM 1999 (1999)
8. Lecomte, T., Burdy, L., Leuschel, M.: Formally checking large data sets in the railways. CoRR, abs/1210.6815 (2012)
9. Leuschel, M., Butler, M.: ProB: a model checker for B. In: Araki, K., Gnesi, S., Mandrioli, D. (eds.) FME 2003. LNCS, vol. 2805, pp. 855–874. Springer, Heidelberg (2003)
10. OpenTrack simulator. http://www.opentrack.ch/

11. Abo, R., Voisin, L.: Formal implementation of data validation for railway safety-related systems with OVADO. In: Counsell, S., Núñez, M. (eds.) SEFM 2013. LNCS, vol. 8368, pp. 221–236. Springer, Heidelberg (2014)
12. RailSys simulation platform. http://www.rmcon.de
13. TPTP. Thousands of Problems for Theorem Provers. www.tptp.org/

Verification of Railway Interlocking - Compositional Approach with OCRA

Christophe Limbrée[1]([✉]), Quentin Cappart[1], Charles Pecheur[1], and Stefano Tonetta[2]

[1] Université catholique de Louvain, Louvain-la-Neuve, Belgium
{christophe.limbree,quentin.cappart,charles.pecheur}@uclouvain.be
[2] Fondazione Bruno Kessler, Trento, Italy
tonettas@fbk.eu

Abstract. In the railway domain, an electronic interlocking is a computerised system that controls the railway signalling components (e.g. switches or signals) in order to allow a safe operation of the train traffic. Interlockings are controlled by a software logic that relies on a generic software and a set of application data particular to the station under control. The verification of the application data is time consuming and error prone as it is mostly performed by human testers.

In the first stage of our research [3], we built a model of a small Belgian railway station and we performed the verification of the application data with the NUSMV model checker. However, the verification of larger stations fails due to the state space explosion problem. The intuition is that large stations can be split into smaller components that can be verified separately. This concept is known as compositional verification. This article explains how we used the OCRA tool in order to model a medium size station and how we verified safety properties by mean of contracts. We also took advantage of new algorithms (k-liveness and ic3) recently implemented in NUXMV in order to verify LTL properties on our model.

1 Introduction

In the railway domain, an interlocking is a signalling subsystem that controls the routes, the switches and the signals before allowing a train through a station. Computer-based interlockings are configured based on a set of application data particular to each station. The safety of the train traffic relies on the correctness of the application data. Usually, the application data are prepared manually and are thus subject to human errors. For example, some prerequisites to the clearance (e.g. green light) of the origin signal of a route can be missing. This kind of error can easily be discovered by a code review or by testing on a simulator. However, errors caused by concurrent actions (e.g. route commands) are much harder to find. In this case, the combination of possible concurrent actions explodes quickly and testing all possible combinations manually is impracticable. The goal of our research is to develop a method based on model checking in

T. Lecomte et al. (Eds.): RSSRail 2016, LNCS 9707, pp. 134–149, 2016.
DOI: 10.1007/978-3-319-33951-1_10

order to verify the application data. Especially, our approach must scale-up and allow the verification of real size interlocking areas.

In a previous work [3], we built a model of a small Belgian railway station and we performed the verification of the application data with the NUSMV model checker. However the verification of larger stations fails due to the state space explosion problem: the models are too big so that the model checker does not give a result in reasonable time. In this paper, we therefore tackle the problem with a compositional approach. The intuition is that large stations can be split into smaller components that can be verified separately. We report on the usage of the OCRA tool in order to model a medium size station and on how we verified safety properties by mean of contracts. We also took advantage of new algorithms (k-liveness and ic3) recently implemented in NUXMV in order to verify LTL properties on our model.

Outline. The paper is structured as follows. In Sect. 2, we give a brief overview of the formal techniques that have been used in the case study. In the Sect. 3, we describe our model and the new features that we have added compared to our first model. In Sect. 4, we explain our verification strategy for larger stations. In Sect. 5, we discuss the performance of our verification approach and show how counter examples are produced when we insert errors in the application data. References to related work are provided in Sect. 7.

2   Contract Based Verification

2.1   Symbolic Model Checking

Model checking [15] is a method to formally verify that a system is correct. In symbolic model checking [20], a system M is described by a finite set V of variables, the initial states are represented by a formula I over V, while the transitions by a formula T over the variables V and V', where V' represent the value of V after a transition. In the scope of this paper, we consider finite-state systems. Thus, without loss of generality, we can consider V as Boolean variables and formulas in propositional logic.

A state is an assignment to the variables in V. An initial state is a state that satisfies I. A transition is a pair of states that satisfy T. A path is a sequence $\sigma = s_0, s_1, s_2, \ldots$ of states such that s_0 is an initial state ($s_0 \models I$) and, for every $i \geq 0$, s_i, s_{i+1} is a transition ($s_i, s_{i+1} \models T$). A state s is reachable if there is a path $s_0, s_1, s_2, \ldots$ such that $s = s_i$ for some $i \geq 0$.

In this paper, we specify transition systems in SMV [20], the input language of different model checkers such as NUSMV [8] and NUXMV [5]. Safety properties have been formalized by invariants, i.e. formulas over V that must be satisfied by all reachable states. Temporal properties have been formalized into LTL [21], which uses temporal operators to specify the temporal evolution of the transition system. The typical LTL formula we consider is in the form $\mathbf{G}\ (\phi_1 \rightarrow F\phi_2)$, where ϕ_1 and ϕ_2 are state formulas over V. It means that whenever ϕ_1 is true along an execution, ϕ_2 is true in a state that follows along the trace.

2.2   nuXmv: Verification of Components with K-Liveness and IC3

In the case study we use NUXMV to prove invariants and LTL properties. In particular, we use the IC3 algorithm to prove invariants and the k-liveness algorithm for LTL properties.

IC3 [2] is a SAT-based algorithm for the verification of invariant properties of transition systems. Very briefly, the idea of IC3 is to build iteratively a sequence of formulas $F_0, F_1, \ldots, F_k$ such that (i) $F_0 = I$, (ii) for all $i > 0$, F_i is a set of clauses, (iii) $F_i \models F_{i+1}$, iv) $F_i(V) \wedge T(V, V') \models F_{i+1}(V')$, and v) for all $i < k$, $F_i \models P$ where P is the property that we want to verify. The formulas F_i are therefore over-approximations of the state space reachable in up to i transitions. They are iteratively strengthened and extended by generalizing clauses while disproving candidate counterexamples. The procedure terminates when either a counterexample is found or when $F_i = F_{i+1}$ for some i so that F_i is an inductive invariant that proves P.

In [7], IC3 has been integrated with *predicate abstraction* (PA) [18]. The approach leverages *Implicit Abstraction* (IA) [23], which allows to express abstract transitions without computing explicitly the abstract system, and is fully incremental with respect to the addition of new predicates.

k-liveness [13] reduces liveness to a sequence of invariant checking. It uses a standard approach to reduce LTL verification for proving that a certain signal f is eventually never visited ($\mathbf{F} \, \mathbf{G} \, \neg f$). The key insight of k-liveness is that, for finite-state systems, this is equivalent to find a K such that f is visited at most K times, which in turn can be reduced to invariant checking. k-liveness is therefore a simple loop that increases K at every iteration and calls a subroutine safe to check the invariant. In particular, the implementation in [13] uses IC3 as safe and exploits the incrementality of IC3 to solve the sequence of invariant problems in an efficient way.

2.3   OCRA: Contract-Based Compositional Approach

In this paper, we adopt a compositional contract-based approach and we use the framework supported by the OCRA tool [10]. In particular, we specify component interfaces in terms of Boolean data ports and LTL contracts.

The OCRA input language is a component-based description of the system architecture where every component is associated with one or more contracts. Each contract consists of an assumption and a guarantee specified as LTL formulas. The assumption represents a requirement on the environment of the component. The guarantee represents a requirements for the component implementation to be satisfied when the assumption holds.

When a component S is decomposed into subcomponents, the contract refinement ensures that the guarantee of S is not weakened by the contracts of the subcomponents while its assumption is not strengthened. This is checked independently from the actual implementation of the components and is verified by means of a set of proof obligations in LTL, which are discharged with model checking techniques [12].

OCRA allows to associate to a component a behavioral model representing its implementation. The language used for the behavioral model is SMV. OCRA checks if the SMV model is a correct implementation of the specified component simply calling NuSMV to verify if the SMV model satisfies the implication $A \to G$ for every contract $\langle A, G \rangle$ of the component.

3   System and Model Description

In this section, we describe the station, the model, and two new features of our model that are the directional locking and the sequential release.

3.1   The Station

Braine l'Alleud station, shown in Fig. 1, is a medium size Belgian railway station comprising 32 routes, 12 switches, 12 signals, and 4 platforms (101-104). A platform is a section of pathway, alongside rail tracks at a railway station, metro station or tram stop, at which passengers may board. A route is a line of railway track between two signals on a rail system (e.g. route R_CC_102 from signal CC to track ▮102▮ - signal JC). The station can be decomposed into two separate nearly symmetrical parts comprising 16 routes each: $M1$ and $M2$.

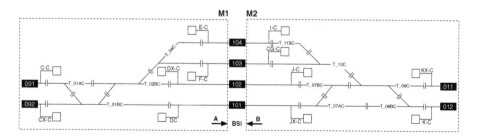

Fig. 1. Track layout of Braine station

3.2   Composite System

The two parts of the station (i.e. $M1$ and $M2$) are not totally independent but have interfaces. These interfaces materialize a mutual exclusion mechanism preventing two trains to head for a platform in opposite direction at the same time (e.g. routes CC_101 and KC_101). Such routes are called conflicting routes. The exercise then consists in defining the system and its components, the interaction among the components, and try to prove some global properties on the system by making assumptions on the environment of each component.

The cuts (i.e. $M1$ and $M2$) are chosen so-that: (1) the number of interface variables is minimum, and (2) it sticks to the principle of distribution between interlockings applied in larger stations. The same principle will be applied to two interlockings sharing a section. As shown in Fig. 2, the system is made of three components: $M1$, $M2$, and $C1$. Partial Listing 1.1 shows how the components, and the interfaces are defined in OCRA. The components: $M1$, $M2$, and $C1$ are implemented in SMV language.

```
1   COMPONENT BraineLL system
2
3   REFINEMENT
4
5     SUB BraineLeft   : M1;
6     SUB BraineRight  : M2;
7     SUB Controller   : C1;
8
9   CONNECTION BraineLeft.BSIB_101 := BraineRight.BSIB_101;
10  ...
11
12  COMPONENT M1
13
14  INTERFACE -- From Environment
15    INPUT PORT BSIB_101: boolean;
16  ...
17
18  COMPONENT M2
19
20  INTERFACE -- From Environment
21    OUTPUT PORT BSIB_101: boolean;
22  ...
```

Listing 1.1. System definition in OCRA

The components are defined by means of the SUB keyword. The interfaces are defined as $INPUT$ or $OUTPUT$ (e.g. BSIB_101 is an output for $M1$ and an input for $M2$). The $INPUT$ and $OUTPUT$ are connected by mean of the $CONNECTION$ keyword.

Figure 2 shows how the components are connected by interfaces. The L_CS OUTPUT variable (=TRUE) is an output of the system and states that the route is set and the origin signal at proceed aspect (e.g. the route R_CC_102 is set and signal CC is green). The Controller outputs the cmdR variable stating that the controller has issued a route command. The Rongo{1,2} INPUT variable provides an acknowledgement that the route command has been properly processed by the interlocking. The two $M1$ and $M2$ interlocking components exchange the state of the platform track-circuits and the state of the BSI. A track-circuit is an electrical circuit that detects the presence of train in a block of track. The four track-circuits at the platform can be occupied by a train running in either $M1$, or $M2$. The BSI variable allows for mutual exclusion of conflicting routes leading to the same platform. The principle of functioning of the BSI is explained in Sect. 3.4.

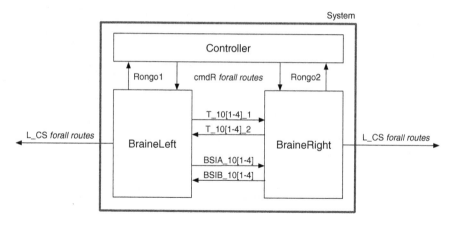

Fig. 2. Architecture of the composite system

3.3 $M1$ and $M2$ Models

Figure 3 depicts the internal architecture of the M{1,2} component. Each component is implemented in an SMV model. All the modules represent a function achieved by the interlocking except for the train module. In fact the train module allows to simulate the interact of the interlocking with its environment.

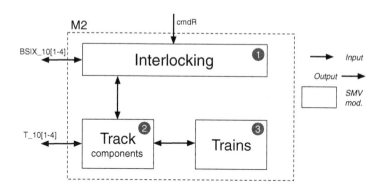

Fig. 3. Architecture of the SMV interlocking model

The interlocking module is directly translated from the application data by mean of a translator tool described in [3] and models the routes and the locking logic of the switches. Upon a route request, the interlocking (1) verifies that the route can be set and then controls the track components accordingly. A proceed aspect (e.g. green) is sent to the origin signal of the route when the switches are locked in correct position and the track-circuits are clear (i.e. no other train is present on the route). Finally the interlocking detects the trains movement, releases the route and unlocks the resources used by the route. The track components (2) record the status of the track-side objects. For example:

for a switch upon a command, the instance verifies that it is not locked before allowing the transition from one position to the other (e.g. left to right). The train modules (3) rely on the track layout of the station. When a signal is at proceed aspect, it simulates a train movement by actuation of the track components. This module is built independently of the application data by mean of a DSL (Domain Specific Language). The train module is local to M{1,2} as it is built based on the track layout of its component.

3.4   BSI Interface Explained

In order to prevent head to head train collisions, the interlocking use a locking mechanism (i.e. *BSI* - Blocage du sens intermittent in French) that prevent two train to head for the same platform in opposite direction. Figure 4 illustrates how the *BSI* variables are actuated upon a route command.

For each platform, two locking variables are used (e.g. BSIA_102 and BSIB_102 for platform 2). When no route is set towards platform 102, the two variables have a permissive value (Free). Upon a route command (e.g. *R_CC_102*), the *BSIA_102* variable is set in a restrictive state (Locked). The routes in opposite direction (e.g. KC_102) are thereby blocked and the signal KC can never be commanded to a proceed aspect (e.g. green). The BSIA_102 variable regains its permissive value when the train has reached platform 102.

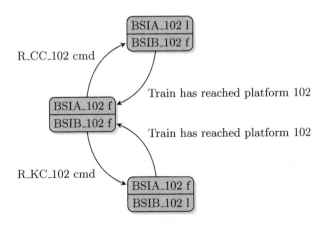

Fig. 4. Directional locking for platform 102

3.5   Sequential Release

When the interlocking grants access to a route, it locks all the resources that will be run through by the train: typically all the switches and the track-circuits. This prevents different routes that share those resources to be set at the same time. Such routes are called conflicting routes. Normally those resources are unlocked when the train has completely run through the route. They then become available for other routes. In large stations, it might be interesting to unlock the resources sequentially allowing them to be used by other routes before the train has totally run through. This contributes to improve the train traffic.

The principle of sequential release is illustrated in Fig. 5: the first route R_DXC_091 is set and prevents the second route R_DXC_092 to be set. The following switches are locked: P1A: left, P2B: right, and P3: right. According to the sequential release principle, the second route is set when the train T_2 is on the track-circuit T_01AC and when the track-circuit T_02BC is free.

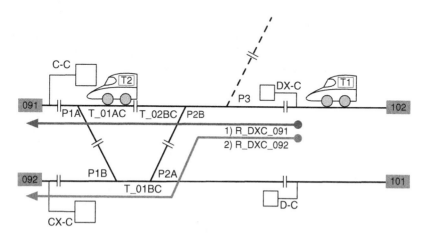

Fig. 5. Sequential release example

4 Verification

The decomposition of one interlocking into several components allows to perform the verification on smaller models (one for each component) and thus limits the so-called state space explosion problem. Therefore we have used two different methods to verify the application data of Braine station: the first takes advantage of the OCRA compositional verification tool and the second uses the NUXMV tool to verify local properties.

The compositional verification applies to the safety properties that imply an interaction between the two components. Those properties are expressed by mean of contracts. An example of contract is given in Listing 1.2.

A second set of properties are verified straight on each component (i.e. $M1$ and $M2$) with NUXMV. Several instances of NUXMV can be started at the same time in order to reduce the computation time of the verification.

4.1 Compositional Verification

Conflicting Routes Controlled by Two Different Components. The routes R_CC_101 and R_KC_101 are conflicting because they share the same platform as a destination and the corresponding safety property is expressed by the formula: $P = G!(R\_CC\_101\_LCS \ \& \ R\_KC\_101\_LCS) - routesTowards\_101$ in Listing 1.2. Equation (4.1) shows how this property is verified by composition of the $M1$ and $M2$ modules. The first premise states that when the route R_CC_101 is set and origin signal is clear (i.e. R_CC_101_LCS is true), the mutual exclusion property (!BSIA_101 & BSIB_101) is true. The second premise states the same property (P_2) for the route R_KC_101. P_1 and P_2 are respectively CC_101_OK and KC_101_OK in Listing 1.2. OCRA performs the verification of these two properties with NUXMV. The third premise states that the first two premises entail the global property P. Finally when all three premises are true, the composition of the components $M1$ and $M2$ verifies the global property P.

In other words, if each component (i.e. $M1$ and $M2$) properly blocks the access to a shared platform when it controls a route, then the other component will not be able to control a conflicting route for the same platform.

$$
\begin{array}{c}
(\text{Premise 1}) \ M_1 \models P_1 \\
(\text{Premise 2}) \ M_2 \models P_2 \\
(\text{Premise 3}) \ P_1 \wedge P_2 \models P \\
\hline
M_1 \| M_2 \models P
\end{array}
$$

Equation 4.1: Compositional verification of conflicting routes property involving the M_1 and M_2 components

```
1    CONTRACT routesTowards_101
2      assume: always TRUE;
3      guarantee: always (R_KC_101_LCS -> !R_CC_101_LCS );
4
5    CONTRACT routesTowards_101
6      REFINEDBY M1.CC_101_OK, M2.KC_101_OK;
7
8    CONTRACT CC_101_OK
9      assume: TRUE;
10     guarantee: always (R_CC_101_LCS -> (!BSIA_101 &
           BSIB_101));
11   CONTRACT KC_101_OK
12     assume: TRUE;
13     guarantee: always (R_KC_101_LCS -> (!BSIB_101 &
           BSIA_101));
```

Listing 1.2. Contract definition for conflicting routes towards platform 101 involving the $M1$ and $M2$ components

Listing 1.2 illustrates how the conflicting routes contract for the routes R_KC_101 and R_CC_101 is specified. First a top level contract (routesTowards_101) specifies that the two routes cannot be set at the same time. The top level contract is then refined by two contracts that apply on $M1$ and $M2$: KC_101_OK and CC_101_OK respectively. These two contracts allow to verify that the $M1$ and $M2$ components handle the BSI locking mechanism properly. The syntax of the language is given in [11].

4.2   Local Safety Properties

The term *Local Properties* designates the properties that are not influenced by the environment of the component on which they are verified. Those properties are verified on each component SMV model with NUXMV. Due to the space limitation, those properties will not be explained in detail but examples are provided in Listing 1.3. They are expressed in two different ways:

– By mean of invariants (lines 1 to 5)
– By mean of LTL formulas and especially by using the ic3 algorithm (lines 6 and 7)

```
1   check_invar -p "!(M1.t1.front = derailed)"
2   check_invar -p "!(M1.t1.front = M1.t2.front)"
3   check_invar -p "!((M1.T_01AC.st = o) & M1.P_01AC.willMove)"
4   check_invar -p "(M1.R_CXC_103.L_CS -> !M1.R_EC_091.L_CS)"
5   check_invar -p "(M1.f1.U_CXC_13C.st=1 -> (M1.f1.U_13C_15C.
        st = 1 xor M1.f1.U_13C_DXC.st = 1))"
6   check_ltlspec_klive -p "G (M1.U_IR_01AC.st = 1 -> ((M1.
        P_01AC.posi = cdr -> X M1.P_01AC.posi = cdr) & (M1.
        P_01AC.posi = cdn -> X M1.P_01AC.posi = cdn)))"
7   check_ltlspec_klive -p "G((M1.T_01AC.st = o & M1.TRP_CC.krc
        = s) -> X (!M1.R_CC_101.L_CS & !M1.R_CC_102.L_CS & !M1.
        R_CC_103.L_CS & !M1.R_CC_104.L_CS))"
```

Listing 1.3. Local properties

Explanation of the properties:

– Line 1: the train never derails. A derailment happens when a train takes a trailing point in reverse direction.
– Line 2: two trains never collide. This is done by verifying that their front never reaches the same track segment at the same time.
– Line 3: a point never move when its home track-circuit is occupied.
– Line 4: conflicting routes are not set at the same time. This formula verifies the same property as the contracts defined in OCRA.
– Line 5: the sub-routes are released in the correct sequence.
– Line 6: a point never moves when its latching variable is in restrictive state. These formulas are checked by mean of k-liveness (see [14])
– Line 7: signal replacement. The origin signal of a route is immediately commanded to red (replaced) when the train occupies the first track-circuit of the route and has triggered the first passage sensor. This prevents a second train to use the same authorization (i.e. signal green).

5   Results and Performance

In this section, we discuss the performance of our verification approach based on composition and local verification. We also illustrate how we validate the model and the properties by error seeding.

5.1   Performance

The tests were performed on 2.3 GHz i7 MacBookPro with 4 GB of RAM running under OS 10.11. Tables 1, 2, and 3 illustrate the results (in terms of computation time), which we achieve using different methods and different models. "BDD" refers to the fix-point algorithm using BDDs (see [15]); "SAT(ic3)" refers to the ic3 algorithm using a SAT solver as backend (see [2]); "SMT(ic3)" refers to the ic3 algorithm integrated predicate abstraction using an SMT solver as back-end (see [7]).

Table 1. Performance of the verification of invariants on monolithic models

Model		Tool	Method	Properties	Duration
1	Monolithic model	NuSMV	BDD	Invariants	$> 1\ day$
2	Partial monolithic model	NuSMV	BDD	Invariants	$> 1\ day$
3	Monolithic model	NuXMV	SAT(ic3)	10 × Invariants	123 s
4	Monolithic model	NuXMV	SMT(ic3)	10 × Invariants	80 s

Table 1 reports the performance of the verification of the application data for the station described in Sect. 3. Line 1 shows that NUSMV could not terminate in one day. After reducing the size the state space by allowing only 16 routes to be commanded, NUSMV could build the reachable state space in 6 days and verify invariants (line 2). One of the features of OCRA is to allow to rebuild a monolithic (32 routes) model based on the definition of the system. The verification of invariants is therefore possible. The results clearly show that ic3 with predicate abstraction performs better than plain ic3, and that both outperform the BDD-based algorithm on this case study.

Table 2. Performance of the verification of the contracts by OCRA

Model		Tool	Method	Properties	Duration
5	Contract refinement	OCRA	-	4 × Contracts	$7,34$ s
6	Implementation M1	OCRA	ic3	4 × Contracts	$5,6$ s
7	Implementation M2	OCRA	ic3	4 × Contracts	$14,94$ s
8	Composite monolithic	OCRA	ic3	4 × Contracts	1242 s

Table 2 illustrates the performance of the verification of the contracts and their implementation. Line 5 corresponds to the verification of the premise 3 of

Eq. (4.1) $(P_1 \wedge P_2 \models P)$. Lines 6 and 7 are respectively related to the verification of the premisses 1 and 2 ($M1 \models P_1$ and $M2 \models P_2$). The sum of the duration of these 3 tasks gives the time needed by OCRA to check the coherence between the contracts and their implementation in the SMV models (i.e. ≤ 28 s). This time is to be compared with the *1242* s needed by OCRA to verify the same contracts and implementations on a monolithic model.

Table 3. Performance of the verification of the local properties

Model		Tool	Method	Properties	Duration
9	M1	NuXMV	BDD	197 × Invariants	*123 s*
10	M2	NuXMV	BDD	199 × Invariants	*424 s*
11	M1	NuXMV	SAT(ic3)	12 × LTL	*960 s*
12	M1	NuXMV	SMT(ic3)	12 × LTL	*20 s*
13	M2	NuXMV	SAT(ic3)	12 × LTL	*1036 s*
14	M2	NuXMV	SMT(ic3)	12 × LTL	*740 s*

Finally Table 3 illustrates the verification of the local safety properties on the $M1$ and $M2$ components. Two approaches are used: first some invariants are verified with NUXMV and the standard BDD and second 12 LTL properties are verified with the ic3 algorithm. An order file based on [26] is used to optimize the BDD structure. ic3 with abstraction and the SMT MathSAT solver outperforms ic3 with MiniSAT in this context in an order of magnitude close to 50.

5.2   Error Seeding

In order to gain confidence in our model and properties, we have seeded errors in the model by removing some safety conditions in the route proving conditions[1]. As expected, OCRA could not prove the safety property and produced a counterexample. Listing 1.4 shows that the property is false (line 1) because the route R_KXC_101 is set (line 30) whereas the BSIB_101 is TRUE (line 5).

```
1  LTL spec G (R_KXC_101_LCS         9       -> State: 2.2 <-
       -> (!BSIB_101 &              10          R_KXC_101.cmd = TRUE
       BSIA_101)) is false          11  ...
2  Trace Description: IC3           12       -> Input: 2.3 <-
       counterexample               13          cmdR = R_KXC_103
3     -> State: 2.1 <-              14       -> State: 2.3 <-
4     ...                           15          R_KXC_101.st = s
5        BSIB_101.st = TRUE         16  ...
6     ...                           17       -> State: 2.4 <-
7     -> Input: 2.2 <-              18          U_IR_09C.st = 1
8        cmdR = R_KXC_101           19          U_IR_07BC.st = 1
```

---

[1] Conditions to give a proceed aspect on origin signal of the route.

```
20        BSIA_101 = TRUE              28        T_101.st = c
21        U_IR_07AC.st = 1             29        T_101_1 = FALSE
22        U_16C_JXC.st = 1             30        R_KXC_101_LCS = TRUE
23        U_18C_16C.st = 1                        (Route is set)
24        U_KXC_18C.st = 1             31        KXCopen = TRUE
25        ...
26        -> State: 2.5 <-
27        R_KXC_101.st = rsu
```

Listing 1.4. Error trace generated after error seeding in the model

6 Related Work

Many works applied model checking to interlocking systems. One of the first work dates back to 1998 and is described in [6]. However, as also concluded in [17], although small scale interlocking systems can be addressed by model checking, interlockings that control medium or large railway needs to tackle the state-space explosion problem. As shown also in [9], a single approach is often not sufficient to prove all properties and sometimes a combination of approach may dramatically improve the performance.

Compositional approach is one method to reduce the complexity of the verification but is not the only one. For instance, Cappart et al. [4] introduced a method based on discrete event simulations. The idea is to do not verify all the states but to limit the verification to a set of likely scenarios. However this method does not provide enough confidence that all the errors in the application data will be detected.

In [19,25], Winter shows how to compute optimized variable and transition orderings in order to speed-up the symbolic model checking of railway interlockings with NuSMV. She also reported on her findings on how to set the threshold for cluster.

In [26], Winter et al. modelled the interlocking by means of the formal notation ASM that are more readable. The formal model is translated in NuSMV code and the Safety requirements are expressed in CTL.

In [16], Peter Duggan (Siemens Rail Automation, UK) and Arne Borälv (Prover Technology AB, Sweden) have demonstrated that the Prover[2] tools were successfully used to generate and test the configuration data of a realistic size UK station.

In [24], Haxthausen et al. detailed how they modelled an ETCS level 2 compatible Danish interlocking with the RT-Tester. The state space, the transition relation and the safety properties are efficiently evaluated by the SMT solvers that support bit vector and integer arithmetic. The model also include the sequential release feature.

In [27], Xu et al. verifies hybrid safety properties of Automatic Collision Avoidance System (ACAS) in the European Train Control System (ETCS). They verify those properties using Compositional Verification rules based on weakly monotonic time extension.

---

[2] http://www.prover.com.

In [1], Antoni et al. have developed a SIL4 interlocking that uses the Petri Nets as application data. In [22], Dutilleul et al. have also used the Petri Nets in order to define a model pattern of railway interlocking.

7 Conclusions and Future Work

Conclusions. The verification of medium and large interlocking data is still a challenge due to the state space explosion problem affecting the model checking process. Our main contribution was to achieve the verification of the application data of a medium size railway interlocking by mean of compositional verification. In order to do that, we modelled our case study interlocking as a composite of smaller interlocking components in OCRA and SMV language. The verification of the safety properties (expressed as contracts) was performed with OCRA and NUXMV tools.

We have also added the sequential release functionality into our interlocking model. This functionality allows to increase the throughput of the railway network by releasing the route components earlier.

Finally, we have achieved the verification of LTL properties in efficient time thanks to the usage of the new ic3 algorithm implemented into NUXMV. The verification of the local components can be paralleled by running several instances of NUXMV at the same time.

Future work. In our future work, we will continue to refine the structure of the interlocking composite into adequate components (e.g. train). Our goal is to be able to verify safety properties on a network of interlockings by mean of compositional verification.

We will continue to develop the automatic translator tool in order to convert the application data of a network of interlockings into OCRA language.

Another goal is to develop a model of an IL/ETCS installation in order to verify safety properties related to the train dynamic characteristics (i.e. speed and position). In order to do that we will extend our train module in order to make it continuous.

References

1. Antoni, M., Ammad, N.: Formal Validation Method and Tools for French Computorized Railway Interlocking Systems, pp. 1–10, June 2008
2. Bradley, A.R.: SAT-based model checking without unrolling. In: Jhala, R., Schmidt, D. (eds.) VMCAI 2011. LNCS, vol. 6538, pp. 70–87. Springer, Heidelberg (2011)
3. Busard, S., Cappart, Q., Limbrée, C., Pecheur, C., Schaus, P.: Verification of railway interlocking systems. In: Proceedings 4th International Workshop on Engineering Safety and Security Systems, ESSS 2015, Oslo, Norway, June 22, 2015, pp. 19–31 (2015). http://dx.doi.org/10.4204/EPTCS.184.2
4. Cappart, Q., Limbrée, C., Schaus, P., Legay, A.: Verification by discrete simulation of interlocking systems. In: Proceedings of the 29th Annual European Simulation and Modelling Conference, EUROSIS, October 2015

5. Cavada, R., et al.: The NUXMV symbolic model checker. In: Biere, A., Bloem, R. (eds.) CAV 2014. LNCS, vol. 8559, pp. 334–342. Springer, Heidelberg (2014)
6. Cimatti, A., Giunchiglia, F., Mongardi, G., Romano, D., Torielli, F., Traverso, P.: Formal verification of a railway interlocking system using model checking. Formal Aspects Comput. **10**, 361–380 (1998). doi:10.1007/s001650050022
7. Cimatti, A., Griggio, A., Mover, S., Tonetta, S.: IC3 modulo theories via implicit predicate abstraction. In: Ábrahám, E., Havelund, K. (eds.) TACAS 2014 (ETAPS). LNCS, vol. 8413, pp. 46–61. Springer, Heidelberg (2014)
8. Cimatti, A., Clarke, E., Giunchiglia, E., Giunchiglia, F., Pistore, M., Roveri, M., Sebastiani, R., Tacchella, A.: NuSMV 2: an opensource tool for symbolic model checking. In: Brinksma, E., Larsen, K.G. (eds.) CAV 2002. LNCS, vol. 2404, pp. 359–364. Springer, Heidelberg (2002)
9. Cimatti, A., Corvino, R., Lazzaro, A., Narasamdya, I., Rizzo, T., Roveri, M., Sanseviero, A., Tchaltsev, A.: Formal verification and validation of ERTMS industrial railway train spacing system. In: Madhusudan, P., Seshia, S.A. (eds.) CAV 2012. LNCS, vol. 7358, pp. 378–393. Springer, Heidelberg (2012)
10. Cimatti, A., Dorigatti, M., Tonetta, S.: OCRA: A tool for checking the refinement of temporal contracts. In: ASE, pp. 702–705 (2013)
11. Cimatti, A., Dorigatti, M., Tonetta, S.: Ocra: Othello Contracts Refinement Analysis Versions 1,3. FBK (2015)
12. Cimatti, A., Tonetta, S.: Contracts-refinement proof system for component-based embedded systems. Sci. Comput. Program. **97**, 333–348 (2015)
13. Claessen, K., Sörensson, N.: A liveness checking algorithm that counts. In: FMCAD, pp. 52–59. IEEE (2012)
14. Claessen, K., Sorensson, N.: A liveness checking algorithm that counts. In: Formal Methods in Computer-Aided Design, FMCAD 2012, Cambridge, UK, October 22–25, 2012, pp. 52–59 (2012). http://ieeexplore.ieee.org/xpl/articleDetails.jsp?arnumber=6462555
15. Clarke, J.E.M., Grumberg, O., Peled, D.A.: Model Checking. The MIT Press, Cambridge (1999)
16. Duggan, P., Borälv, A.: Mathematical proof in an automated environment for railway interlockings. IRSE News Issue 217, Institution of Railway Signal Engineers, 2–6 December 2015. www.irse.org
17. Ferrari, A., Magnani, G., Grasso, D., Fantechi, A.: Model checking interlocking control tables. In: FORMS/FORMAT, pp. 107–115 (2010)
18. Graf, S., Saïdi, H.: Construction of abstract state graphs with PVS. In: Grumberg, O. (ed.) CAV 1997. LNCS, vol. 1254, pp. 72–83. Springer, Heidelberg (1997)
19. Johnston, W., Winter, K., van den Berg, L., Strooper, P., Robinson, P.: Model-based variable and transition orderings for efficient symbolic model checking. In: Misra, J., Nipkow, T., Sekerinski, E. (eds.) FM 2006. LNCS, vol. 4085, pp. 524–540. Springer, Heidelberg (2006)
20. McMillan, K.L.: Symbolic Model Checking. Kluwer Academic Publishers, Norwell (1993)
21. Pnueli, A.: The temporal logic of programs. In: FOCS, pp. 46–57 (1977)
22. Sun, P., Collart-Dutilleul, S., Bon, P.: A model pattern of railway interlocking system by Petri nets. In: 2015 International Conference on Models and Technologies for Intelligent Transportation Systems (MT-ITS), pp. 442–449, June 2015
23. Tonetta, S.: Abstract model checking without computing the abstraction. In: Cavalcanti, A., Dams, D.R. (eds.) FM 2009. LNCS, vol. 5850, pp. 89–105. Springer, Heidelberg (2009)

24. Vu, L.H., Haxthausen, A.E., Peleska, J.: Formal modeling and verification of interlocking systems featuring sequential release. In: Artho, C., Ölveczky, P.C. (eds.) FTSCS 2014. CCIS, vol. 476, pp. 223–238. Springer, Heidelberg (2015). http://dx.doi.org/10.1007/978-3-319-17581-2_15
25. Winter, K.: Optimising ordering strategies for symbolic model checking of railway interlockings. In: Margaria, T., Steffen, B. (eds.) ISoLA 2012, Part II. LNCS, vol. 7610, pp. 246–260. Springer, Heidelberg (2012). http://dx.doi.org/10.1007/978-3-642-34032-1_24
26. Winter, K., Robinson, N.J.: Modelling large railway interlockings and model checking small ones. In: Oudshoorn, M. (ed.) Twenty-Fifth Australasian Computer Science Conference (ACSC 2003), pp. 309–316 (2003)
27. Xu, T., Tang, T., Gao, C., Cai, B.: Logic verification of collision avoidance system in train control systems. In: 2009 IEEE Intelligent Vehicles Symposium, pp. 918–923, June 2009

Safety Verification of Heterogeneous Railway Networks

Paulius Stankaitis$^{(\boxtimes)}$ and Alexei Iliasov

Centre for Software Reliability, Newcastle University,
Newcastle upon Tyne, UK
{paulius.stankaitis,alexei.iliasov}@ncl.ac.uk

Abstract. Formal verification of safety-critical systems is crucial for demonstrating their safety to the certification bodies. In particular, the railway network validation requires rigorous analyses and the use of formal methods to meet railway standards. This student paper outlines objectives and the current progress of the work on verification of complex railway networks consisting of the areas with different signalling and interlocking.

1 Introduction

1.1 Background and Motivation

The modernisation of railway systems is concerned with many improvement aspects like capacity, energy or interoperability, however, one requirement has to be preserved for any kind of development - safety. Railway certification standards require applying semi-formal or formal methods for description of the system and even correctness validation [1]. The most popular formal description languages used in the railway industry for modelling and requirement specification are UML, B-Method and Petri Nets, whereas in the academic community Communicating Sequential Processes (CSP) and Event-B have been used more widely for railway modelling. The industry has been successfully applying these formal techniques for safety reasoning for some time now with many application examples currently in operation. Perhaps the finest example was the use of the B-method in major railway projects including a Paris metro line and a more complex New York Canarsie line [2].

In spite of formal methods success in the railway domain simulation techniques are still extensively used by railway industry to ensure that safety standards are met within the system [3]. The simplicity of the simulation method is the main driving force for its use, therefore, simulation tools like OpenTrack [4] or RailSys [5] are widely used in the industry to design and analyse railway systems. Even though, simulation tools are becoming more powerful nowadays and even capable of mixed-signalling simulation the main drawback of this technique is a small state-space coverage. On the contrary the formal safety verification of railway networks is a complicated process, which requires expertise in the mathematical modelling, however, it provides techniques to guarantee

© Springer International Publishing Switzerland 2016
T. Lecomte et al. (Eds.): RSSRail 2016, LNCS 9707, pp. 150–159, 2016.
DOI: 10.1007/978-3-319-33951-1_11

safety for a complete state-space. A significant effort has been made by an academic research projects like SafeCap [6] to hide mathematical complexity and allow railway engineers to use formal methods. In this particular project, formal methods are being applied together with capacity, energy optimisation techniques to improve railway networks. Despite of formal methods complexity, the approach is increasingly receiving more attention from the industry. One of the best examples is a company [7], which developed a formal methodology for the railway network safety verification that has been applied in real projects.

European Union's initiative to unify railway signalling systems and therefore enhance interoperability aims to reduce the complexity of networks in the future. However, replacing current systems will be done gradually due to financial and time constraints, therefore, creating tangled railway networks with heterogeneous signalling systems. The Crossrail Project [8] is just one of the examples, where high capacity requirements will need to be met in a complex multi-signalling network consisting of three different signalling types.

On the other hand, as it was demonstrated by Koning [9] specific layouts or sections of the network are more suited with a particular signalling system, therefore, railway networks can also benefit from the mixed-signalling in terms of increased capacity.

Because of the high importance and close relation to our research in the next subsection we provide an additional information about the academic project, SafeCap, which aims to address many of optimisation, modelling and verification issues in the railway domain.

1.2 SafeCap Project

The SafeCap project was started with the objective to overcome railway capacity problems without weakening safety constraints. The key outcome of the first stage of the project was a SafeCap tooling environment, which not only allowed railway engineers to design and analyse railway junctions/stations, but also to formally and automatically verify safety. The SafeCap platform was designed to be easily configurable and extensible, so it could be used in various railway optimisation and capacity assessment exercises.

At the core of the SafeCap framework is a compact and simple domain-specific language, which was designed to enable railway engineers to use formal techniques by hiding complexity of formal methods. The SafeCap domain-specific language is used to define topological and logical properties for reasoning about operational safety. A huge advantage of this language is the compatibility with various automatic verification tools like a model-checker ProB or SMT constraint solvers. The SafeCap project, also has strong industrial links and closely collaborates with industrial partners like Siemens Rail Automation to improve tooling environment to fulfil industry needs.

2   Research Aim and Technical Objectives

The aim of this PhD study is to a create a methodology and tool support for modelling and verification of heterogeneous railway networks. In order to successfully achieve our aim we will need to make following advances: extend theoretical foundations, improve verification and simulation techniques.

Theoretical foundations are needed for modelling complex heterogeneous railway networks. Significant progress was achieved by Iliasov *et al.* [10], where a domain-specific language was developed to demonstrate multi-agent system's operational safety. The objective of this work package is to build on this domain-specific language and extend it to enable reasoning about heterogeneous railway networks safety. The main challenge is discovering additional functionality requirements for the extension of the domain-specific language.

The safety verification of complex models like mixed-signalling railway networks is a grand challenge and requires the state-of-the-art tool support. Railway industry has been using simulation techniques to demonstrate that safety standards are preserved, however, these techniques cannot ensure safety for complete state-space. The objective of this work package is to develop a verification tool, which exploits modern automated reasoning techniques and would allows us to demonstrate that even for railway networks with mixed-signalling we can verify safety conditions for a complete state-space.

Last technical objective is to design a new flexible and expressive simulation suite, which one could use to design existing or exotic signalling systems. Since, the aim of the research is to enable us modelling a multi-signalling systems a signalling library is vital. Therefore, a developed simulation tool will be used to create a signalling library with multiple existing train control systems. Furthermore, the development process of the signalling library will also help us to identify additional features, which are needed for extending theoretical foundations.

We aim to evaluate our research by demonstrating multiple examples of the complete cycle of modelling and verification of artificial and real-world heterogeneous railway networks using data received from our industrial partners. In particularly, we are interested in applying our methodology and tools to major railway projects like the Crossrail or Thameslink.

All technical research outcomes will be integrated into the SafeCap platform, which after the modifications will have a framework to support the design, analysis and verification of heterogeneous railway systems. The SafeCap platform also allows capacity and energy assessments, which could further support our motive to investigate complex heterogeneous systems and their benefits.

3   Research Plan

In this section we provide a detailed research plan, which is visually represented in the diagram below. Figure 1 illustrates connections and possible parallelism between technical objectives we set in the previous section as well as particular development tasks we need to complete. In the diagram we highlighted two essential design tasks in this research, which are discussed in greater detailed and results are presented in this publication.

3.1 Theoretical Foundations: Unified Train Driving Policy

In the previous section we established a necessity to extend the current railway modelling language, called Unified Train Driving Policy. Contrary to other general modelling languages like [11,12] the UTDP language was developed with a objective to target specifically railway engineers. Therefore, the syntax of the formalism is easily readable and can be interpreted by railway engineers without prior knowledge of formal methods. However, the current version of the language is not capable of capturing complex heterogeneous railway network models, hence, a significant effort will be put to modify the language, and also, to prove the soundness and correctness of the new extended formal language.

From Fig. 1 we can see that work on extending this modelling language depends on results from the simulation part. Throughout, the design of multiple train control systems we hope to identify additional formalism features.

3.2 Verification Techniques: Concept of the Tool

Heterogeneous railway network safety verification will require a cutting edge tool support to validate these complicated models. In the introduction we discussed a problem of inadequate railway safety verification in the industry using simulation techniques. In Sect. 2 we set an objective to address this problem by developing a new tool, which uses modern state-of-the-art theorem proving techniques to tackle the issue. Below we describe the concept of the plug-in and the implementation plan.

Considering, a huge effort put and progress achieved in automated theorem proving area by companies like Microsoft Research [13] and universities like Manchester University [14], it was decided to tackle this complexity and scalability problem by utilising leading theorem provers. Currently, there exists more

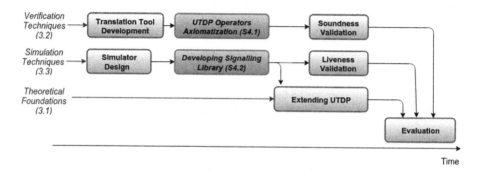

Fig. 1. Visual representation of the research plan

than a dozen of different theorem provers, which are different in many aspects e.g. input notation, performance. Although, this can be seen as advantage as hosting a collection of them would increase the range of problems and success rate of proving a safety condition, creating a link to each of them could be a challenging task. Therefore, the foremost task is to address this problem and create a tangible link between SafeCap platform and multiple theorem provers.

We decided to use a popular tool, called Why3 [15], which has been used fairly widely in automated reasoning community to exploit multiple theorem provers by providing a common interface. It has a straightforward input notation as well as an additional library to support SMT-LIB solvers. An important feature of the tool is the capability to import additional libraries, hence, allowing defining other not built-in types or functions. We will use this tool property to define new set-theoretic operators, which are used in the SafeCap platform modelling language.

Theorem proving is a computationally intensive exercises, where success of discharging a condition highly correlates with machines capabilities. Therefore, we intend to support our verification tool with a cloud technology, which allows computationally intensive tasks to be done remotely. Because of, cloud parallelism capabilities this could yield significant improvements in terms of verification time, also increase the number of discharged verification conditions.

Visual concept of the complete system is shown in Fig. 2, where we combine the theorem proving and cloud technologies to enhance our verification capabilities. The verification process is as follows: the SafeCap platforms generated safety conditions in internal set-theoretic modelling language are translated to Why3 input notation using our plug-in. The translated goals are then parsed to the multiple theorem provers and results are collected, and transferred back to the SafeCap platform.

The essential part of the tool development will be defining new set-theoretic operators and axiomatizing them in Why3 language, we conjecture that it has the most significant effect on discharging a safety conditions. The ongoing work and results regarding this challenge are described in Sect. 4.1.

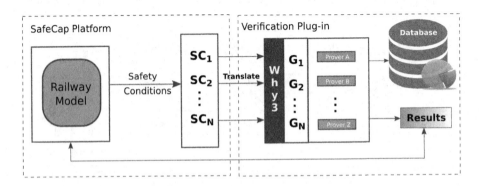

Fig. 2. Visual concept of the verification plug-in

3.3   Simulation Techniques: Simulator and Signalling Library Design

The important and challenging technical objective of this research is the development of the expressive railway simulator, which would provide a framework for developing train control systems. Technical advances in this work will include the development of expressive simulation tool and a signalling library.

First of all, existing rigid event-based SafeCap simulator, which currently only supports a single route-based train control system needs to be replaced by more flexible and expressive time-slicing simulator. The purpose of the new simulator is to enable us designing different types of signalling systems in order to create heterogeneous railway networks. Expressiveness of the tool will provide us with a framework to develop not only existing signalling systems like ETCS or CBTC, but also some more exotic and unconventional interlocking systems. The multiple developed signalling systems will form a SafeCap signalling library, which we will be used model and experiment with multi-signalling railway systems.

3.4   Research Evaluation

Methodology and tool evaluation will be the final step in our research, where we intend to use a combination of artificial and existing heterogeneous railway networks to assess our developed tools and methodology. Nonetheless, before the evaluation we need to assert a set of aspects under which we will be evaluating our research. To easy research evaluation, we can divide the procedure into three main parts with respect to technical objectives.

An extended theoretical semantics must be able to capture railway networks with the mixed-signalling and also must be proved to be sound, and correct. To validate this we can experiment with a variety of signalling system combinations as well as real-world heterogeneous networks like Crossrail or Thameslink to deduce if theoretical basis is adequate to create formal system models.

The evaluation of verification tool support will be completed by proving multiple heterogeneous models with a developed verification plug-in and comparing results with already existing SafeCap verification tool set. Even though, many can argue that a complete automation of verification process in particularly of complex models is hardly achievable, we conjecture that with the modern state-of-the-art provers we can achieve complete automation for at least the railway domain. Furthermore, during the verification tool evaluation we can detect missing operator axiomatisation properties and improve tool by including new premises.

Finally, we will evaluate the simulation technique part of the research on the basis of expressiveness and stability of the new simulator during the development of signalling systems.

4   Ongoing Work and Results

In this section we present and discuss current progress and some of the results with particular focus on the SafeCap modelling language operator axiomatisation and a moving-block train control system development. We choose to exclude discussion and results of programming tasks like development of verification and simulation tools as they have little relevance to this conference.

4.1   Verification Techniques: Set-Theoretic Operator Axiomatisation

Significant research effort was concentrated on defining set-theoretic operators of the SafeCap platforms modelling language in the Why3 notation. The verification tool will use these definitions to reason about safety conditions, therefore, it is essential to have a sound and sufficient library of definitions. However, we recognise that is arguably achievable to have a complete set of definitions, hence, we leave the library open for further extensions in the future.

In order to demonstrate the importance and the function of axiomatisation in a verification process, lets consider an example below. In Eq. 1, we define a typical railway model topological constraint, which states that a route must be non-empty [3]. A condition below contains an operator card, which represents a cardinality operator. A cardinality, or else set size is a function, which takes a set and returns the number of elements in that set.

$$\forall r \cdot r \in R \rightarrow card(fst(r)) = card(lst(r)) = 1 \qquad (1)$$

In order to satisfy this condition we need to have a set of definitions about cardinality operator in our library. In the example below, we show a fragment of our operator library, which describes a set size function. To define an operator one needs to specify parameters like input/output type, function name. Then, using axioms define its properties, i.e. output of cardinality is greater or equal to zero if the set is finite.

```
function card (set 'a) : int

axiom card_def0:
forall s: set 'a. finite s -> card s >= 0
```

We successfully defined all set-theoretic operators from the internal modelling language, which resulted in a library with in total 78 functions and predicates. To further define those operators in more detail we wrote 78 axioms and 115 lemmas.

The verification tool is already at the state, where it can translate safety conditions generated by the SafeCap tool to the Why3 input notation and discharge a significant number of verification conditions.

4.2   Simulation Techniques: Moving-Block Signalling Development

In this subsection we report on progress achieved in developing and experimenting with signalling systems with particular focus on designing a moving-block train control system using newly developed time-slicing simulator.

The biggest effort in the development of a moving-block control system was the design of the abstract algorithm. We applied a top-down approach and in the initial step the algorithm was divided into two main parts: analysis and operation. Analysis part of the algorithm was responsible for examining the static information i.e. the layout topology, train parameters, timetable. Furthermore, it was responsible for scheduling trains over shared resources like, points. Operation stage of the algorithm used information generated in the analysis part together with dynamic information like train speed, position, direction of points to control the actors of the system (e.g. train speed, point direction). In order to use a new simulator an abstract algorithm had be to translated into programming language, which can be interpreted by the new simulator. At the moment, the new time-slicing simulator only supports Java input.

To demonstrate the current implementation of the algorithm we use a small single-line bridge scenario, where a fragment of the network is shown in Fig. 3. At this development stage we are mostly concerned with testing algorithms analysis part and refinement of the train speed control. In the current version of the algorithm a train speed is adjusted to satisfy following condition:

– to maintain a safe train separation distance
– to cross points at allowed speed and in the scheduled order

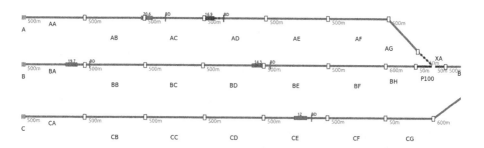

Fig. 3. A fragment of single-line bridge layout with a moving-block signalling

In this experiment we introduced a small disturbance to test re-activeness of the system, which made a one of the trains to slow down for a period of time. We expected other trains to respond to this disturbance and respectively reduce the speed in order to satisfy established conditions above. In Fig. 4 we project the speed profiles of this experiment. As one can see from the figure below, the chain reaction of the reducing speeds starts after the first trains starts to slow down at around 80s. The second important point to take from this figure is deceleration of trains before entering the points. It is important to note that we currently at initial stage of the moving-block signalling development and we testing the very basic properties. Nonetheless, we will gradually refine the algorithm and implementation to represent a more realistic, and optimal train control mechanism.

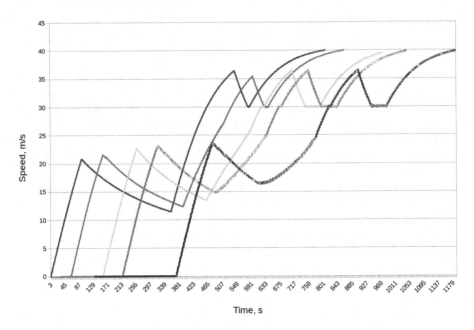

Fig. 4. Speed profiles of trains under developed control system

4.3   Future Work

In our future work we will mostly concentrate on developing multiple railway signalling systems and extending our theoretical foundations. On the short-term, the foremost objective is completing design of a moving-block train control system. A collection of developed signalling systems will enables us to identify required additional theoretical functionality, thus, we will proceed our work on extending theoretical foundations after we gained sufficient information from signalling system development.

5   Conclusion

In the introduction authors discussed the initiative and issues of the process to gradually unify signalling systems across Europe, and thus, create complex heterogeneous railway networks. Furthermore, we raised an issue of insufficient verification methods such as simulation technique used by the railway industry to demonstrate systems safety to certification bodies.

In this research we set the aim to address these problems by developing a methodology and tool support for modelling and formal verification of these multi-signalling railway systems. We established three main technical advances in theoretical, verification and simulation areas we need make in order to complete the study goal and provided a detailed technical description of how we plan to achieve this.

Finally, the paper presented current results on axiomatisation of set-theoretic operators and the progress on the development of a moving-block train control system. Authors decided not to include and discuss some of the technical advances related to the tool development due to little relevance to the topic of the conference.

Acknowledgements. This work is supported by the RSSB SafeCap+ project. We are grateful to our colleagues from Siemens Rail Automation for invaluable feedback.

References

1. Cimatti, A., Corvino, R., Lazzaro, A., Narasamdya, I., Rizzo, T., Roveri, M., Sanseviero, A., Tchaltsev, A.: Formal verification and validation of ERTMS industrial railway train spacing system. In: Madhusudan, P., Seshia, S.A. (eds.) CAV 2012. LNCS, vol. 7358, pp. 378–393. Springer, Heidelberg (2012)
2. Essamé, D., Dollé, D.: B in large-scale projects: the canarsie line CBTC experience. In: Julliand, J., Kouchnarenko, O. (eds.) B 2007. LNCS, vol. 4355, pp. 252–254. Springer, Heidelberg (2006)
3. Iliasov, A., Romanovsky, A.: SafeCap domain language for reasoning about safety and capacity. In: Workshop on Dependable Transportation Systems at the Pacific-Rim Dependable Computing Conference, Niigata, Japan (2012)
4. OpenTrack simulator. http://www.opentrack.ch/
5. RailSys simulation platform. http://www.rmcon.de
6. SafeCap Project. http://www.safecap.co.uk
7. Prover Company. http://www.prover.com/
8. Crossrail Project. http://www.crossrail.co.uk/
9. Koning, J.A.: Comparing the performance of ERTMS level 2 fixed block and ERTMS level 3 moving block signalling systems using simulation techniques. In: Proceedings of Eighth International Conference on Computers in Railways, pp. 43–52 (2002)
10. Iliasov, A., Lopatkin, I., Romanovsky, A.: Unified train driving policy. In: Formal-Methods Applied to Complex Systems, pp. 447–473 (2014)
11. Abrial, J.-R.: Modelling in Event-B. Cambridge University Press, Cambridge (2010)
12. Bjørner, D., Jones, C.B.: The Vienna Development Method: The Meta-Language. LNCS, vol. 61. Springer, Heidelberg (1978)
13. de Moura, L., Bjørner, N.S.: Z3: an efficient SMT solver. In: Ramakrishnan, C.R., Rehof, J. (eds.) TACAS 2008. LNCS, vol. 4963, pp. 337–340. Springer, Heidelberg (2008)
14. Riazanov, A., Voronkov, A.: Vampire. In: Ganzinger, H. (ed.) CADE 1999. LNCS (LNAI), vol. 1632, pp. 292–296. Springer, Heidelberg (1999)
15. Filliâtre, J.-C., Marché, C., Paskevich, A.: Why3: shepherd your herd of provers. In: Boogie : First International Workshop on Intermediate Verification Languages, pp. 53–64 (2011)

Comparing Formal Verification Approaches
of Interlocking Systems

Anne Elisabeth Haxthausen[1], Hoang Nga Nguyen[2],
and Markus Roggenbach[3(✉)]

[1] DTU Compute, Technical University of Denmark, Kongens Lyngby, Denmark
[2] Centre for Mobility and Transport, Coventry University, Coventry, UK
[3] Swansea Railway Verification Group, Swansea University, Wales, UK
`M.Roggenbach@Swansea.ac.uk`

Abstract. The verification of railway interlocking systems is a challenging task, and therefore several research groups have suggested to improve this task by using formal methods, but they use different modelling and verification approaches. To advance this research, there is a need to compare these approaches. As a first step towards this, in this paper we suggest a way to compare different formal approaches for verifying designs of route-based interlocking systems and we demonstrate it on modelling and verification approaches developed within the research groups at DTU/Bremen and at Surrey/Swansea. The focus is on designs that are specified by so-called control tables. The paper can serve as a starting point for further comparative studies.

1 Introduction

An interlocking system is responsible for guiding trains safely through a given railway network. It is a vital part of any railway signalling system and has the highest safety integrity level (SIL4) according to the CENELEC 50128 standard [3].

Conventionally, the development and verification process of interlocking systems is informal and mostly manual.

Adding Automated Verification. The left-hand picture in Fig. 1 provides some detail as to how a conventional design process of interlocking systems is typically realised. Concretely it shows the process as implemented by our industrial partner Siemens Rail Automation, UK, in the form of a UML activity diagram. The client provides a CAD plan of the track plan and routes. Independently, the regulator provides a set of design rules. Based on these, the routes are signalled, i.e., various tables are developed. This scheme plan (i.e., track plan plus various tables, e.g., control tables) undergoes thorough manual checks before the tables are used to implement an interlocking. These checks are part of quality control: motivated on the one hand to detect mistakes early, already in the design phase, on the other hand to adhere to development standards required by the authorities as part of a certification process.

© Springer International Publishing Switzerland 2016
T. Lecomte et al. (Eds.): RSSRail 2016, LNCS 9707, pp. 160–177, 2016.
DOI: 10.1007/978-3-319-33951-1_12

As the manual checks are time-consuming, costly, and error-prone, automated verification of interlocking systems is an active research topic. The right-hand picture in Fig. 1 shows a lightweight integration of automated verification (AV) into the traditional work-flow. It includes an automated check of the scheme plan for safety conditions. Only if a scheme plan has been proven to be safe, the costly manual checks are performed. Here, we deliberately refrain from replacing the manual checks. One reason is that safety covers only part of them. Furthermore, academic tools often have not been certified to the tool qualification levels required in safety cases. Finally, the railway domain is conservative: replacing traditional checks by different methods would require additional arguments in safety cases.

Automated Verification of Interlocking Designs. It is still an open research question as how to perform safety checks on interlocking designs. The challenge is how to cope with the complexity of the problem: the state space grows exponentially in the size of the scheme plan to be verified. Several research groups, see e.g. [1,2,4,6–13,15,16,20,23,27–29], have been addressing this challenge and have developed a number of different modelling and verification approaches.

The modelling part of such approaches usually consists of "transformations" of how to derive a (formal) model from informal rail descriptions as used in rail industry such as a track plan (e.g., as a CAD drawing) enriched by various tables (e.g., a control table). Similarly, the verification part usually states a safety condition (e.g., no train collision) and expresses this as a (formal) property (e.g., as a logical formula). Finally, an (automated) verification tool is utilised to provide an answer if the property holds in the model.

Different groups apply different design rules for signalling, country specific rail standards, utilising various modelling languages, employing different verification tools. This leads to the natural, however, fundamental question: how can these many modelling and verification approaches be related with each other? This question comes in at least three, interconnected forms: (i) how to relate the input of these modelling approaches? (ii) how to relate the formal models? (iii) how to relate the verification results?

Relating Automated Verification Approaches. In this paper we suggest a general way of how to compare different formal verification approaches for interlocking systems and demonstrate it on modelling and verification approaches developed within our respective research groups at DTU/Bremen and at Surrey/Swansea. We see this comparison as pioneering work, to which we hope – in the long run – other groups will contribute as well by running their verification approaches through the very same exercises, i.e., this paper can serve as a start for a benchmark for railway verification.

While the focus of our comparison is on verification, to a certain extent we also address the other two questions posed above. Concerning input, we define a common core – see Sect. 2 – and discuss group specific extensions. Concerning the models, for a start we attempt to present the modelling approaches in a uniform way – see Sect. 3. The development of a general questionnaire on models

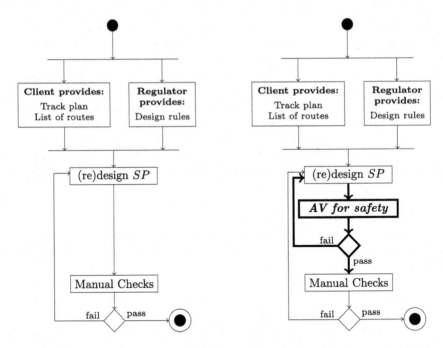

Fig. 1. Incorporating automated verification (AV) in a design & check cycle for a scheme plan *SP*.

will require more experience, including analysing work by further groups. Concerning relating verification, we are confident to propose a practicable and useful approach.

To the best of our knowledge, we are the first to address the question of how different verification approaches for interlocking systems relate. This question is important for various reasons: to advance the field, it will be necessary to better understand work from other groups and to learn from each other; from a company's point of view it is important to be able to evaluate different techniques when choosing one to be included in an interlocking design cycle.

Our comparison focuses on the safety claims that different approaches make. Rather than directly comparing models or properties, we look into the ability of verification approaches to detect errors in the design tables of an interlocking system. Starting with a correct rail design, we inject an error (e.g., by altering the entry of a table), and see if – under a given modelling and verification approach – the injected error is caught. As rail designs can be fault tolerant, here it is necessary to work with "minimal" designs, i.e., such designs, where an injected error actually can be caught. When comparing now two verification approaches, we say that an approach has more distinguishing power than another one, if the first flags the same errors as the second and possibly more.

Our comparison draws on ideas from testing theory. Yu and Lau prove a number of theorems on the error detecting capabilities of various coverage criteria for testing logical decisions [30]. Their set-up consists of several elements: the logical decision to be tested needs to be in a normal form – corresponding to our minimal designs, see Sect. 2; they define a number of syntactic errors (e.g., adding or forgetting a negation, confusing a logical and with a logical or) – we will define a number of error types, see Sect. 4; they establish theorems that characterise the kind of errors that will be detected via testing provided a test suite has been constructed to minimally fulfil a certain coverage criterion – we will compare two verification approaches by defining and performing a number of experiments, see Sect. 5.

Organisation of the Paper. First, in Sect. 2, we introduce basic notions of the railway domain, including the notions of scheme plan, track plan, and control table. Then, in Sect. 3, we provide a descriptive comparison between the two different modelling and verification approaches by DTU/Bremen and Surrey/Swansea, where both approaches are described using a similar scheme. In Sect. 4 we identify a number of error types that might happen during the design of a control table. Finally, in Sect. 5, we report on experimental results demonstrating that all these errors can be detected by both formal methods, the one from DTU/Bremen as well as the one from Surrey/Swansea.

2   Railway Scheme Plans

A railway scheme plan consists of a track plan and various tables, e.g., control tables.

Track Plans. A railway network consists of a number of track-side elements of different types, for instance linear sections, points, and either marker boards (for ETCS level 2 systems) or physical signals (for legacy systems). The track plan in Fig. 2 shows an example layout of a railway network having six linear sections (b20, t20, b10, t10, t13, b13, t23, b23), two points (t11, t12), and eight marker boards (mb10, . . . , mb30). A linear section is a section with up to two neighbours. A point can have up to three neighbours: one at the stem, one at the plus end, and one at the minus end, e.g., point t12 in Fig. 2 has t11, t13, and t30 as neighbours at its stem, plus, and minus ends, respectively. Linear sections and points are collectively called detection sections, as they are used by interlocking systems to detect the presence of trains in a railway network. A point can be switched between two positions: PLUS and MINUS. When it is in the PLUS (MINUS) position, traffic can run from its stem to its plus (minus) end and vice versa. A marker board is installed along a section, and it is used as reference location for an intended travel direction that it is facing, e.g. mb20 in Fig. 2 is installed along section b20, and it is intended for travel direction towards t20. Contrary to legacy systems, in ETCS Level 2, there are no physical signals, but virtual signals associated with marker boards. A virtual signal can be OPEN or CLOSED, respectively, allowing or disallowing traffic to pass the associated marker board. For simplicity, the terms virtual signals, signals, and marker boards are used interchangeably throughout this paper. Our approach

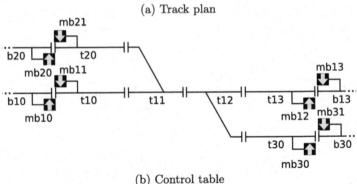

(a) Track plan

(b) Control table

Route name	From	To	Route path	Point positions
r1	mb10	mb12	t10;t11;t12;t13	t11:p;t12:p
r2	mb10	mb30	t10;t11;t12;t30	t11:p;t12:m
r3	mb13	mb11	t13;t12;t11;t10	t11:p;t12:p
r4	mb13	mb21	t13;t12;t11;t20	t11:m;t12:p
r5	mb20	mb12	t20;t11;t12;t13	t11:m;t12:p
r6	mb20	mb30	t20;t11;t12;t30	t11:m;t12:m
r7	mb31	mb11	t30;t12;t11;t10	t11:p;t12:m
r8	mb31	mb21	t30;t12;t11;t20	t11:m;t12:m

Fig. 2. Scheme plan "Twist".

can be used for both, systems using marker boards and classical systems having physical signals.

Control Tables. An interlocking system monitors constantly the status of track-side elements, and sets them to appropriate states in order to allow trains travelling safely through the given railway network. A control table specifies the routes in the given network layout and the conditions for setting these routes. A route is a path from a source signal to a destination signal.

In railway signalling terminology, setting a route denotes the process of allocating the resources – i.e. sections, points, signals – for the route, and then locking it exclusively for only one train when the resources are allocated. The specification of a route and conditions for setting and releasing it includes the following information – c.f. the control table shown in Fig. 2: the name of the route (e.g. r1), at which marker board it starts (e.g. mb10) and ends (e.g., mb12), a list of the detection sections in the route's path (e.g. t10;t11;t12;t13) and the required positions of points used by the route (e.g. t11:p;t12:p). Here p and m stands for PLUS and MINUS, respectively.

Note that – for the sake of comparison – we restrict the control table format as illustrated in Fig. 2 to those parts common to both modelling and verification approaches to be discussed in this paper. In general, the DTU/Bremen approach utilises an extended control table discussed in Sect. 3.2. In contrast, the Surrey/Swansea approach includes release tables which will be described in Sect. 3.3. In Sect. 5 on error injection we will discuss how the two different approaches deal with errors injected in the common part. Additionally we will also demonstrate the effect of errors in the extended control tables and in release tables within the DTU/Bremen approach and the Surrey/Swansea approach, respectively.

In order to prevent collision and derailment of trains, route-based interlocking systems employ a basic principle: a route is locked exclusively for use of one train at a time.

In this setting, we consider three safety properties:

1. **collision-freedom** excludes two trains occupying the same track;
2. **run-through-freedom** says that whenever a train enters a point, the point is set to cater for this; e.g., when a train travels from track t20 to track t11, point t11 is set so that it connects t20 and t12 (and not t10 and t12);
3. **no-derailment** says that whenever a train occupies a point, the point does not move.

The correct design for the control table is safety-critical: mistakes can lead to a violation of any of the three safety properties and thus lead to death or serious injury to people, or loss or severe damage to equipment.

3   A Descriptive Comparison Between the Modelling and Verification Approaches of DTU/Bremen and Surrey/Swansea

3.1   Commonalities of both Approaches

The DTU/Bremen and the Surrey/Swansea approach share as common starting points:

Assumption. We assume track equipment (signals, points, track circuits) to function without mistake, i.e., both our modelling and verification approaches target normal operation.

Narrative. As reference point for our modelling we take standard literature on railway signalling such as the book by Kerr and Rowbothan [18], interact with industry, and discuss our models with railway engineers. Communication with practitioners is essential, as the literature is written in jargon and not always as concise as one would wish for as the following quote might illustrate: "When a valid route is received, the interlocking first checks the availability of each set of points in the route and overlap. Points are deemed to be available if they are already lying the correct way, or are not locked the other way." [18].

3.2   DTU/Bremen Specialities

This section gives an overview of the verification framework developed by DTU/Bremen as part of the RobustRailS research project[1]. For details of this framework, see [5, 25–27].

---

[1] http://www.imm.dtu.dk/~aeha/RobustRailS/index/.

Overall objectives. The framework provides support for an automated 3 step verification and testing approach: (1) First a *static check* is performed on the input scheme plan, (2) then a formal, behavioural system model is automatically generated and *model checked*, (3) and finally *model based testing* of the implemented system is done using test cases, test oracles etc. automatically generated from the formal model. The static check is able to catch errors in scheme plans and in particular in the control tables. The model checking is used to check that the system model is safe and can be used to catch errors in the designed control algorithms as well as to catch errors in the control table if these have not already been found by the static checker. The reason for having the extra static check is to catch as many errors as possible before the more time consuming model checking. The testing is used to catch errors in the *implemented* system. Below we will provide some more details of the two first steps, but not on the testing as that is outside the scope of this paper.

DSL specification of scheme plans. The CAD plan and the control table are represented in a DSL. The DTU/Bremen DSL, called Interlocking Configuration Language (ICL), has been formally specified in RSL, and an XML representation has been implemented. An ICL representation can be created manually, or exported from computer-aided design tools supporting the XML format. Alternatively, the user can use the graphical user interface [5] to specify the scheme plan by drawing the track plan and type in the control table via an editor implemented as an Eclipse plug-in. The editor can then export the specification to the XML format. As an option the user may not explicitly provide a control table, but only a track plan and then get a complete control table created automatically from the track plan.

Static check of scheme plans. A static checker validates that the track plan and control tables are well-formed, and in case there are errors, it suggests what might be wrong and in some cases also how this can be fixed. The checker validates for instance that any route path in the control table is a connected path in the track plan and that required point positions are correct. It is out of the scope of this paper to list all kinds of checks as there are about 55 of them.

Specification of generic system models. For each product family of interlocking systems, a second input is needed: a formal, generic system model. This is given in Interlocking Dynamic Language (IDL), which is another DSL, specially designed for the DTU/Bremen framework. Specifications in this language are similar to RSL-SAL transition system specifications (Kripke model representations consisting of variable declarations and state transition rules) with some additional built-in types and operators. State transition rules for different kind of entities, e.g. the interlocking system controller and track side elements, are placed in different modules and combined by non-deterministic choice (possibly including a prioritization of the transition rules) at the top level.

Automated creation of instantiated system models. A system model is automatically created by instantiating the generic IDL system model with data from the ICL scheme plan. Hence, an instantiated model does not include a scheme plan. The resulting instantiated IDL system model is automatically converted to the internal model representation of the RT-Tester tool [21,24]. Here is an example of an IDL transition rule expressing that when the actual state of a virtual signal s differs from its commanded state, the actual aspect of the signal is updated to the commanded aspect:

```
s.ACT ≠ s.CMD ⟶ s.ACT' = s.CMD
```

Verification properties. The verification properties are automatically created by instantiating a description of generic properties with data from the ICL scheme plan. The resulting verification properties are expressed in RT-Tester as invariants in propositional logic over the state variables of the system model.

Example: For the specific model we used for the experiments reported in this paper, there were no explicit train objects. Instead, train behaviour was implicitly modelled via the occupancy status of track detection sections. This was chosen as it captures behaviours corresponding to all possible numbers of trains, each train having an arbitrary length. The train occupancy of a linear track section t is captured by two integer variables $t.D2U$ and $t.U2D$, one for each of the two travel directions (called down-to-up and up-to-down) through the section. If no train is driving on t in direction down-to-up/up-to-down $t.D2U/t.U2D$ is zero. Hence, there is no head-to-head collision on t, if at least one of the two variables is zero, and this can therefore be expressed as the following invariant:

```
t.D2U * t.U2D = 0
```

Verification in step 2

> **Verification task (what):** It is verified that the invariants hold in all reachable system states of the system model instance.
>
> **Verification technique (how):** Model checking, more specifically by *k-induction using bounded model checking*. If the system model does not satisfy the invariants, counter-examples will be generated. An interface for visualising the counter-examples at the DSL (ICL) level is integrated into the editor in Eclipse, see [5].
>
> **Verification tool:** The bounded model checker of the RT-Tester tool.

3.3 Surrey/Swansea Specialities

This section gives an overview of the verification framework developed by Surrey/Swansea as part of their SafeCap and Ditto research projects[2]. For details of this framework, see [14,15].

Overall objective is to verify if a control table is safe w.r.t. a track plan.

---

[2] http://www.cs.swan.ac.uk/~csmarkus/ProcessesAndData/ditto.

Architecture. All verification shall be performed by a model checker. This means that also checks that could be performed by some static analyser are encoded as model checking problems. These checks concern conditions on well-formedness of the tables. These lead to two further safety properties, additionally to the three properties listed in Sect. 2, namely:

- "no train on a route with a green signal" – this encodes the check that the route path of the clear table covers all detection sections between two marker boards; and
- "no deviation from the designated route" – this encodes the check that all points on a route path are in the right position to guide the train from the start marker board to the end marker board of a route.

Specification Language for the system model is CSP‖B [22], a combination of the process algebra CSP and the B specification language that allows for a combination of event-based and state-based modelling.

We use event-based modelling to capture state changes, e.g., a train moves from one track to the other is represented as `move.A.B`; we use state-based modelling to represent the rules that guide the behaviour of the interlocking, e.g., the conditions under which a route can be set or cancelled.

Modelling – DSL. The CAD plan and the tables are first represented in a Domain Specific Language (DSL) before being encoded in CSP‖B. This intermediate step allows to implement the whole modelling process as a model transformation in our tool OnTrack [17].

Modelling – Track-plan, tables are represented in dedicated data types in CSP‖B.

Modelling – Entities. A speciality of the Surrey/Swansea modelling approach is that it directly represents railway entities as part of the specification, i.e., there is a controller, there is an interlocking, there are trains. This allows to observe these identities in simulations, i.e., one can directly see how the train moves, how the state of the interlocking changes, which route requests come from the controller. Besides being helpful in the validation of the modelling approach, this helps to reflect about the model: Surrey/Swansea have proven a number of theorems on their modelling approach, see e.g. [13].

Modelling – System dynamics. Active entities, i.e., entities which are able to initiate a system change, are modelled as CSP processes. These are the controller (who can request or cancel route) and the trains (which can move along the track or remain). The interlocking as a passive component, i.e., it reacts to train movements or controller requests, is modelled in B.

For each event that the controller or the trains initiate, the interlocking updates its status and the track equipment according to the dynamic rules as stated in [18]. E.g., a route can be released provided the entry signal of this route is green, all locks of the route are still there, and there is no train in front of the entry signal.

Encoding of the safety conditions. The verification properties are encoded as invariants in the specification language B, see the below code representing when there is a collision between two trains on a detection section t.

```
Collision(t) == #(t1,t2).(t1 : TRAIN & t2 : TRAIN
```

```
& t1 /= t2 & t1:dom(pos) & t2:dom(pos)
& (dom({pos(t1)}) = {t}) & (dom({pos(t2)}) = {t}));
```

Verification Technology. Model checking with the ProB tool [19]; the tool checks that the invariant holds in all system states.

4 Error Injection

Interlocking applications are developed according to the CENELEC standard EN50128 [3] and to processes prescribed by Railway Authorities. For the UK, Network Rail's *Governance for Railway Investment Projects* (GRIP) provides such a process. The first four GRIP phases define the track plan and routes of the railway to be constructed, while phase five – the detailed design – is contracted to a signalling company such as Siemens Rail Automation, UK, which chooses appropriate track equipment, adds control tables to the track plan, and implements the interlocking. Thus, in such a process the track plan is developed first. Only in a second step signalling engineers enrich the track plan with a control table. It is for exactly this second step, namely for the design of a control table that our paper discusses support in terms of formal methods. As track plan and routes come from earlier phases, actually the control table is the element that needs verification.

Track plans can have a considerable size, comprising of hundreds of track-side elements such as linear sections, points, marker boards. This makes control tables complex due to their sheer size measured in numbers of entries needed in the various columns. The control table of Langley – a station which signalling engineers consider to be a small one – has about 160 entries, c.f. [13]. To guarantee safety, every single entry in the control table needs to be correct, none can be forgotten or wrong. To manually check all these entries is a challenging task with a high error probability. It is for that reason, that at Siemens Rail Automation, UK, there are at least three different people who independently perform these checks.

Signalling engineers are well trained to apply various sets of design rules to systematically develop control tables. Thus, one can assume that they have the correct design in mind, however, that due to the sheer number of entries to be produced it is likely that they make a mistake due to an oversight. Consequently, in this paper we inject errors of "syntactic type" into an originally correct control table, i.e., a control table which we have proven to be safe w.r.t. a given track plan. More precisely we start with a correct control table and apply one of the following error types (ET) to it:

ET1 – leave out one of the track ids in the route path column.
ET2 – exchange one "p" with an "m" or vice verse in the point positions column.
ET3 – delete one point entry in the point positions column.

Then we check if this altered control table still is safe.

Adding elements to the table would not effect safety: as we presume the original control table to be safe anyway, an added element would only further constrain the possible train behaviour – as the original set of train behaviours was already safe, there won't be any safety violations to be found in the reduced set of behaviours.

In the next section on error detection, we will consider various scenarios: we will systematically explore the effects of errors on a number of scheme plans.

5   Error Detection

Both, the DTU/Bremen and the Surrey/Swansea approach, verify safety for the given table of "Twist" as shown in Fig. 2 – and for the tables of two more scheme plans "Mini" and "Cross" shown in Figs. 3 and 4 in Sect. 5.4. Thus, starting with a proven to be correct control table, we can perform experiments where errors are injected into the control table.

5.1   Injecting a Single Error into "Twist"

As the network is double symmetric, i.e., all eight routes are built in the same way, we decided to inject errors only into the row concerning route r1:

Route name	From	To	Route path	Point positions
r1	mb10	mb12	t10;t11;t12;t13	t11:p;t12:p

For route r1 this results in total into eight different errors:

ET1 Four errors $e_1, \ldots e_4$, each by forgetting one track section in the route path.
ET2 Two errors e_5, e_6, each by requiring one point to be in the wrong position.
ET3 Two errors e_7, e_8, each by forgetting a point position.

DTU/Bremen Approach. For error e_1 – forgetting t10 in the route path column – the static checker provides the error message: `In route r1, two consecutive segments, b10 and t11, are not connected.` Similar outputs are produced for e_2 and e_3. For error e_4 – forgetting the last section, t13, in the route path column such that the route does not end at the exit signal – the error message is: `The exit signal is not placed at the end of the last section of route r1.` For error e_5 – set t11 in wrong position (m rather than p) – the static checker provides the error message: `For route r1, point t11 is set to MINUS, but it should have been set to PLUS.` Similarly for e_6.

For error e_7 – forgetting to set point t11 – the static checker provides the following error message: `For route r1, point t11 is not given a point position.` Similarly for e_8.

All eight errors have been detected. Note that all errors have been detected by static checking, including a suggestion on what the error might be.

Surrey/Swansea Approach. For error e_1 – forgetting t10 in the route path column – the ProB tool finds an invariant violation and provides a counter example trace leading to the violating state:

```
request.r1.yes, move.albert.offUnit.b10, nextSignal.albert.b10.green,
move.albert.b10.t10, request.r1.yes, release.r1.yes, request.r4.yes,
move.albert.t10.nullUnit, run-through
```

I.e., in step 6 it is possible to release route r1 although train `albert` is currently on track t10; this allows it to set route r4, which moves point t11 to minus; thus, in step 7, train `albert` moves onto a point set in the wrong direction. The tool detects a **run-through**. Similar counter example traces are found for $e_2, e_3, e_4,$ – where a collision is detected.

For error e_5 – set t11 in wrong position (m rather than p) – the ProB tool finds an invariant violation and provides as last step of the counter example trace the event `move.albert.t10.nullUnit`, indicating that train `albert` enters point t11 at the plus end while t11 is connecting the minus end. Also, for error e_6 – set t12 in wrong position (m rather than p) – the ProB tool finds an invariant violation and provides as last two steps of the counter example trace the events `move.bertie.offUnit.b30`; `move.albert.t30.b30` – i.e., the two trains `bertie` and `albert` collide on section b30.

Similarly, for e_7 – forgetting to set point t11 – ProB comes up with a counter example trace where train `albert` enters the point t11 at the plus end while t11 is connecting the minus end. For e_8 – forgetting to set point t12 – ProB comes up with a counter example trace ending with a collision section b30.

All eight errors have been detected. Note that all errors have been uncovered by model checking where the counter example trace provides an insight into the nature of the first fault detected. Note that further faults might be possible – the tool provides just the first counter example trace found during state exploration.

5.2   Injecting Multiple Errors in "Twist"

Naturally, it is also possible to inject several errors into one table. Therefore, as in good testing practice, we experiment with at least one scenario including two mistakes at the same time, namely

ET2 – e_6 – set t12 in wrong position (m) and
ET3 – e_7 – forget to set point t11.

In the *DTU/Bremen approach* the static checker find both errors:

```
For route r1, point t11 is not given a point position.
For route r1, point t12 is set to MINUS, but it should have been
set to PLUS.
```

In the *Surrey/Swansea approach* the model checker provides a counter example trace classifying the safety violation as a **run-through**.

5.3   Further Errors in the Parts Different in both Modellings

As discussed earlier, the control table used above is common to both approaches. However, thanks to national differences and also different suppliers, they both have a richer input format. In the following we experiment with errors outside of the shared input.

DTU/Bremen Approach. The DTU/Bremen approach has an extended control table that also includes a list of conflicting routes. In case one forgets to include route r2 in the list of conflicting routes for route r1, the static checker highlights this with the message:

```
Routes r1 and r2 are in conflict, but route r2 is not listed in
the conflicts of route r1. Reasons to be in conflict:
Non-concatenated routes with shared elements: t10, t11, t12.
```

Yet another column consists of protecting signals that must be closed when setting a route. When one forgets mb11 (on track t10) in the list of protecting signals for route r1, the static checker flags this with the message:

```
For route r1, signal mb11 at section t10 should have been listed
as a protecting signal.
```

Another type of error is to forget to set a point that should provide flank protection for the route. Such errors will be caught by the static checker and suggestions for fixing that will be presented. However, this type of error can't be illustrated for the twist network as there are no such cases.

Surrey/Swansea Approach. The Surrey/Swansea approach has as a further input a collection of so-called release tables. These tables determine when the locks on points can be released.

One interesting case is when one releases point t11 too early and forgets to include t11 into the route path. Here, the model checker finds the following counter example trace:

```
move.bertie.offUnit.b10, request.r1.yes nextSignal.bertie.b10.green,
move.bertie.b10.t10, move.albert.offUnit.b10, move.bertie.t10.t11,
request.r1,yes, nextSignal.albert.b10.green, move.albert.b10.t10,
move.albert.t10.t11, collide
```

The trains `albert` and `bertie` collide on point t11. This happens as route r1 is wrongly set in step 7: as t11 is not in the route path, the interlocking does not check if this track is free; as t11 is released early, there is also no lock on the point t11.

5.4   Error Injection in Further Scheme Plans

In this section we consider error injections in the tables of the two scheme plans shown in Figs. 3 and 4.

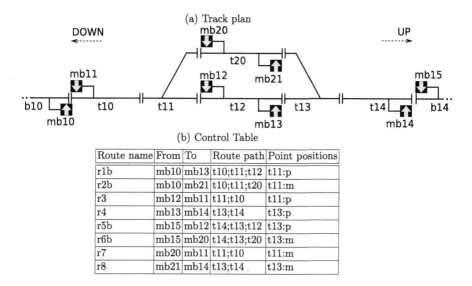

(a) Track plan

(b) Control Table

Route name	From	To	Route path	Point positions
r1b	mb10	mb13	t10;t11;t12	t11:p
r2b	mb10	mb21	t10;t11;t20	t11:m
r3	mb12	mb11	t11;t10	t11:p
r4	mb13	mb14	t13;t14	t13:p
r5b	mb15	mb12	t14;t13;t12	t13:p
r6b	mb15	mb20	t14;t13;t20	t13:m
r7	mb20	mb11	t11;t10	t11:m
r8	mb21	mb14	t13;t14	t13:m

Fig. 3. Scheme plan for "Mini"

Mini. For symmetry reasons it is enough to consider route r1b (an entry route) with five errors:

- three of type ET1 (forget t10, t11, and t12, respectively)
- one of type ET2 (set point t11 in wrong position)
- one of type ET3 (forget to set point t11)

and route r4 (an exit route) with four errors:

- two of type ET1 (forget t13 and t14, respectively)
- one of type ET2 (set point t13 in wrong position)
- one of type ET3 (forget to set point t13)

Cross. For symmetry reasons it is enough to consider routes r1b with five errors:

- three of type ET1 (forget t10, t11, and t12, respectively)
- one of type ET2 (set point t11 in wrong position)
- one of type ET3 (forget to set point t11)

and route r2 with eight errors:

- four of type ET1 (forget t10, t11, t21 and t22, respectively)
- two of type ET2 (set points t11 and t21 in wrong position, respectively)
- two of type ET3 (forget to set points t11 and t21, respectively)

and route r4b with five errors

- three of type ET1 (forget t20, t21, and t22, respectively)
- one of type ET2 (set point t21 in wrong position)
- one of type ET3 (forget to set point t21)

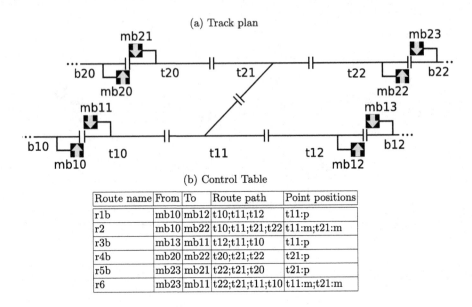

(a) Track plan

(b) Control Table

Route name	From	To	Route path	Point positions
r1b	mb10	mb12	t10;t11;t12	t11:p
r2	mb10	mb22	t10;t11;t21;t22	t11:m;t21:m
r3b	mb13	mb11	t12;t11;t10	t11:p
r4b	mb20	mb22	t20;t21;t22	t21:p
r5b	mb23	mb21	t22;t21;t20	t21:p
r6	mb23	mb11	t22;t21;t11;t10	t11:m;t21:m

Fig. 4. Scheme plan for "Cross"

Results. Both verification approaches find all errors, in case of the DTU/ Bremen approach the static checker provides error messages as illustrated above, in case of the Surrey/Swansea approach the ProB model checker finds counter example traces.

6   Summary

This paper presented a first systematic comparison of rail modelling and verification approaches developed by different research groups, in our case the research groups at DTU/Bremen and at Surrey/Swansea.

In order to relate the input of these modelling approaches we defined a common core and discussed differences. In order to relate the formal models, we attempted to present the modelling approaches in a uniform way. In order to relate the verification results we proposed a practicable and useful approach in the form of a testing equivalence: though input and output of both approaches are different, however, both approaches catch the same errors.

For the research community we see this comparison as pioneering work, to which we hope – in the long run – other groups will contribute as well by running their verification approaches through the very same exercises, i.e., this paper can serve as a starting point for a benchmark for railway verification.

In future work we would like

- to consolidate the common input core by including work from further group.
- extend the benchmark with further and larger scheme plans. However, note that in general safety properties of scheme plans are local. This has been

exploited by several authors, e.g., for testing and for compositional reasoning [13]. Therefore, one would not expect that considering larger scheme plans would provide new insights into the error detection capabilities of verification approaches.

- to develop a systematic questionnaire for comparing modelling and verification approaches
- to compare actual models by (1) highlighting the different assumptions made for the formal model, i.e., what are the chosen abstractions (e.g., with respect to train length, speed, behaviour of trains, and whether shunting is considered etc.) and (2) highlighting differences in the approaches to route allocation and release (e.g., whether sequential release is used)
- to cover performance aspects such as (1) their scalability, i.e., the limits for the size of track plans and control tables that the approaches can deal with and (2) verification speed, i.e., how long time does it take to verify? For such a comparison to be fair, it needs to be measured for models of the *same* system, but such data is not currently available.

Acknowledgements. The DTU/Bremen research has been funded by the RobustRailS project granted by Innovation Fund Denmark. The Surrey/Swansea research has been funded by the SafeCap and the DITTO research projects granted by EPSRC and RSSB. The authors would like to thank Linh Hong Vu for providing the benchmark of scheme plans and the drawings of the track plans.

References

1. Banci, M., Fantechi, A., Gnesi, S.: Some experiences on formal specification of railway interlocking systems using statecharts. In: TRain Workshop at SEFM (Software Engineering and Formal Methods) (2005)
2. Cao, Y., Xu, T., Tang, T., Wang, H., Zhao, L.: Automatic generation and verification of interlocking tables based on domain specific language for computer based interlocking systems. In: CSAE, pp. 511–515. IEEE (2011)
3. C. European Committee for Electrotechnical Standardization: EN 50128:2011 – railway applications – communications, signalling and processing systems – software for railway control andprotection systems (2011)
4. Ferrari, A., Magnani, G., Grasso, D., Fantechi, A.: Model checking interlocking control tables. In: Schnieder, E., Tarnai, G. (eds.) FORMS/FORMAT. Springer, Heidelberg (2010)
5. Foldager, A.: A graphical domain-specific language for railway interlocking systems. Master's thesis, Technical University of Denmark, DTU Compute (2015)
6. Haxthausen, A.E.: Towards a framework for modelling and verification of relay interlocking systems. In: Calinescu, R., Jackson, E. (eds.) Monterey Workshop 2010. LNCS, vol. 6662, pp. 176–192. Springer, Heidelberg (2011)
7. Haxthausen, A.E.: Automated generation of formal safety conditions from railway interlocking tables. Int. J. Softw. Tools Technol. Transf. (STTT) **16**(6), 713–726 (2014). Special Issue on Formal Methods for Railway Control Systems
8. Haxthausen, A.E., Le Bliguet, M., Kjær, A.A.: Modelling and verification of relay interlocking systems. In: Choppy, C., Sokolsky, O. (eds.) Monterey Workshop 2008. LNCS, vol. 6028, pp. 141–153. Springer, Heidelberg (2010)

9. Haxthausen, A.E., Peleska, J., Kinder, S.: A formal approach for the construction and verification of railway control systems. Formal Aspects Comput. **23**(2), 191–219 (2011). Special issue in Honour of Dines Bjørner and Zhou Chaochen on Occasion of their 70th Birthdays

10. Haxthausen, A.E., Peleska, J., Pinger, R.: Applied bounded model checking for interlocking system designs. In: Counsell, S., Núñez, M. (eds.) SEFM 2013. LNCS, vol. 8368, pp. 205–220. Springer, Heidelberg (2014)

11. Iliasov, A., Lopatkin, I., Romanovsky, A.: Practical formal methods in railways - the safecap approach. In: George, L., Vardanega, T. (eds.) Ada-Europe 2014. LNCS, vol. 8454, pp. 177–192. Springer, Heidelberg (2014)

12. James, P., Lawrence, A., Roggenbach, M., Seisenberger, M.: Towards safety analysis of ERTMS/ETCS level 2 in real-time maude. In: Artho, C., Ölveczky, P.C. (eds.) Formal Techniques for Safety-Critical Systems. Springer, New York (2016)

13. James, P., Moller, F., Nga, N.H., Roggenbach, M., Schneider, S.A., Treharne, H.: Techniques for modelling and verifying railway interlockings. STTT **16**(6), 685–711 (2014)

14. James, P., Moller, F., Nguyen, H.N., Roggenbach, M., Schneider, S., Treharne, H.: Decomposing scheme plans to manage verification complexity. FORMS/FORMAT (2014)

15. James, P., Moller, F., Nguyen, H.N., Roggenbach, M., Schneider, S.A., Treharne, H.: On modelling and verifying railway interlockings: tracking train lengths. Sci. Comput. Program **96**, 315–336 (2014)

16. James, P., Roggenbach, M.: Encapsulating formal methods within domain specific languages: a solution for verifying railway scheme plans. Math. Comput. Sci. **8**(1), 11–38 (2014)

17. James, P., Trumble, M., Treharne, H., Roggenbach, M., Schneider, S.: Ontrack: an open tooling environment for railway verification. In: Brat, G., Rungta, N., Venet, A. (eds.) NFM 2013. LNCS, vol. 7871, pp. 435–440. Springer, Heidelberg (2013)

18. Kerr, D., Rowbothan, T.: Introduction to Railway Signalling. Institution of Railway Signal Engineers, London (2001)

19. Leuschel, M., Bendisposto, J., Dobrikov, I., Krings, S., Plagge, D.: From Animation to Data Validation: The ProB Constraint Solver 10 Years On, pp. 427–446. Wiley, Hoboken (2014)

20. Mirabadi, A., Yazdi, M.B.: Automatic generation and verification of railway interlocking control tables using fsm and nusmv. Transp. Prob. **4**(1), 103–110 (2009)

21. Peleska, J.: Industrial-strength model-based testing - state of the art and current challenges. In: Petrenko, A.K., Schlingloff, H. (eds.) Proceedings 8th Workshop on Model-Based Testing, Rome, Italy, Electronic Proceedings in Theoretical Computer Science, vol. 111, pp. 3–28. Open Publishing Association (2013)

22. Schneider, S., Treharne, H.: CSP theorems for communicating B machines. Formal Aspects Comput. **17**(4), 390–422 (2005)

23. Tombs, D., Robinson, N., Nikandros, G.: Signalling control table generation and verification. In: Proceedings of Cost Efficient Railways through Engineering (CORE), pp. 415–425. Railway Technical Society of Australasia (2002)

24. Verified Systems International GmbH: RT-Tester Model-Based Test Case and Test Data Generator - RTT-MBT - User Manual (2013)

25. Vu, L.H.: Formal development and verification of railway control systems - in the context of ERTMS/ETCS Level 2. Ph.D. thesis (2015)

26. Vu, L.H., Haxthausen, A.E., Peleska, J.: A domain-specific language for railway interlocking systems. In: Schnieder, E., Tarnai, G. (eds.) FORMS/FORMAT 2014– 10th Symposium on Formal Methods for Automation and Safety in Railway and Automotive Systems, pp. 200–209. Got best-paper-award, Institute for Traffic Safety and Automation Engineering, Technische Universität Braunschweig (2014)

27. Vu, L.H., Haxthausen, A.E., Peleska, J.: Formal modeling and verification of inter-locking systems featuring sequential release. In: Artho, C., Ölveczky, P.C. (eds.) FTSCS 2014. CCIS, vol. 476, pp. 223–238. Springer, Heidelberg (2015)

28. Winter, K.: Optimising ordering strategies for symbolic model checking of railway interlockings. In: Steffen, B., Margaria, T. (eds.) ISoLA 2012, Part II. LNCS, vol. 7610, pp. 246–260. Springer, Heidelberg (2012)

29. Winter, K., Johnston, W., Robinson, P., Strooper, P., van den Berg, L.: Tool support for checking railway interlocking designs. In: Proceedings of the 10th Australian Workshop on Safety Critical Systems and Software, SCS 2005, vol. 55, pp. 101–107. Australian Computer Society Inc., Darlinghurst (2006)

30. Yu, Y.T., Lau, M.F.: A comparison of MC/DC, MUMCUT and several other cov-erage criteria for logical decisions. J. Syst. Softw. **79**(5), 577–590 (2006). Quality Software

Predictive Reasoning and Machine Learning for the Enhancement of Reliability in Railway Systems

Luke J.W. Martin[(✉)]

Centre for Software Reliability, Newcastle University,
Newcastle upon Tyne, UK
luke.burton@newcastle.ac.uk

Abstract. The real-time prediction of train movements in time and space is required for ensuring the reliability in operational management and in the information that is relayed to passengers. In practice, however, accurate predictions of train arrival times are very difficult to achieve, given the nature of uncertainty and unpredictability in train movements. This is often due to truly random delay causes that results in a constantly changing probability distribution in delay events as the effects of those causes. The overall consequence is less reliable estimates in train arrival times being made, which can potentially reduce the ability of traffic controllers to effectively plan and respond to disruptions. This paper presents a series of methods that are currently being applied for developing a preliminary working prototype of a future rail advisory system, which is the main objective of an ongoing PhD research project. The system prototype is expected to be capable of relaying advice to a traffic controller with the goal of minimising the effects of a disruption as much as possible and to potentially avoid future disruptions, for which accurate train movement and delay predictions using methods in predictive reasoning and machine learning are vital.

Keywords: Predictive reasoning · Artificial intelligence · Machine learning · Reliable systems · Railway traffic · Data analytics · Train describer

1 Introduction

The quality and dependability of a reliable rail service depends heavily on accurate predictions of future train movements and delays that may occur, since it is important for ensuring proactive and anticipative real-time control of railway traffic [1]. These are also highly beneficial in ensuring that traffic operations may be controlled effectively by taking actions that can either prevent or considerably minimise the impact of delays. In practice, however, predictions of train arrival times are performed according to the experience and intuition of a dispatcher based on last known delays that were recorded and with limited computational support. According to several studies [1–8], this method is inadequate since these predictions do not account for partial recovery from a delay or extended delays due to conflicts. Although more precise predictions can be achieved through a microscopic analysis, the complexity and computational requirements for this do not allow for predictions to be produced on demand, particularly for large and dense

© Springer International Publishing Switzerland 2016
T. Lecomte et al. (Eds.): RSSRail 2016, LNCS 9707, pp. 178–188, 2016.
DOI: 10.1007/978-3-319-33951-1_13

network areas [6]. Part of this complexity is largely attributed to the uncertainty and unpredictability of delays and train process times. In the literature, stochastic models that have been developed for real-time prediction of train movements have placed considerable emphasis in addressing this complexity, particularly with respect to train rescheduling and delay handling [4]. Although these approaches have been successful in solving complex instances in real-time, they have done so under assumptions that perfect deterministic knowledge of the traffic state exists [3] and that the probability distributions, required for realising uncertainty, of train process times are fixed [8]. These are considerable limitations as complete knowledge of the current state is not possible since traffic controllers are only aware of the state of a network within a small geographical area. Delayed trains that enter this area may have an impact, which is unknown, or a train within the area may become suddenly delayed due to earlier disruptions. Some studies [1, 3, 4, 7] attribute these phenomena to an evolving nature of delays, in which the probability distribution changes continuously and therefore the uncertainty of delay events are difficult to realise completely.

The approach that this study considers is one that aims to utilise readily available data streams for describing the current state in two ways: the first is to collect a sufficient amount of historical data that would be analysed to develop various data models that describe train delays in terms of causes and effects. This is to be used to create and train a Bayesian Network. The second, is to analyse data online as a continuous stream and to make predictions of this data using the trained Bayesian Network to forecast a potential future state, where domain specific knowledge, such as train movement behaviour, can also be incorporated in an effort to improve the accuracy of the predictions. This essentially serves to enhance reliability in the sense that traffic operators can develop better situational awareness through complex computational support, which can aide in providing better planning and preventive procedures.

This paper therefore presents a series of techniques and methods that are currently being investigated as part of an ongoing PhD research project, which aims to develop a working prototype of a rail advisory system that may be used as a future tool in rail operations. The paper is structured as follows: Sect. 2 details a brief, high-level overview of the current proposal for the design of the rail advisory system and how it is expected to operate. Section 3 discusses the data mining processes of the current state of the rail network in terms of the source where data will be extracted from and how this will be used in generating a historic data base. Section 4 briefly details some of the main methods that are being investigated in modelling the data as a stochastic process and justifies the use of Bayesian Networks for real-time predictions. Section 5 will provide a brief summary of how impact of a delay can be modelled and assessed. Finally, Sect. 6 concludes the paper through a summary of current work and planned directions of study.

2   Design of Real-Time Rail Advisory System

The rail advisory system project is the current focus of an ongoing sponsored PhD, which is supported by Siemens Rail Automation, The Engineering and Physical Sciences Research Council (EPSRC) and Newcastle University. The goal of the system is to provide advice concerning traffic movements to a rail network operator, where improved degrees of operational reliability and network dependability and resilience can be achieved. A detailed description of the high-level concept of the advisory system is explained in Martin et al. [7], however, this section provides a very brief summary of the system design and its expected functionality. Figure 1 illustrates a high-level architectural design of the proposed advisory system, which is expected to work as an extension to existing traffic control systems, such as the European Train Control System (ETCS):

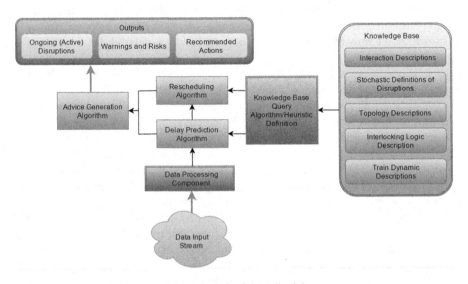

Fig. 1. High-level design of the rail advisory system

From this design, the system extracts data via a continuous data stream, which is assumed to exist as part of the ETCS as it retrieves data from the interlocking at a constant rate to display the current state of the network to the network operator. For the purposes of this study, the data is provided through open data policies that are detailed in Sect. 3. This data is processed using a data analytics tool, such as SparkXD, to provide the parameters necessary for producing a prediction, such as current train speed profiles, train positions, source and destination points, the current schedule, etc. The parameters are passed into the prediction algorithm which is to determine if there are any ongoing disruptions or there is a likely risk of a disruption taking place based on the evidence of delay causes that may have been reported. If the prediction computes a positive result, the rescheduling algorithm is queried to identify a possible solution, where it aims to identify a route for each train in an affected area that has the lowest cost of impact, which is briefly explained in more detail in Sect. 5.

It is expected that the final advice would produce details of ongoing disruptions and the effects of these; warnings of potential disruptions – based on last known delays and reported causes - and the effects of these and finally a proposed rescheduling solution to (partially) minimise the impact and/or prevent an anticipated delay. The scope of this paper is mostly concerned with the preliminaries of developing a solution for a prediction algorithm that is capable of applying reasoning techniques, such as Bayesian inference, to identify the following: if a delay is ongoing and to predict the possible effects; if events that are known to result in delays have been reported and predict the possibility of delays from this; if there is a risk that current train movements may impede on the movements of other trains (i.e. conflicts) and finally to determine if trains within the network area are likely to reach a station on time based on its current movement patterns and with respect to the previous points. The prediction algorithm therefore represents a critical part of the advisory system since it provides the predictions that are used to generate a significant part of the advice.

3 Data Mining

Data mining is applied in this study to extract data that describes actual train movements within a specified area of the railway network. As a case study, a very small section of the Great Western Rail line have been considered and are currently being monitored. This area is of particular interested as it is one of the UK's largest and oldest railway lines that has recently undergone substantial modernisation, where there is now much diversity in the density of the lines, the types of traffic and modes of signalling.

Typically, extracting data of current train movements is achieved through a train describer system, which exists to provide live data feeds of train positions in discrete steps over its route, based on train numbers and messages that are received from the interlocking [5]. In the UK, train describer data is available through various sources, where this study refers to the Network Rail data feed, which is provisioned and maintained for public use by Network Rail [12]. The system has six data feeds that a user may subscribe to, which is summarised in Table 1. The feeds are accessible through one of two channels: the first being a real-time (RT) channel that publishes data as JSON messages on ActiveMQ topics that are extracted via a Stomp client; and the second is a semi-static (SS) channel, which publishes large data batches daily into Amazon S3 buckets and extracted through authenticated HTTP GET requests [12].

The ActiveMQ topics are listed by all signalling areas that divide the British railway network, where messages are received over the Stomp protocol. To date, it has been possible to extract, filter, store and interpret data from these feeds, which has enabled a preliminary set of results to be generated that are presented in Sect. 6. However, since this work is currently ongoing, it has not yet been possible to accumulate a final set of results given the time period that is to be covered. The current focus, therefore, is to continue with data collection and interpretation over a longer period, where it may then be fully analysed for the purpose of generating stochastic models that provide detailed descriptions of the evolution of delays and the effect that statistically significant factors have in triggering this.

In particular, some works refer to the application of multiple variable regression analysis for understanding factors in which punctuality is dependent, where it is noted in [11] that the length of carriage, distance previously covered, track layout and driver behaviour are often cited as statistically significant factors in this. Thus, based on significant characteristics of the train, which influence its runtime performance, it is

Table 1. Data feeds available through the Network Rail Open Rail Data system. **Source:** http://nrodwiki.rockshore.net/index.php/About_the_feeds

Data feed	Description	Channel type
Train movements	The train movements feed provides train positioning and movement event data including incident and delay reporting messages	RT
TD	The Train Describer (TD) feed provides train positioning data at signal berth level	RT
VSTP	The Very Short Time Planning (VSTP) feed provides schedule records via the VSTP process	RT
RTPPM	Real-time Public Performance Measure (RTPPM) show the performance of trains against the timetable, measured as the percentage of trains arriving at destination	RT
TSR	Temporary Speed Restrictions (TSR) data as published in Weekly Operation Notice	Low-volume
SCHEDULE	The Schedule feed is an extract of train schedules from the Integration Train Planning System (ITPS)	SS

possible to develop a train behaviour patterns and probability distributions of a train arriving at each control point, which is central to the idea of describing a train run as a stochastic process [2], which allows analytical probability models of delay propagation to be established by describing delays based on its effect in train movement.

A point of caution is that the data is not expected to provide complete information of many of the statistically significant factors that dispatchers would be aware of, since the data is generally limited to capturing train movements and operational activities that take place within the track. The Delay Attribution Guide, which is provided to dispatchers, is a document that provides an extensive summary of the known significant causes of delays both internally and externally of the track. It includes instances such as changes in weather patterns, behaviour of passengers, incidents involving death or serious injury, various blockages on the track and so on. This shortcoming in the data can be remedied through the establishment of regular behavioural patterns of train movements, where sudden and unexpected changes within these patterns would trigger a diagnosis of a potential problem, given the information that is available both from confirmed statistically significant factors from the analysed data and from the Delay Attribution Guide. For example, suppose a train suddenly slowed down to a stop while travelling on a high speed line and was not approaching a signal or a station. The logical conclusion, based on the evidence available, would be an obstruction on the line, where trains that are approaching this same area are at considerably high risk of also being delayed due to the obstruction and the stopped train. In other words, the advisory system doesn't need to be aware of the probabilities of all the likely causes of the delays, since this would result in noisy, practically useless advice resulting in potentially inaccurate predictions, but once a cause has resulted in an immediate effect, the continuing effects should be predicted given evidence that a likely cause has occurred. The evidence is thus accumulated through sudden and unexpected changes in known train behaviour patterns.

4   Stochastic Prediction of Train Delays in Real-Time Using Bayesian Reasoning

This section has largely been inspired by the works of Kecman [4, 5], in which it was proposed that given a stochastic model of a train run, it would be possible to determine the probable likeliness of a train arriving at the next control point on its route on time, and the resulting effect this would have on other trains that would soon approach the same point later in time. The approach taken in this study is somewhat similar in that train runs are to be described as an independent stochastic process. Although such an approach neglects the fact that multiple train runs are often interdependent as they use the same infrastructure or have scheduled passenger transfers and so on, the modelling of these interdependencies is a considerably complex task since it requires detailed knowledge of train routes and departure orders which are often not available in the data [10]. Therefore, not enough information is available to build the detailed models that were dominant in previous approaches for delay prediction [4] and hence the reason why a stochastic approach that models the uncertainty of train event times is more favourable. Likewise with Kecman, this study presents a train run as a dynamic sequence of discrete arrival and departure events, where these events are connected by the corresponding running and dwell processes [5]. The number of events corresponds to the number of scheduled arrivals and departures. A through event can be separated into the arrival and departure events that occur simultaneously. The events occur in a fixed sequence $j \rightarrow k$, where $k = j + 1$, $j = 1, 2, \ldots, n - 1$, and n is the total number of events in the train run. This way a train run can be modelled by knowing only the events scheduled by the timetable. The variable of the system is a train delay that may change at every event. As delays are random in nature, it is assumed that no intermediate information is available, resulting in the final system being event-driven.

With these definitions, a train run can be defined using a *Bayesian Network*. A Bayesian Network is a directed acyclic graph model, $G = (V{:}E)$, that represents, as its vertices, a set of random variables, $V = \{X_1, \ldots, X_n\}$, and, as its edges, the conditional dependencies of each random variable [3]. It is a model used for reasoning about the likeliness of events occurring under uncertainty. The direction of the edge reflects the causality relationship between two vertices, where the event that is represented by the child vertex can only occur on the condition that the event represented by the parent vertex has occurred. This property is defined in joint probability distribution, $P(X_1, \ldots, X_n)$ of the network which is informally given by [3]:

$$P(X_1, \ldots, X_n) = \prod_{i=1}^{n} P(X_i | parents(X_i))$$

In the instance of a train run, a train t, is described as either arriving at a control point or departing from one, where a and d respectively denote arrival and departure events. The probability of a train arriving at a control point on time is given by $P(t_a)$ and departure is given by $P(t_d | t_a)$. For multiple trains 1 and 2, the following network would be constructed:

$$P(t_{a_1})P(t_{d_1}|t_{a_1})P(t_{a_2}|t_{a_1},t_{d_1})P(t_{d_2}|t_{d_1},t_{a_2})$$

This network is based on common reasoning as well as initial results of some preliminary data that identifies a train coming into the station at a specific platform, would do so under the condition that a previous train had both arrived and left. Thus, the probability that the train would arrive on time, would depend on the probability that the previous train had left on time. However, this isn't necessarily the complete picture as factors that may have delayed arrival other than the activities of a previous train would also need to be taken into account, which can be achieved when constructing a network that includes various causes and sub-causes of delays as nodes and computing the conditional probability distributions for each node. These probabilities can be inferred directly from evidence in the data through either a diagnostic or causal inference. In the event that causes are inferred based on observed effects of a known impact, it then becomes theoretically possible to predict the possible impact of further effects that are likely to occur and also the likeliness of such effects occurring, where such deductions are needed to determine the costs of a route to enable rescheduling decisions to be made to ensure that a train chooses a route with the lowest possible cost, which is briefly detailed in the next section.

5   Measuring Potential Impact

As discussed, the main purpose of the prediction algorithm is to identify if a delay is ongoing and to determine the likely effects of this within a given time period, as well as to infer the likeliness of delays based on observed activities that could be identified as potential causes. This section essentially describes the types of output that may be deduced based on the results of the prediction, which is then expected to provide a series of key parameters used in developing a solution for a rescheduling algorithm that aims to find the route with the lowest cost for each train. When describing cost, it is defined in this study in terms of time spent to travel between two points and energy consumed in travelling, where the most desirable route is the optimal value of one of these based on some preference. We therefore provide a highly simplified definition of cost accordingly:

$$c = a \cdot t + b \cdot e$$

where t is time, e is energy and a and b are preference constants. For simplicity, it is assumed that the value of a and b can assume one of two binary values: 0 to denote that it is not preferred and 1 for preferred. As the study develops, so the definition for preference will be subject to improvement. It is argued that such constants are needed as optimal travel time and optimal energy savings are typically regarded as tradeoffs [2, 7]. To determine cost with respect to a deadline, we refer to the following definition [9]:

$$c(t) = a(t - d)^2$$

where a cost function, c, can be defined as the time of arrival, t, relative to a deadline, d with respect to some preference a. This definition can be applied to construct a formula for an overall expected cost in time when travelling from a start point, i, to a single end point, j, with respect to a fixed distance between the two points, f, and a random duration required to cover that distance, x. The expected cost definition of arriving from one point to another, is thus defined as follows [9]:

$$EC(t) = \int_0^\infty f_{ij}(x) \cdot c(a(t-d))dx$$

This is further expanded to account for the total approximate time it would take to complete a journey, where a traveler must continuously reach each point within its route until it reaches its final destination. The new function for the expected cost in time, $EC_p(t)$, is thereby derived by determining the overall probability of duration between two points for every point in the route, against the total observed duration [9]:

$$EC_p(t) = \int_0^\infty \prod_{i=1}^r f_{ij}(x) \cdot c\left(a(t + \sum_{i=1}^r x_i)\right) \ldots dx_i$$

With delays, travel time is increased to a large variance, where it is not possible to predict precisely how long a journey may take, leading to an overall lack of reliability and subsequently, lack of confidence from passengers, which in itself carries economic consequences [3]. One such consequence is the increasing difficulty to optimise energy consumption in which delays can particularly have an impact on train driving styles as drivers are more likely to adopt higher speeds in an attempt to make some recovery. Such reactions are noted to result in inefficient energy consumption, especially in dense networks, as sharper or earlier braking is required to decelerate back to the speed limit when approaching junctions. Optimising the overall cost of energy consumption is more complex to define, since driver behaviour would need to be considered, which is an area that will be briefly touched upon later in the research project, however, it is currently beyond the scope of this work. Currently, we refer to a more general definition of energy consumption in an effort to define some cost of energy:

$$E(t) = \int_0^{tf} (T(v) - B(v)) \cdot v(t)dt$$

where $T(v)$ is tractive effort, $B(v)$ is the braking force, v is velocity and tf is the travelling time [2]. It is planned that a final formula will be developed to provide a robust and accurate description of cost in these terms in the developing phases of this work, however, what has been described provides a brief outline for the overall strategy.

6 Ongoing and Future Work

There are several topics that are currently being investigated throughout the second year of study, which focus on improving the current level of understanding in the types of techniques and methods that may be applied in developing working modules of the advisory system. As detailed in Sect. 3, the primary focus is in ensuring the successful collection of train movement, scheduling and performance data from the live Network Rail data feed. As noted, this is a cornerstone achievement as the development of the data processing and delay prediction components depend heavily on the completion of this task. After a sufficient historic sample has been collected, with the current target at approximately 4 months, the data will be analysed using well established statistical methods and techniques, such multiple regression analysis, modelling of uncertainty and identification of probability distribution of arrival/departure times. This is necessary for progressing into stochastic analysis, which will focus on describing train delays and train movement patterns as stochastic processes, namely using a Markov chain, which can then be applied to the design of a Bayesian Network – the basis of the prediction algorithm – and can also be used in training the Network.

In terms of the data processing component, many frameworks and tools for data stream processing and analysis currently exist, namely those that have been developed by Apache, such as Samza, SparkXD and Hive. While these provide powerful solutions in real-time data processing online using remote cloud servers, there is a concern about the suitability of these working on a localhost and the feasibility of this when considering the development of a potential industrial tool intended for existing systems, which is currently under investigation.

6.1 Preliminary Results

The preliminary results that have been accumulated detail consecutive delays that occur in a train's arrival and departure times. The data has been considerably detailed in the sense that various codes are attributed to certain actions, but limited in the sense that the times are not in a standard date/time format and are instead expressed as timestamps. This is problematic as it is difficult to attribute delays that occurred with the same time frame (i.e. within an hour) or on the same day, which limits abilities in tracing through and analyzing delays quite considerably. This prevents queries for collecting departures that occur within particular times of the day, such as off-peak times or comparing the delays of consecutive trains. This has somewhat been remedied by extracting information from additional sources, such as trains.im, which do display exact arrival and departure times of each train in a correct format, where data from the feed provide additional levels of detail as the train and station IDs (which is available in both sets of data) can easily be used to map the two sets and clearly identify the trains that arrived at a particular station at a particular time. This is then used to trace the causes and effects of the delay from both data sets and the timings that were involved.

At this stage of the analysis, it has been identified, from Fig. 2, that times and days of the week have an influence on the likeliness of delays occurring and can therefore be considered as statistically significant factors. It has been noted, from Fig. 3, that conditional probabilities for an on time arrival, change as a train arrives at each consecutive station and as a previous train departs from that station, where we can easily conclude that longer journeys are more likely to result in a higher likeliness of delays and that if a train is late departing from a station, this will immediately affect the next train due to arrive, with a higher likeliness of effected every other train arriving at that station thereafter. This simply confirms various findings that have been discussed in previous works, such as [1, 2, 6], but are nevertheless useful in developing predictive methods.

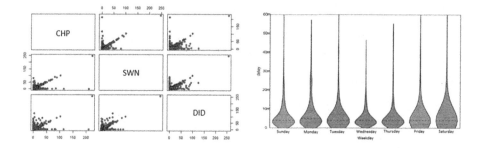

Fig. 2. Correlation between delays in different stations of the same journey

Fig. 3. Distribution of delays of days of the week

6.2   Future Work

Currently, there are several areas for developing this work further in the short-term which include: continue to develop a working stream data processing solution that is able to utilise real-time, simulation and historic data sets that provide essential heuristics for the machine learning algorithm for producing predictions in real-time; to finalise an approach in determining the risk of delays in relation to probability distributions and expected impact, so as to provide a core mechanism for an advisory process and to incorporate both the machine learning algorithm and risk assessment mechanism to develop a preliminary model for an advisory system that can later be further enhanced and developed during the third year of study.

Acknowledgements. This work is sponsored by EPSRC and Siemens Rail Automation within the industrial conversation CASE project on developing train advisory systems of the future. The author would also like to thank Dr. William Blewitt for his advice and feedback and to Newcastle University for their support.

References

1. Berger, A., Gebhardt, A., Müller-Hannemann, M., Ostrowski, M.: Stochastic delay prediction in large train newtorks. In: 11th Workshop on Algorithmic Approaches for Transportation Modelling, Optimization and Systems, pp. 100–111 (2011)
2. Bergström, A., Krüger, N.: Modelling Passenger Train Delay Distributions – Evidence and Implications. Karlstad University Working Paper in Economics, Karlstad University (2013)
3. Friedman, N., Geiger, D., Goldszmidt, M.: Bayesian network classifiers. Mach. Learn. **29**, 131–163 (1997)
4. Kecman, P., Corman, F., Meng, L.: Train delay evolution as a stochastic process. In: 6th International Conference on Railway Operations Modelling and Analysis, Springer, New York (2015)
5. Kecman, P., Goverde, R.M.P.: An online railway traffic prediction model. In: 5th International Seminar on Railway Operations Modelling and Analysis. Springer, Berlin (2013)
6. Keyhani, M.H., Schnee, M., Weihe, K., Zorn, H.P.: Reliability and delay distributions of train connections. In: 12th Workshop on Algorithmic Approaches for Transportation Modelling, Optimization and Systems, pp. 35–46 (2012)
7. Martin, L., Romanovsky, A., Blewitt, W.: Design and development of train advisory systems for the future. In: 13th International Railway Engineering Conference (2015)
8. Peng, Z., Lyu, Y., Miller, A., Johnson, C., Zhao, T.: Risk assessment of railway transportation systems using timed fault trees. Qual. Reliab. Eng. Int. (2014)
9. van Hinsbergen, C.P.I.J., Hegyi, A., van Lint, J.W.C., van Zuylen, H.J.: Bayesian neural networks for the prediction of stochastic travel times in urban networks. IET Intel. Transport Syst. **5**(4), 259–265 (2011). doi:10.1049/iet-its.2009.0114
10. Yaghini, M., Khoshraftar, M.M., Seyedabadi, M.: Railway passenger train delay prediction via neural network model. J. Adv. Transp. **47**(3) (2013). doi:10.1002/atr.193
11. Yuan, J.: Stochastic Modelling of Train Delays and Delay Propagation in Stations. Doctoral thesis, Delft University of Technology, Eburon Academic Publishers (2006)
12. Network Rail Data Feeds Developer Pack, V2.0, Published by Network Rail. https://odmcr.files.wordpress.com/2012/06/developer-pack-for-network-rail-data-feeds.pdf
13. Network Rail Strategic Business Plan. Schedule 8. http://www.networkrail.co.uk/browse%20documents/strategicbusinessplan/cp5/supporting%20documents/financing%20and%20funding/schedule%208.pdf
14. Kang, M.O.: A GA based algorithm for creating energy-optimum train speed trajectory. J. Int. Counc. Electr. Eng. **1**(2), 123–128 (2011). doi:10.5370/JICEE.2011.1.2.123

Verification and Validation

Applying Abstract Interpretation to Verify EN-50128 Software Safety Requirements

Daniel Kästner$^{(\boxtimes)}$ and Christian Ferdinand

AbsInt GmbH, Science Park 1, 66123 Saarbrücken, Germany
{kaestner,ferdinand}@absint.com

Abstract. Like other contemporary safety standards EN-50128 requires to identify potential functional and non-functional hazards and to demonstrate that the software does not violate the relevant safety goals. Examples of safety-relevant non-functional hazards are violations of resource bounds, especially stack overflows and deadline violations, as well as run-time errors and data races. They can cause erroneous and erratic program behavior, invalidate separation mechanisms in mixed-criticality software, and even trigger software crashes. Classical software verification methods like code review and testing with measurements cannot really guarantee the absence of errors. Abstract interpretation is a formal method for static program analysis which supports formal soundness proofs (it can be proven that no error is missed) and which scales. This article gives an overview of abstract interpretation and its application to compute safe worst-case execution time and stack bounds, and to find all potential run-time errors, and data races. We discuss the tool qualification of abstract interpretation-based static analyzers and describe their contribution with respect to EN-50128 compliant verification processes. We also illustrate their integration in the development process and report on practical experience.

1 Introduction

A failure of a safety-critical system may cause high costs or even endanger human beings. With the unbroken trend towards growing software size in embedded systems more and more safety-critical functionality is implemented in software. Preventing software-induced system failures becomes an increasingly important task.

Contemporary safety norms – including DO-178B, DO-178C, IEC-61508, ISO-26262, and EN-50128 – require to identify potential functional and non-functional hazards and to demonstrate that the software does not violate the relevant safety goals. *Functional* program properties can be addressed by automatic and model-based testing, or by model checking and theorem proving. Examples of safety-relevant *non-functional* software requirements are adherence to resource bounds, especially worst-case execution time bounds and stack size, as well as freedom of run-time errors (e.g. division by zero, invalid pointer accesses, arithmetic overflows) and data races (concurrent accesses by two threads to the same

T. Lecomte et al. (Eds.): RSSRail 2016, LNCS 9707, pp. 191–202, 2016.
DOI: 10.1007/978-3-319-33951-1_14

memory location without proper mutex locking). Violations of resource bounds, run-time errors, and data races can corrupt memory, cause erroneous and erratic program behavior, invalidate separation mechanisms in mixed-criticality software, and even trigger software crashes. The term 'non-functional' is traditionally used but misleading: in fact, satisfying non-functional requirements is an essential part of functional safety. The explosion of the Ariane 5 [15] and the unintended acceleration of the 2005 Toyota Camry [2,24] illustrate potential consequences of such errors.

The non-functional program properties cannot be directly mapped to test cases, e.g. a test case for stimulating the worst-case stack usage typically is not known. Identifying a safe end-of-test criterion is a hard problem since failures usually occur in corner cases and full test coverage – which for these properties would require full control and data coverage – typically cannot be achieved on industry-size applications. In consequence the required test effort is high and the results are not complete.

Abstract interpretation is a formal methodology for static program analysis which is well suited to analyze non-functional software properties. It supports formal soundness proofs (it can be proven that no error is missed) and scales to real-life industry applications. Abstract interpretation-based static analyzers provide full control and data coverage and allow conclusions to be drawn that are valid for all program runs with all inputs. Such conclusions may be that no timing or space constraints are violated, or that run-time errors or data races are absent: the absence of these errors can be guaranteed. Nowadays, abstract interpretation-based static analyzers that can detect stack overflows and violations of timing constraints [23] and that can prove the absence of run-time errors [6], are widely used in industry. From a methodological point of view, abstract interpretation-based static analyses can be seen as equivalent to testing with full data and control coverage. They do not require access to the physical target hardware, can be easily integrated in continuous verification frameworks and model-based development environments, and they allow developers to detect run-time errors as well as timing and space bugs in early product stages. For validating non-functional program properties they define the state-of-the-art technology.

In the following we will give an overview of the CENELEC EN-50128 with a focus on the requirements for non-functional software properties and verification methodology. Then we will give a brief overview of the theory of abstract interpretation and present three exemplary tools: aiT for worst-case execution time analysis, StackAnalyzer for stack usage analysis and Astrée for finding run-time errors and data races. Industrial experience is summarized in Sects. 5 and 6 concludes.

2   CENELEC EN-50128

The European norm CENELEC EN-50128 is based on the norm IEC-61508; its latest revision dates from 2011 [4]. It specifies the requirements with which the development, deployment and maintenance of any safety-related software intended for railway control and protection applications shall comply.

The non-functional software properties are listed among the software requirements to be specified and verified throughout all development stages. Timing constraints are listed among the properties that have to be specified for the system in which the software is embedded (clause 4.1). Resource bounds in general are addressed by clause 7.2.4.2 which considers capacity and response time performance to be necessary functional requirements. Like IEC-61508 and ISO-26262, also EN-50128 states that the entire software is subject to the highest safety integrity level used unless freedom of interference ("evidence of independence") can be demonstrated between the components of different integrity levels (clause 7.3.4.9). Sources of interference can be memory corruption like stack overflows, run-time errors and data races, and timing effects. Clause 7.3.4.19 explicitly demands that time constraints and memory bounds have to be addressed by the software interface description. Also the existence of synchronization mechanisms between functions and the definition of allowed and forbidden value ranges for data from and to the interfaces are demanded. In the testing and verification stage this implies demonstrating, e.g., that the synchronization is effective, i.e. that no data races can occur, that the feasible value ranges are respected, and that the resource constraints are met. In the integration stage one objective is to demonstrate that "software and hardware interact correctly to perform their intended functions" (7.6.1.2) which, again, includes meeting resource constraints and avoiding memory corruption.

The verification and testing methods are summarized in Table A.5 of EN-50128. In general, formal proof is recommended for SIL1/SIL2 and highly recommended for SIL3/SIL4. Static analysis in general is highly recommended for SIL1-SIL4. Performance testing addresses response time and memory constraints and is highly recommended for all safety integrity levels. Table A.21 addresses test coverage for code. Here path coverage is recommended for SIL1/SIL2 and even strongly recommended for SIL3/SIL4. Path coverage typically cannot be achieved by testing for industry-size code, but is always achieved by abstract interpretation based static analyzers.

The EN-50128 categorizes software tools in three classes T1, T2, T3. All tools discussed in this article belong to the class T2 which covers tools supporting the "test or verification of the design or executable code, where errors in the tool can fail to reveal defects but cannot directly create errors in the executable software" (cf. clause 3.1.43).

3   Abstract Interpretation

The theory of abstract interpretation [5] is a mathematically rigorous formalism providing a semantics-based methodology for static program analysis. The semantics of a programming language is a formal description of the behavior of programs. The most precise semantics is the so-called concrete semantics, describing closely the actual execution of the program. Yet in general, the concrete semantics is not computable. Even under the assumption that the program terminates, it is too detailed to allow for efficient computations. The solution is to introduce an abstract semantics that approximates the concrete semantics of the program and is efficiently computable. This abstract semantics can be chosen as the basis for a static analysis. Compared to an analysis of the concrete semantics, the analysis result may be less precise but the computation may be significantly faster.

A static analyzer is called *sound* if the computed results hold for any possible program execution. Abstract interpretation supports formal correctness proofs: it can be proved that an analysis will terminate and that it is sound, i.e., that it computes an over-approximation of the concrete semantics. Imprecision can occur, but it can be shown that they will always occur on the safe side. In runtime error analysis, soundness means that the analyzer never omits to signal an error that can appear in some execution environment. If no potential error is signaled, definitely no runtime error can occur: there are no false negatives. If a potential error is reported, the analyzer cannot exclude that there is a concrete program execution triggering the error. If there is no such execution, this is a false alarm (false positive). This imprecision is on the safe side: it can never happen that there is a runtime error which is not reported. In WCET and stack usage analysis soundness means that the computed WCET/stack bound holds for any possible program execution. The only imprecision occurring is overestimation: the WCET and the maximal stack height will never be underestimated.

Abstract Interpretation, like model checking and theorem proving, is recognized as a formal verification method and recommended by the DO-178C and other safety standards (cf. Formal Methods Supplement [21] to DO-178C [22]).

3.1 Stack Usage Analysis

In embedded systems, the run-time stack (often just called "the stack") typically is the only dynamically allocated memory area. It is used during program execution to keep track of the currently active procedures and facilitate the evaluation of expressions.

Precisely determining the maximum stack usage before deploying the system is important for economical reasons and for system safety. Overestimating the maximum stack usage means wasting memory resources. Underestimation leads to stack overflows: memory cells from the stacks of different tasks or other memory areas are overwritten. This can cause crashes due to memory protection violations and can trigger arbitrary erroneous program behavior, if return addresses or other parts of the execution state are modified. In consequence stack overflows are typically hard to diagnose and hard to reproduce, but they are a potential cause of catastrophic failure. The accidents caused by the unintended acceleration of the 2005 Toyota Camry illustrate the potential consequences of stack overflows: the expert witness' report commissioned by the Oklahoma court in 2013 identifies a stack overflow as probable failure cause [2, 24].

StackAnalyzer. The tool StackAnalyzer [14] employs a global abstract interpretation-based static program analysis to compute safe upper bounds on the maximal stack usage of tasks. The main input of StackAnalyzer is the binary executable. The analysis does not require any code modification and does not rely on debug information. The results are independent from flaws in the debug output and refer to exactly the same code as in the shipped system. First, the control-flow graph (CFG) is reconstructed from the input file, the binary executable. Then a static value analysis computes value ranges for registers and address ranges for instructions accessing memory. By concentrating on the value of the stack pointer during value analysis, StackAnalyzer computes how the stack increases and decreases along the various control-flow paths. This information can be used to derive the maximum stack usage of the entire task. StackAnalyzer takes the entire application into account and interprocedurally analyzes each call site with its precise stack height. The results of StackAnalyzer are presented as annotations in a combined call graph and control-flow graph. It shows the critical path, i.e., the path on which the maximum stack usage is reached which gives important feedback for optimizing the stack usage of the application under analysis.

3.2   Worst-Case Execution Time Analysis

Demonstrating timing correctness requires showing that all real-time tasks meet their deadlines, or that deadline violations do not compromise the safety of the system. To demonstrate deadline adherence the worst-case response times (WCRT) of the real-time tasks in the system have to be determined. The WCRT of a task is based on its worst-case execution time (WCET) and takes additional overhead caused, e.g., by task preemptions and task blocking into account.

Due to the characteristics of modern hardware and software architectures determining the WCET of a task has become a challenge. Embedded control software tends to be large and complex. At the hardware level modern microprocessors use hardware features like caches, pipelines, branch prediction, and prefetching which cause the execution behavior of the instructions to depend on the execution history. Small changes in the program code or program input may lead to significant changes in the timing behavior [26].

The widely used classical methods of predicting execution times are not generally applicable. Software monitoring, trace-based measurements, and dual-loop benchmarks modify the code, which in turn changes the cache behavior. Hardware simulation, emulation, or direct measurement with logic analyzers can only determine the execution time for some fixed inputs. They cannot be used to infer the execution times for all possible inputs in general.

In contrast, abstract interpretation can be used to efficiently compute a safe approximation for all possible cache and pipeline states that can occur at a program point in any program run with any input. These results can be combined with ILP (Integer Linear Programming) techniques to safely predict the worst-case execution time and a corresponding worst-case execution path. A survey of methods for WCET analysis and of WCET tools is given in [25].

aiT WCET Analyzer. The timing verifier aiT [7, 20] computes a safe upper bound for the WCET of a task. The main input of aiT is the binary executable. Like StackAnalyzer the analysis does not require any code modification and does not rely on debug information. aiT determines the WCET of a program task in several phases, which makes it possible to use different methods tailored to each subtask. First, the control-flow graph (CFG) is reconstructed from the input file, the binary executable. Then value analysis computes value ranges for registers and address ranges for instructions accessing memory; a loop bound analysis determines upper bounds for the number of iterations of simple loops. Subsequently, a cache analysis classifies memory references as cache misses or hits and a pipeline analysis predicts the behavior of the program on the processor pipeline. Finally the path analysis determines a worst-case execution path of the program. To validate the underlying hardware model automatic trace validation can be applied which allows a cycle-accurate validation of the model down to the level of individual pipeline events and bus signals, based on the automatic processing of trace files created on the real hardware [11].

The results of aiT are reported as annotations in call graphs and control-flow graphs, and as report files in text format and XML format. The overall WCET bounds for sequential code pieces can also be communicated to the system-level analyzer SymTA/S [8], which computes worst-case response times from the sequential WCETs, taking into account interrupts and task preemptions.

aiT is available for a wide range of 16-bit and 32-bit microcontrollers. In general, the availability of safe worst-case execution time bounds depends on the predictability of the execution platform. Especially multi-core architectures may exhibit poor predictability because of essentially non-deterministic interferences on shared resources which can cause high variations in execution time. Reference [13] gives a more detailed overview and suggests example configurations for available multi-cores to support static timing analysis.

3.3 Run-Time Errors and Data Races

Run-time errors are errors that occur during run-time of the software. In this section we will mainly focus on run-time errors which correspond to undefined or unspecified behavior with respect to the semantics of the programming language. This class of errors is of particular interest for the programming language C since it includes many common problems which cannot be detected by the compiler or prevented during run-time. Examples are arithmetic exceptions (e.g. divide by zero), overflows, and validity of addresses for pointers or array bound errors. The C99 standard provides a list of unspecified and undefined behaviors in Section J of ISO/IEC 9899:1999 (E). In addition, errors induced by concurrent execution can be considered run-time errors, most notably data races and thread synchronization errors. A data race is caused by concurrent accesses from two threads to the same memory location without appropriate protection (e.g. mutex locking). Values subject to a data race depend on the timing or process sequencing, resulting in erratic behavior and sporadic crashes.

Depending on their effects run-time errors can be grouped in two categories. The first category of run-time errors is related to conditions in which the source semantics is undefined. After such a run-time error the actual execution will do something unknown. Examples are invalid array or pointer accesses which might corrupt memory and destroy the data integrity of the program. It can even happen that the program code is dynamically modified resulting in erratic behavior, or that the program crashes with segmentation faults or bus errors. Further examples of errors from that class are integer division by zero, floating-point overflows and invalid operations without mathematical meaning which might cause the program to be stopped by an interrupt.

The second category of run-time errors is due to unspecified but implementation-defined behavior; here it is predictable what will happen after the error has occurred. Examples are integer overflows or invalid shifts for which the actual computations are quite different from the expected mathematical meaning.

Astrée. Astrée [3,14] is an abstract interpretation-based sound static analyzer which reports program defects caused by unspecified and undefined behaviors according to the C99 standard, program defects caused by invalid concurrent behavior, and violations of user-specified programming guidelines. Supported error categories include invalid pointer accesses and manipulations, arithmetic overflows, division by zero, out-of-bounds array accesses, etc. Astrée also permits users to specify their own functional properties to be checked with an assertion mechanism (similar to C's assert command), and will report any violation. Finally, Astrée includes a rule checker that supports MISRA C:2004 and MISRA C:2012 and can be extended for customer-specific rule sets.

Astrée uses abstractions to represent and manipulate efficiently over-approximations of program states. As no single abstraction is sufficient to obtain sufficiently precise results, Astrée is actually built by combining a large set of efficient abstractions, e.g., the octagon domain [16]. Some of them, such as abstractions of digital filters [9], have been developed specifically to analyze control-command software as these constitute an important share of safety-critical embedded software. In addition to numeric properties, Astrée contains abstractions to reason about pointers, pointer arithmetic, structures, and arrays. Finally, to ensure precision, Astrée keeps a precise representation of the control flow, by performing a fully context-sensitive, flow-sensitive (and even partially path-sensitive) inter-procedural analysis.

Astrée enables its users to fine-tune the precision of the analyzer to the software under analysis by inserting formal analysis directives to focus precision on specific program parts and specific variables. Also assumptions about the environment such as input value ranges can be specified by Astrée directives. The formal language AAL [1] makes it possible to locate them in the abstract syntax tree without modifying the source code — a prerequisite for analyzing automatically generated code. To deal with evolving software Astrée provides a mechanism to detect whether AAL annotations are still placed at the intended location after structural code changes [12].

Handling Concurrency. Whereas previous Astrée versions have been limited to sequential C software, Astrée has been extended by a novel low-level concurrent semantics [17] which provides a scalable abstraction covering all possible thread interleaving. The interleaving semantics enables Astrée, in addition to the classes of run-time errors found in sequential programs, to report data races and lock/unlock problems, i.e., inconsistent synchronization. In addition to the range of each variable at each program point, Astrée reports the set of shared variables it discovers, together with the set of threads accessing these variables, the kinds of operations performed (reads or writes), and their range of values.

In the simplest case the software runs directly on the hardware, in which case the environment is limited to a set of volatile variables, i.e., program variables that can be modified by the environment concurrently, and for which a range can be provided to Astrée by formal directives as described above. More often, the program is run on top of an operating system, which it can access through function calls to a system library. When analyzing a program using a library, one possible solution is to include the source code of the library with the program. This is not always convenient (if the library is complex), nor possible, if the library source is not available, or not fully written in C, or ultimately relies on kernel services (e.g., for system libraries). An alternative is to provide a stub implementation, i.e., to write, for each library function, a specification of its possible effect on the program. Astrée provides stub libraries for the ARINC 653 standard, the OSEK/AUTOSAR standards, and for POSIX threads. More details on these models are available in [18]. They make it possible to perform a completely automatic OS aware whole-program analysis [19].

4   Tool Qualification

To provide high confidence in the correct functioning of a tool it is necessary to demonstrate that the tool works correctly in the operational context of its users. This is a common requirement of most current safety standards. The correct functioning of a tool might be affected by the OS version, system libraries installed, software patch levels, etc. Moreover, depending on the user's development process structure and tool landscape the probability for detecting tool errors may vary. Therefore taking into account the operational context of tool usage is essential for tool qualification. From the perspective of a tool user, qualifying a software tool causes considerable effort. The functional requirements of the tool have to be specified, a test plan has to be developed, tests have to be executed and documented. Moreover the qualification effort has to be repeated for each development project to be certified. This makes it very desirable to do automate the tool qualification process. Such an automatic tool qualification can be done by dedicated Qualification Support Kits (QSKs) as shipped as a part of a software tool. Qualification kits are available for aiT, StackAnalyzer, and Astrée. They consist of a report package and a test package. The report package lists all functional requirements (tool operational requirements report) and contains a verification test plan describing one or more test cases to check each functional requirement. The test package contains an extensible set of test cases and a scripting system to automatically execute all test cases and evaluate the results. Along with the tool operational requirements report and the verification test plan the generated result report can be submitted to the certification authority as part of the certification package. In particular, all requirements of the EN-50128 regarding tool validation are met (cf. clause 6.7.4.5).

5   Practical Experience

In recent years tools based on static analysis have proved their usability in industrial practice and, in consequence, have increasingly been used by avionics, automotive and health care industries. In the following we report some experiences gained with aiT WCET Analyzer, StackAnalyzer and Astrée. All of them have been successfully used for certification according to various safety standards.

StackAnalyzer results are usually precise for any given program path. Statements about the precision of aiT are hard to obtain since the real WCET is usually unknown for typical real-life applications. For an avionics application running on MPC 755, Airbus has noted that aiT's WCET for a task typically is about 25 % higher than some measured execution times for the same task, the real but non-calculable WCET being in between [23]. Trace-based measurements at AbsInt have indicated overestimations ranging from 0 % (cycle-exact prediction) till 15 % on LEON2, MPC565, MPC5566, M32C, TMS320C33, TriCore TC1197/TC1797/1796, MPC6474F, and C166/ST10 [10,11].

In the following we briefly summarize some experimental results with Astrée for industry applications of different domains. Column *Model* describes the execution model: *sync* stands for a cyclic executive with fully static schedule, *async* denotes a concurrent execution model under control of an operating system compliant to ARINC-653, OSEK, or AUTOSAR. Column *LOC* is the number of lines of preprocessed code without empty lines and without comments, *Alarms* gives the number of code locations with alarms about potential runtime errors, *Data Races* gives the number of variables subject to a potential data race. Column *Memory* indicates the amount of main memory used for the analysis.

Domain	Model	LOC	Alarms	Data races	Time	RAM [GB]
Railway	sync	79.163	39	–	8 min	0.5
Avionics 1	sync	755.197	0	–	6 h	6
Avionics 2	async	225.093	377	119	32 min	2.4
Automotive 1	async	177.574	774	6	30 min	2.6
Automotive 2	async	2.574.481	702	1481	1d 8h	28.4

In all projects investigated the alarm rate is very low, demonstrating high analysis precision. In the *Avionics 1* project no alarms were raised at all so the absence of run-time errors could be proven completely automatically. The six data races reported for project *Automotive 1* were all confirmed to be true data races, i.e., there was no false alarm regarding data races in this example. In the project *Automotive 2* 1481 data races are reported which are not all true data races; some of them are false alarms. The main reason for the high number of data races in that project is that two concepts are not fully supported in Astrée yet: task chaining and the Priority Ceiling Protocol (PCP). Since the PCP can cause task priorities to change, priorities are currently ignored in OSEK/AUTOSAR code by Astrée to get conservative results. Furthermore the scheduling ensures that initialization tasks are not interrupted by regular cyclic tasks. Astrée currently assumes that all tasks run at the same time, which causes spurious data race alarms. Still it is interesting to note that there are only 702 alarms about potential run-time errors: if, e.g., a data race leads to an arithmetic overflow this overflow is reported as a regular run-time error alarm. So in spite of the high number of data races there are only very few actual run-time errors caused by them, which can be explained by the fact that most of them are due to spurious interferences with initialization tasks as explained above. In the upcoming Astrée release both limitations, i.e., regarding PCP and task chaining will be removed, which will further reduce the number of spurious data races.

In general the results show that even software projects consisting of millions of line of code can be analyzed by Astrée in short time with very low alarm rates. To our knowledge there is no other tool available which can detect all potential data races in software projects of comparable sizes.

6   Summary

The quality assurance process for safety-critical embedded software is of crucial importance. The cost for system validation grows with increasing criticality level to constitute a large fraction of the overall development cost. The problem is twofold: system safety must be ensured, yet this must be accomplishable with reasonable effort.

Contemporary safety standards require to identify potential functional and non-functional hazards and to demonstrate that the software does not violate the relevant safety goals. Tools based on abstract interpretation can perform static program analysis of embedded applications. Their results are determined without the need to change the code and hold for all program runs with arbitrary inputs. Especially for non-functional program properties they are highly attractive, since they provide full data and control coverage and can be seamlessly integrated in the development process. We have presented three exemplary tools in this article: aiT allows inspecting the timing behavior of program tasks. It takes into account the combination of all the different hardware characteristics while still obtaining tight upper bounds for the WCET of a given program in reasonable time. StackAnalyzer calculates safe upper bounds on the maximum stack usage of tasks and can prove the absence of stack overflows. Astrée can be used to prove the absence of runtime errors and data races in C programs. Industrial synchronous real-time software from the avionics industry could be successfully analyzed by Astrée with zero false alarms.

aiT, StackAnalyzer and Astrée can be used as analysis tools for the certification according to safety standards like EN-50128, or DO-178B/C. The tool qualification process can be automatized to a large extend by dedicated Qualification Support Kits.

Acknowledgement. The work presented in this paper has been supported by the European FP7 project INTERESTED, and is supported by the European ITEA3 project ASSUME and the German BMBF (FORTISSIMO project).

References

1. AbsInt. The Static Analyzer Astrée – User Documentation for AAL Annotations (2015)
2. Barr, M.: Bookout v. Toyota, 2005 Camry software Analysis by Michael Barr (2013). http://www.safetyresearch.net/Library/BarrSlides_FINAL_SCRUBBED.pdf
3. Blanchet, B., Cousot, P., Cousot, R., Feret, J., Mauborgne, L., Miné, A., Monniaux, D., Rival, X.: A static analyzer for large safety-critical software. In: Proceedings of the ACM SIGPLAN Conference on Programming Language Design and Implementation (PLDI 2003), pp. 196–207, San Diego, California, USA, 7–14 June 2003. ACM Press (2003)
4. CENELEC EN 50128. Railway applications - Communication, signalling and processing systems - Software for railway control and protection systems (2011)
5. Cousot, P., Cousot, R., Abstract interpretation: a unified lattice model for static analysis of programs by construction or approximation of fixpoints. In: 4th POPL, pp. 238–252. ACM Press, Los Angeles (1977)
6. Delmas, D., Souyris, J.: Astrée: from research to industry. In: Riis Nielson, H., Filé, G. (eds.) SAS 2007. LNCS, vol. 4634, pp. 437–451. Springer, Heidelberg (2007)
7. Ferdinand, C., Heckmann, R.: Worst-case execution time - a tool provider's perspective. In: Proceedings of the International Symposium on Object-Oriented Real-Time Distributed Computing (ISORC), pp. 340–345. IEEE Computer Society, Orlando, May 2008
8. Ferdinand, C., Heckmann, R., Jersak, M., Martin, F., Richter, K.: Integrating system-level and code-level timing analysis for dependable system development. In: 4th European Congress ERTS Embedded Real Time Software, Toulouse, France, January 2008
9. Feret, J.: Static analysis of digital filters. In: Schmidt, D. (ed.) ESOP 2004. LNCS, vol. 2986, pp. 33–48. Springer, Heidelberg (2004)
10. Gebhard, G.: Static Timing Analysis Tool Validation in the Presence of Timing Anomalies. PhD thesis, Saarland University (2013)
11. Kästner, D., Pister, M., Gebhard, G., Schlickling, M., Ferdinand, C.: Confidence in Timing. Safecomp 2013 Workshop: Next Generation of System Assurance Approaches for Safety-Critical Systems (SASSUR), September 2013
12. Kästner, D., Pohland, J.: Program analysis on evolving software. In: Roy, M. (ed.) CARS 2015 - Critical Automotiveapplications: Robustness & Safety, Paris, September 2015
13. Kästner, D., Schlickling, M., Pister, M., Cullmann, C., Gebhard, G., Heckmann, R., Ferdinand, C.: Meeting real-time requirements with multi-core processors. Safecomp 2012 Workshop: Next Generation of System Assurance Approaches for Safety-Critical Systems (SASSUR), September 2012

202 D. Kästner and C. Ferdinand

14. Kästner, D., Wilhelm, S., Nenova, S., Cousot, P., Cousot, R., Feret, J., Mauborgne, L., Miné, A., Rival, X.: Astrée: Proving the Absence of Runtime Errors. Embedded Real Time Software and Systems Congress $ERTS^2$ (2010)
15. Lions, J., et al.: ARIANE 5, Flight 501 Failure. Report by the Inquiry Board (1996)
16. Miné, A.: The octagon abstract domain. Higher-Order Symbolic Comput. **19**(1), 31–100 (2006)
17. Miné, A.: Static analysis of run-time errors in embedded real-time parallel C programs. Logical Methods Comput. Sci. (LMCS) **8**(26), 63 (2012)
18. Miné, A., Delmas, D.: Towards an industrial use of sound static analysis for the verification of concurrent embedded avionics software. In: Proceeding of the 15th International Conference on Embedded Software (EMSOFT 2015), pp. 65–74. IEEE CS Press, October 2015
19. Miné, A., Mauborgne, L., Rival, X., Feret, J., Cousot, P., Kästner, D., Wilhelm, S., Ferdinand, C.: Taking Static Analysis to the Next Level: Proving the Absence ofRun-Time Errors and Data Races with Astrée. Embedded Real Time Software and Systems Congress $ERTS^2$ (2016)
20. NASA Engineering and Safety Center. Technical Support to the National Highway Traffic Safety Administration (NHTSA) on the Reported Toyota Motor Corporation (TMC) Unintended Acceleration (UA) Investigation (2011)
21. Radio Technical Commission for Aeronautics. Formal Methods Supplement to DO-178C and DO-278A (2011)
22. Radio Technical Commission for Aeronautics. RTCA DO-178C. Software Considerations in Airborne Systems and Equipment Certification (2011)
23. Souyris, J., Pavec, E.L., Himbert, G., Jégu, V., Borios, G., Heckmann, R.: Computing the worst case execution time of an avionics program by abstract interpretation. In: Proceedings of the 5th International Workshop on Worst-case Execution Time (WCET 2005), Mallorca, pp. 21–24 (2005)
24. Transcript of Morning Trial Proceedings had on the 14th day of October 2013 Before the Honorable Patricia G. Parrish, District Judge, Case No.CJ-2008-7969, October 2013. http://www.safetyresearch.net/Library/Bookout_v_Toyota_Barr_REDACTED.pdf
25. Wilhelm, R., Engblom, J., Ermedahl, A., Holsti, N., Thesing, S., Whalley, D., Bernat, G., Ferdinand, C., Heckmann, R., Mitra, T., Mueller, F., Puaut, I., Puschner, P., Staschulat, J., Stenström, P.: The worst-case execution-time problem–overview of methods and survey of tools. ACM Trans. Embedded Comput. Syst. **7**(3), 1–53 (2008)
26. Wilhelm, R., Grund, D., Reineke, J., Pister, M., Schlickling, M., Ferdinand, C.: Memory hierarchies, pipelines, and buses for future time-critical embedded architectures. IEEE TCAD **28**(7), 966–978 (2009)

The PERF Approach for Formal Verification

Nazim Benaissa, David Bonvoisin, Abderrahmane Feliachi[(✉)],
and Julien Ordioni

RATP, ING/STF/QS, 54 rue Roger Salengro, 94724 Fontenay-sous-Bois, France
{Nazim.Benaissa,David.Bonvoisin,Abderrahmane.Feliachi,
Julien.Ordioni}@ratp.fr

Abstract. In order to analyse extensively the safety of the deployed railway software systems, RATP rely on rigorous verification methodologies based on formal methods. During the past few years, RATP has developed a new formal verification method called PERF, supported by a rich proof tool-chain. The main purpose of this method is to perform a non-intrusive verification on the implemented software. Unlike many formal methodologies, it does not require any intervention in the early stages of the software development.

In this paper, we present the PERF methodology as well as the different part of its supporting tool-chain with some feedback on the its application in some real projects. We also present the ongoing and future work around the PERF tool-chain.

Keywords: Formal methods · Verification tool-chain · Railway safety · PERF

1 Introduction

In order to analyse extensively the safety of the deployed railway software systems and to manage the increasing complexity of railway software, RATP rely on rigorous verification methodologies based on formal methods. The advantage of formal verification, compared to other verification methods such as testing for example, is the exhaustive coverage of the implementation domain of the targeted systems. Formal verification ensures that a software or more generally a system satisfies a given specification. This specification can be described as properties or requirements that the system must satisfy. These properties are divided into two groups: safety properties and liveness properties. Safety properties generally describe undesired events that the system must avoid; e.g. "Two trains should not collide". The liveness property describe the normal behavior the system must follow; e.g. "A train can not remain indefinitely in a station".

Thanks to its exhaustive nature, formal verification can replace classical testing in the classical V-shaped software development cycle. In addition to the verification of systems, formal methods also allow for a better understanding of the system specification and its different properties because of their unambiguous formalization. Formal proof often requires to explicit a number of constraints on the environment

© Springer International Publishing Switzerland 2016
T. Lecomte et al. (Eds.): RSSRail 2016, LNCS 9707, pp. 203–214, 2016.
DOI: 10.1007/978-3-319-33951-1_15

of the system, describing what is called an environment model. This model allows the environment to constrain the verification only to realistic conditions. This also helps to better understand the environment in which the system evolves.

Formal methods include all specification and verification languages and tools defined on mathematical bases. In recent years, a plethora of languages and formal tools were developed for the specification and verification of different types of systems. The formal verification process is built around automatic or assisted provers (proof engines). In addition to the provers, other formal tools are used to assist the verification and the analysis of proof results. Among these tools we note the different editors, static analyzers and counter-examples simulators.

In the past 25 years, RATP has used numerous formal methods for the verification of the critical software of railway systems. This commitment is mostly due to the growing confidence of RATP in these techniques after their successful application in various projects. In the meanwhile, the expertise of RATP in the industrial application of formal methods has been continuously increasing, resulting in the development of an innovative verification methodology (PERF) supported by a rich tool-chain. This paper reports the different applications of formal methods by RATP and gives a picture on the current and future developments around the PERF verification methodology and its supporting tool-chain.

This paper is organized as follows. Section 2 draws an overview on the use of formal methods at RATP. The PERF methodology is explained in Sect. 3 and its application in industrial projects is given in Sect. 4. Finally, Sect. 5 enumerates the ongoing and future developments around the PERF tool-chain.

2   RATP, 25 years of Formal Verification

RATP, with the suppliers Matra/Siemens, Ansaldo and Alstom, has promoted the use of formal proof since the beginning of the 1990s. Today a strong railway community is built not only with these suppliers and Thales, but also with major contributors like Clearsy, Systerel, SafeRiver, Prover Technology and Ikos for providing formal tools and expertise.

Besides railway, other industrial sectors have applied this approach for a long time, such as energy, semiconductors or IT systems security industries. The aeronautics sector, which was held back for a long time by its standards that did not recognize the use of formal proof, should also take the leap, since the publication of version C of the D0178 standard [2]. Nowadays formal proof is widely used. In 2010 for instance, the Japanese Ministry of Industry published a decree encouraging the use of formal proof in all sectors of industry. There is an increasing number of examples around us, and in the rail industry most European manufacturers now offer products developed or verified using formal methods. The current trend is clearly to take more and more into account formal methods for the industrial development or verification processes.

At RATP, everything started more than 25 years ago with the development of the new automatic train protection system SACEM (RER A) in 1989. The use of formal methods revealed 10 safety bugs that had not been detected using testing. This experience initiated a confidence at RATP in the importance of formal methods in the verification process. As a consequence, RATP required the application of formal methods in the development and verification of its systems by any supplier. This led to the development of the first automatic driver-less metro line in Paris (Line 14) in the METEOR project operating since 1998. The development of this system, realized by an external supplier, was entirely based on the formal B method. This means that the refinement proof allowed the supplier to avoid all the unit tests and be sure nevertheless to deliver a safe system. This safety was confirmed during the complementary testing phases (validation tests, integration tests, etc.) since no bugs were found on this system. In addition to the safety assurance, this method was cost effective which is a very important advantage comparing to the classical methodology.

Since the 2000s, the CENELEC standard EN 50128 [6] and RATP highly recommend the suppliers to use formal methods to develop or verify railway critical software. Despite this recommendation, the suppliers are free to use the methods they want to build their safety cases. Consequently, RATP wanted to provide means to perform the formal verification, *a posteriori*, of a product that was not developed using a proof based process.

According to its internal safety policy and in order to assess the safety of software systems independently of the contracted supplier, RATP developed and procured a Formal Proof tool-chain based on a tried-and-tested proof engine combining Model Checking and inductive proof techniques. With this configuration, the formal verification, with all its benefits, can be applied independently of the system development method. This proof tool-chain only impacted the rising part of the V-shaped software development cycle, after the design and coding stages. This technique, designated as an "ex post facto" proof, was the starting point of the PERF methodology [5].

By the end of year 2010, several CBIs (Computer-Based Interlocking) had been developed and validated by their manufacturer for RATP. The formal methods with *Prover Certifier* was the cornerstone of the verification process. In 2011, a transfer of competence was organized and RATP became capable to deploy the CBI "product" on its own and independently of any contracted supplier (specific application, safety validation and safety assessment). This transfer of competence was a success and enabled RATP to deploy the CBIs in complete safety and to maintain and increase its knowledge of formal methods. Using all this knowledge in this domain, RATP worked on a feasibility study on the OCTYS L5 on-bord critical software to assess it regardless the supplier. The success of this study encouraged RATP to continue this way; the PERF methodology was born. It has been, since then, applied to several systems in internal and external projects.

3   The PERF Methodology

PERF (**P**roof **E**xecuted over a **R**etro-engineered **F**ormal model) is a formal proof methodology performed after the development of a system [5]. Unlike formal development techniques (such as the B method for instance) where the proof drives the different development and refinement phases of the system, the PERF verification technique is only applied at the ascending phase of the V-shaped development cycle, all by achieving the same safety requirements as the first method. This technique allows for the application of formal verification even if it was not planned in the early stages of system development. In addition to the independence regarding to the development phase, PERF shares, from a safety point of view, the following strong features with formal development methods:

- The exhaustiveness brought to the verification of considered properties,
- The validation of requirements themselves by means of a formal modeling that reveals any ambiguity or lack of accuracy.

RATP has developed, around the PERF methodology, a complete tool-chain built around a proof engine combining Model-Checking and induction poof techniques. The tool-chain is based on a formal language used to describe, in synchronous languages style, a formal model of the system to be checked. Having fully appreciated the existing potential of using this formal proof tool-chain, RATP decided to widen its scope of application and fully take advantage of its potentialities. This approach presents two major advantages.

First, this tool-chain could prove properties on a software that had already been developed, whether or not it had already been tested; consequently:

- It was possible to produce formal proof of a model, even if the developer had not planned for such formal proof.
- Thanks to the exhaustiveness of the verification of properties by formal proof, this type of verification guaranteed on its own the compliance of properties through the formal model (or the software). This leads to a potentially significant productivity gain during engineering phases of the product.
- Formal proof when performed independently from the development cycle, it could take place concurrently with software test phases.

Additionally, the PERF tool-chain comprises several "elementary building blocks" that can be organized in different ways to address a particular issue. This multi-purpose tool can be used for different types of verification. So the same tool can be used for different project by adapting its use. This means one can capitalize on expertise using a single tool.

Technically, PERF is based on a formal declarative, synchronous, data flow language in the tradition of LUSTRE [10]. Models are defined by a set of streams that can be composed using either temporal or data operators. Temporal operators can be used to describe clock-dependent expressions. The data operators are used to manipulate streams values e.g. arithmetic, logical and array operators. The declarative nature of the language makes it suitable for the definition of formal models as well as safety properties.

The PERF workflow is organized into different steps. First, the source software is translated into a formal model understandable by the proof engine. All or part of the specification is expressed in the same formal language as properties representing safety requirements. The formal model together with the formal properties form a proof setup. This setup might be enriched with constraints or assumptions describing a model of the environment. This environment model can be very useful for eliminating impossible cases and for a better guidance of the proof process. All three models (software, specification and the environment) are input to the proof engine that check if the properties are valid or not. In the case of properly proven properties, the proof engine also provides a certifiable proof log to trace the proof steps that was used to validate the properties. In the case of invalid properties, the proof engine provides counter-examples in which these properties are falsified.

The PERF verification workflow is explained in figure Fig. 1. First, the software is translated to a formal execution model that can be manipulated by the PERF workshop. Environmental constraints and safety requirement are introduced directly in the formal language of PERF. Using all these inputs, the PERF workshop provides either a proof certificate if the properties hold or counter-examples in the other case.

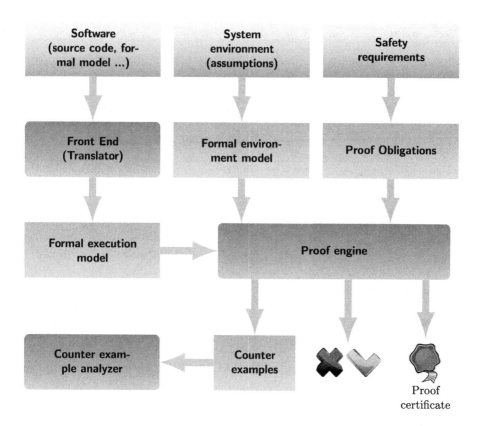

Fig. 1. The PERF verification workflow

4   Feedback and Case Studies

RATP has used or uses formal methods through PERF or other techniques to achieve an independent assessment of critical software for internal or external projects and purposes. The present section gives an overview of some major projects where formal methods were applied. Throughout the projects, different proof workshops were used for the verification activity. This can be seen as a time-line describing the genesis of the PERF approach in order to achieve safety assessment activities, from the coupling of some existing proof workshops.

4.1   For Internal Purposes

The application of formal verification methods for internal RATP projects is summarized in the following table.

Line	System	Dev. method	Proof workshop	Date	Use case
Line 8	CBI (67 routes)	Petri nets	Prover Certifier	2011	Safety Demonstration
Line 12	CBIs (27 &57 routes)	Petri nets	Prover Certifier	2012	Safety Demonstration
Line 4	CBI (38 routes)	Petri nets	Prover Certifier	2013	Safety Demonstration
Line 1	CBIs (52 &76 routes)	Petri nets	Prover Certifier	2013	Safety Demonstration
Line 5	CBTC on-board equipment (100k loc)	Scade 5	PERF	since 2013	Safety Assessment
Line 9	CBTC on-board equipment (100k loc)	Scade 5	PERF	since 2014	Safety Assessment
Line 13	CBTC equipments (6M loc)	Scade 6	PERF	since 2014	Safety Assessment

4.2   For Its External Clients

Formal verification was also applied by RATP for other clients as shown in the following table.

4.3   PERF Feedback

RATP's use of the formal proof workshop (PERF tool-chain) has spotlighted and finally enhanced several strengths:

Client	System	Development method	Proof workshop	Use case
SL (Stockholm - Sweden)	CBI	Synchronous Formal Model (PiSpec)	Prover Certifier	Evaluation of the process and proof tools used for safety demonstrations
USA	CBI	Ladder logic	Prover iLock	Independent safety assessment
RFF (LGV Est - France)	RBC (ERTMS)	Classical process (manually produced Ada)	PERF	Expert opinion on critical software

- The formal language used by the PERF tool-chain is simple. It can be learnt and mastered quickly by new users. Thus RATP can easily mutualise and capitalize knowledge through the team and the different projects.
- The cost of implementing PERF is, for the first shot, equivalent to conventional methodologies based on validation test campaigns. This initial cost is largely due to the necessary adaptation of the tools to the development methodology used by the supplier and the establishment of a suitable process. However, the cost of formal proof falls sharply when dealing with changes (non regression and impact assessments), which makes PERF more advantageous over the lifetime of the project, for example:
  - RATP noticed that the use of PERF instead of validation tests reduced the overall validation workload by roughly 25 % while at the same time significantly improving the confidence level with regards to the safety of software based systems.
  - PERF performed on the SCADE model of on-board equipment revealed a safety-threatening bug 15 days before its deployment. The supplier then proposed a patch that corrects this bug. Thanks to the use of PERF, RATP was able to convince itself of the effectiveness of this patch and the absence of regression caused by this patch in much less time than the supplier needed to replay the subsets of its tests, and the date of deployment was maintained.
  - The abstraction principle [5] allows RATP to assess relatively quickly big and complex components where classical analysis methods would be time consuming and sensitive to human errors.
- When a property is not proven by the tool-chain, the latter exhibits a counter example. This eases the understanding of the scenario that led to the violation of this property. For instance, on a recent major project, not less than 200 potentially unsafe bugs have been revealed this way, enabling their correction before commissioning.
- The formal verification of some properties requires to constrain the environment model of the system under assessment to behave in the expected way, that is, to behave as in real scenarios. This means to formally model some assumptions about the behavior of the environment of the system under assessment. It leads, in fine, to an explicit list of assumptions made to establish the

safety demonstration of the system, i.e. to an explicit list of safe use conditions of the system.

This methodology nevertheless has certain limits: it does not apply to software developed in object languages (C++, Java) if they make use of inheritance or dynamic object creation (which is, in any event, not allowed under standard EN 50128). Lastly, the PERF methodology is easier to implement on software whose development is based on formal methods.

5   The Future of PERF

The successful application of formal verification techniques in the safety assessment of railway software increases the confidence in their usefulness. In order to take more advantage of formal methods, additional extensions and applications are currently developed. In this section, we introduce some of the current and future developments of the PERF tool-chain. This development is organized in two axes which are PERF core extensions and additional applications. In the following, we will give an overview on the currently developed extensions and applications. We will expose at the end of this section our vision for the future of PERF and its applications.

5.1   PERF Extensions

Presently, two kinds of extensions are being developed, covering additional source language support and new proof engine integrations. The goal of the first type of extensions is to make the PERF approach applicable to other new source languages. This should widen the scope of application of PERF to other systems and thus to other users. For instance, an ongoing work is to support B formal models as possible inputs of PERF. The second kind of extensions aims at adding a set of different proof engines in order to have a more complete proof environment. It is well known that no proof engine is perfect for all problems, combining different proof strategies should allow PERF to deal with a variety of systems in the most efficient way. For example, symbolic proof techniques can be used to simplify the addressed proof goals for the SAT or SMT based provers.

5.2   Proof Coverage Application

In addition to the extensions that are intended to enrich the verification tools, new applications are also developed around the PERF tool-chain. The first application consists of the computation of some proof coverage metrics.

The formal verification ensures that the model has been exhaustively covered regarding the proven properties. However, nothing indicates which parts of the source software or model were involved in the proof of these properties. This concept of coverage can be important to determine which parts of the code are covered by which properties and vice versa. The coverage computation offers the following advantages:

- It highlights the parts of the code that guarantee the respect of a given property or requirement. This draws a clear connection between the specification and the code and helps the detection of overly strong assumptions or unspecified behaviors.
- The opposite coverage link between properties and their implementing code parts allows the detection of dead code.
- The coverage metrics can replace test coverage metrics and thus unit testing can be definitely replaced by formal proof.
- The coverage results may be used as support for other tasks, by making the relationship between properties and code entities explicit.
- Finally, the relationships between properties and code entities may help for a more efficient proof rerun by reducing the system, in the proof of a given property, to the parts that are covered by this property.

Inspired from some existing works in the electronics field such as [7–9], an advanced prototype of a proof coverage computation and visualization tool has been developed. The basic coverage criteria considered in this solution is the coverage of stream definitions (variable assignments) by properties and its dual i.e. the coverage of properties by definitions. Using this coverage metrics, number of other coverage criteria can be addressed e.g. modules (components) coverage.

5.3   Non-regression Application

A second application, is the assisted impact analysis and automatic non-regression verification. The goal of this ongoing work is to store additional information from the first verification campaign in order to make explicit causality relations between the software components and the specification properties. The impact of an evolution of the software on the verified properties can then be easily determined and, thus, the non-regression study becomes straightforward.

5.4   GRAAL Application

Another currently studied application is the generalization of software-level properties to system-level properties in the verification process. In the classical V-shaped software life cycle, the descendant phase consists of successive refinement and decomposition steps, starting from a high-level specification and ending with a fine grained software. The goal of GRAAL (The **G**rail obtained by **R**everse-modeling/**A**scendant **A**bstraction **L**evel) is to cover the whole ascendant phase of the cycle with abstraction and generalization proofs. This can be compared to integration and validation testing starting from unit testing in the life cycle bottom. The ultimate goal of this tool is to perform a complete formal verification (and validation) of the entire descendant phase of the life cycle of one subsystem (e.g. on-board or wayside equipment) or the whole system (on-board and wayside) with an integration proof. Technical problems like asynchronous systems or interfaces between emerging models will have to be solved to reach this grail. This means that all the testing process could be replaced with GRAAL.

5.5   Towards an IDE for PERF

In the recent years, some formal proof environments have been developed following, more or less, the trend of integrated development environments (IDE). Integrated platforms (such as Eclipse for example) are widely used nowadays and have demonstrated their usefulness for several activities like modeling, development and testing. The success of these IDEs led the formal methods community to develop similar integrated environment for formal methods and proof engines. Some examples of formal proof environments are Isabelle PIDE [12], Atelier B [1] Rodin [4], FoCaLiZe [11] and Coq PIDE [13].

We are convinced that the idea of an integrated environment for formal verification can be very beneficial in many ways. First, having an integrated extensible environment makes the different formal verification activities easier for the users and thus reduces time and effort. A considerable amount of time can also be reduced by factoring the common tasks of the different involved tools. The environment enforces the harmony of the team work and the capitalization of the overall experience. Finally, it allows for the integration of the different tools and extensions in smooth and transparent way.

A first attempt for developing a proof IDE was made by RATP in the OVADO tool [3] for the validation of critical software data. OVADO is not considered as a part of PERF even though they are complementary. PERF covers the dynamic aspects of a parametrized system when OVADO covers the static data and parameters verification. OVADO offers, in addition to the formal verification component, number of additional tools (e.g. rich editing, quick evaluation, reporting) that ease its usage and make the verification process very productive. The same idea is now under study for the formal verification of software systems using the PERF tool-chain. The overall architecture of the desired IDE is given in Fig. 2. The different components are split in two groups, business components i.e. proof related applications and support components i.e. user assistance applications. Each component might be composed of different applications and must be extensible to support any new tools. For examples, the languages support

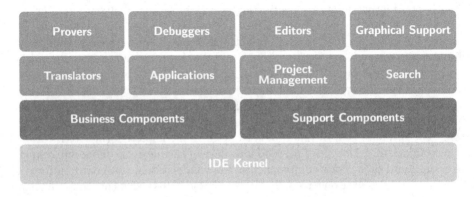

Fig. 2. The PERF IDE architecture

extensions should be included in the translators component and the new proof engines integrated in the provers component. In the debuggers, one can find for example counter example analyzers and simulators.

6   Conclusion

The application of formal proof is increasingly advocated for the verification of critical systems and particularly in railway. Nevertheless, its application in big industrial projects is still limited despite all the potential benefits it offers. This limitation is due, inter alia, to the absence of mechanized solutions that are comprehensive and robust enough to support the formal verification of industrial size systems. Considerable efforts have been employed by RATP to develop a methodology for formal verification. This have led to the PERF formal proof methodology and its supporting tool-chain which has allowed for the application of formal proof in several projects for the verification of safety requirements. With its arsenal of translators, proof engines and counter-example analyzers, the PERF tool-chain is a good environment for formal verification activities.

The applications of formal verification techniques (and more recently PERF in particular) by RATP gave birth to several success stories. Since 2011, the verification of more than 7 internal projects and 3 external ones was conducted using formal methods. The verification revealed at least as many errors as detected in unit testing with higher confidence and more effectiveness. This confirmed the confidence of RATP in formal methods, which led to the development of the PERF tool-chain. The ambition for the present and future of PERF is to enhance and extend the tool-chain with more extensions and applications. This should make it possible to apply the formal verification in other different projects. Finally, the ultimate goal is to build a substantial community of experts and industrial actors in order to build a strong formal environment that can be used by each and every one.

References

1. Atelier, B.: version 3.2, manuel de référence du langage B. GEC Alsthom Transport and Steria Méditerrannée and SNCF and INRETS and RATP (1997)
2. DO-178C, software considerations in airborne systems and equipment certification. Special Committee 205 of RTCA (2011)
3. Abo, R., Voisin, L.: Formal implementation of data validation for railway safety-related systems with OVADO. In: Counsell, S., Núñez, M. (eds.) SEFM 2013. LNCS, vol. 8368, pp. 221–236. Springer, Heidelberg (2014)
4. Abrial, J.R., Butler, M., Hallerstede, S., Hoang, T.S., Mehta, F., Voisin, L.: Rodin: an open toolset for modelling and reasoning in event-B. Int. J. Softw. Tools Technol. Transf. **12**(6), 447–466 (2010)
5. Bonvoisin, D., Benaissa, N.: Utilisation de la méthode de preuve formelle PERF de la RATP sur le projet PEEE. Revue Générale des Chemins de Fer 250 (2015)
6. CENELEC EN-50128: Railway applications - Communication, signalling and processing systems - software for railway control and protection systems (2011)

7. Chockler, H., Kupferman, O., Vardi, M.Y.: Coverage metrics for formal verification. In: Geist, D., Tronci, E. (eds.) CHARME 2003. LNCS, vol. 2860, pp. 111–125. Springer, Heidelberg (2003)

8. Claessen, K.: A coverage analysis for safety property lists. In: Formal Methods in Computer Aided Design, November 2007

9. Das, S., Basu, P., Banerjee, A., Dasgupta, P., Chakrabarti, P., Mohan, C., Fix, L., Armoni, R.: Formal verification coverage: computing the coverage gap between temporal specifications. In: ICCAD, pp. 198–203, November 2004

10. Halbwachs, N., Caspi, P., Raymond, P., Pilaud, D.: The synchronous data flow programming language LUSTRE. Proc. IEEE **79**(9), 1305–1320 (1991)

11. Pessaux, F.: FoCaLiZe: Inside an F-IDE. arXiv preprint arXiv:1404.6607 (2014)

12. Wenzel, M.: Isabelle/jedit – a prover IDE within the PIDE framework. CoRR abs/1207.3441 (2012)

13. Wenzel, M.: PIDE as front-end technology for Coq. CoRR abs/1304.6626 (2013)

Abstract Software Specifications and Automatic Proof of Refinement

Claire Dross and Yannick Moy$^{(\boxtimes)}$

AdaCore, 46 Rue d'Amsterdam, 75009 Paris, France
{dross,moy}@adacore.com

Abstract. It is common practice in critical software development, and compulsory in railway software developed according to EN 50128 standard, to separate software specification from software implementation. Verification activities should be performed to ensure that the latter is a correct refinement of the former. When the specification is formalized, for example in B method, the refinement relation can even be formally proved. In this article, we present how a similar proof of refinement can be performed at the level of the programming language used for implementation, using the SPARK technology. We describe two techniques to specify abstractly the behavior of a software component in terms of mathematical structures (sequences, sets and maps) and a methodology based on the SPARK tools to prove automatically that an efficient imperative implementation is a correct refinement of the abstract specification.

Keywords: Formal methods · Verification and validation · Certification · Dependability · EN 50128

1 Introduction

The railway standard EN 50128 [1] has been the first one in 2001 to recommend formal methods for the development of critical software, an example later followed by other domains such as avionics [17]. In EN 50128, formal methods are recommended at levels SIL 1 and SIL2, and highly recommended at levels SIL3 and SIL4, both for software requirements (table A.2 of EN 50128) and for design and implementation (table A.4 of EN 50128). Among formal methods, formal proof is similarly (highly) recommended at the same levels for verification and testing (table A.5 of EN 50128). Formal proof based on contracts is a particularly good fit to the principles of high integrity software development enumerated at the start of EN 50128 document, as it allows modular verification of individual components with a clear description of dependences between components given by their contract.

Work partly supported by the Joint Laboratory ProofInUse (ANR-13-LAB3-0007, http://www.spark-2014.org/proofinuse) and project VECOLIB (ANR-14-CE28-0018) of the French national research organization.

© Springer International Publishing Switzerland 2016
T. Lecomte et al. (Eds.): RSSRail 2016, LNCS 9707, pp. 215–230, 2016.
DOI: 10.1007/978-3-319-33951-1_16

Subprogram contracts were popularized in the Design-by-Contract approach [20] as a means to separate responsibilities in software between a caller and a callee. The callee's *precondition* states the responsibility of its caller, while the callee's *postcondition* states the responsibility of the callee itself. For example, the following (incomplete) contract for procedure Swap specifies that it should be called with index parameters within the range of the array parameter, and that Swap will ensure on return that the corresponding values in the array have been swapped. Attribute Old in the postcondition is used to refer to values on entry to the subprogram.

```
procedure Swap (A : in out Arr; X, Y : Idx) with
  Pre  => X in A'Range and Y in A'Range,
  Post => A(X) = A(Y)'Old and A(Y) = A(X)'Old;
```

The procedure declaration above is written in SPARK, a subset of the Ada programming language targeted at safety- and security-critical applications. SPARK builds on the strengths of Ada for creating highly reliable and long-lived software. SPARK restrictions ensure that the behavior of a SPARK program is unambiguously defined, and simple enough that formal verification tools can perform an automatic diagnosis of conformance between a program specification and its implementation. The SPARK language and toolset for formal verification has been applied over many years to on-board aircraft systems, control systems, cryptographic systems, and rail systems [5,21]. The latest version, SPARK 2014 [12,19], builds on the new specification features added in Ada 2012 [4], so formal specifications are now understood by the usual development tools and can be executed. SPARK toolset was qualified as a verification tool (tool class T2) in a railway certification project subject to EN 50128 standard.

Compared to previous versions, the latest version of SPARK is used industrially to prove automatically both absence of run-time errors and properties of programs expressed as contracts. Contracts are mostly used to express low-level specifications, close to the actual implementation, like the one on Swap above (although they can be much more complex). In comparison, the B method [2] used in railway industry allows expressing specifications abstractly in terms of mathematical sequences, sets and maps (the abstract machine), while the implementation uses a restricted subset of B called B0 that provides a thin layer over concrete arrays and machine integers/floats (the concrete machine) in order to allow generation of efficient machine code. The proof that the concrete machine refines the abstract machine gives the confidence that the code indeed implements an abstract specification more easily understood by humans and shared among stakeholders. In this article, we show how a similar expression of abstract specifications is possible in SPARK, and that the proof of refinement can be performed automatically.

1.1 SPARK Verification Environment

Key Language Features. The most useful feature in SPARK is the ability to specify a contract on subprograms, given by a precondition and a postcondition as presented on `Swap`. Attribute `Result` in the postcondition of a function is used to refer to the value returned by the function.

Instead of preconditions and postconditions, or in addition to them, subprogram contracts may be specified by a set of disjoint and complete cases. For example, the following contract for procedure `Swap` states separate sub-contracts for the cases where the elements at indexes `X` and `Y` are equal or different. The first case specifies that, if `A(X)` equals `A(Y)` on entry, then `A` should not be modified by the call. The second case specifies that, if `A(X)` is different from `A(Y)` on entry, then `A` should be modified by the call.

```
procedure Swap (A : in out Arr; X, Y : Idx) with
  Contract_Cases =>
    (A(X) = A(Y) => A = A'Old,
     A(X) /= A(Y) => A /= A'Old);
```

Specific kinds of expressions make it easier to express contracts. If-expressions and case-expressions are the expression forms which correspond to the usual if-statements and case-statements. Note that an if-expression without an else-part (`if A then B`) expresses a logical implication of B by A. Quantified expressions (`for all X in A => P`) and (`for some X in A => P`) correspond to the mathematical universal and existential quantifications, only on a bounded domain. Expression functions define a function using a single expression, like in functional programming languages. As expression functions can be part of the specification of programs (contrary to regular function bodies) in SPARK, they provide a powerful way to abstract complex parts of contracts.

The second most useful feature in SPARK (after contracts) is the ability to specify properties of loops. A loop invariant expresses the cumulated effect of the loop up to that point. For example, the following loop invariant expresses that the array `A` has been zeroed-out up to the current loop index `J`, and that the rest of the array has not been modified. Attribute `Loop_Entry` is used to refer to values on entry to the loop.

```
pragma Loop_Invariant
  (for all K in A'Range =>
    (if K <= J then A(K) = 0 else A(K) = A'Loop_Entry(K)));
```

To show loop termination, one can use a loop variant to express that a quantity varies monotonically at each iteration of the loop. For example, the following loop variant expresses that scalar variable `J` increases at each loop iteration.

```
pragma Loop_Variant (Increases => J);
```

For-loops in SPARK are bounded by construction, so this is only needed for while-loops and plain-loops.

Benefits of Executable Contracts. Traditionally, contracts have been interpreted quite differently depending on whether they were used for run-time assertion checking or for formal program verification. For run-time assertion checking, contracts have been interpreted as assertions on entry and exit of subprograms. For formal program verification, assertions have typically been interpreted as formulas in classical first-order logic. This was the situation with SPARK prior to SPARK 2014. Practitioners have struggled with this interpretation, which was not consistent with the run-time assertion checking semantics [8].

SPARK reconciles the logic semantics and executable semantics of contracts, so users can now execute contracts, debug them like code, and test them when formal verification is too difficult to achieve. Furthermore, by keeping the annotation language the same as the programming language, users don't have to learn another language.

All the previously presented contracts and assertion pragmas lead to run-time assertions. If a property is not satisfied at run time, an exception is raised with a message indicating the failing property, for example on procedure Swap:

```
failed precondition from swap.ads:4
```

Another key benefit of executable contracts is that they can be used by other tools working at the level of code. For example, the CodePeer[1] static analysis tool uses contracts and assertion pragmas to issue more precise messages. Most notably, this also allows SPARK users to combine the results of formal verification and testing, when only part of a program is formally analyzed [10].

Key Tool Features. GNATprove is the formal verification tool that analyzes SPARK code. It performs two different analyses: (i) flow analysis of the program and (ii) proof of program properties.

Flow analysis checks correct access to data in the program: correct access to global variables and correct access to initialized data. It is a fast static analysis (analysis time typically comparable with compilation time).

Proof is used to demonstrate that the program is free from run-time errors, and that the specified contracts are correctly implemented. It internally generates mathematical formulas for each property, that are given to the automatic provers Alt-Ergo, CVC4 and Z3. If one of the automatic provers manages to prove the formula in the given time, then the property is known to hold. Otherwise, more work is required from the user to understand why the property is not proved.

As proof requires interactions between the user and the tool until the specification can be proved automatically, the efficiency and the granularity at which the tool can be applied are critical. For efficiency, GNATprove uses a compilation-like model where only those parts that are impacted by a change need to be reanalyzed, and a fast generation of formulas. For convenient interaction, GNATprove allows users to focus on a single unit, a single subprogram inside a unit, or even a single line inside a subprogram.

A very useful feature of GNATprove to investigate unproved properties is its ability to display counterexamples along paths that lead to unproved properties. The counterexample and the path can be displayed in GPS[2] or in Eclipse[3], the two Integrated Development Environments which support SPARK. The user can

---

[1] http://www.adacore.com/codepeer.
[2] http://www.adacore.com/gnatpro/toolsuite/gps/.
[3] http://www.adacore.com/gnatpro/toolsuite/gnatbench/.

also change the parameters of the tool to perform more precise proofs, at the expense of longer analysis time.

Finally, modular verification based on contracts can very easily exploit multi-core architectures, as the generation of Verification Conditions (VCs) for different units, or the proof of different VCs, can both be run in parallel. Typically, projects contain hundreds of units, and lead to the generation of thousands of VCs, which can be run by GNATprove on as many cores as are available. Note also that GNATprove uses file timestamps to avoid re-generating VCs for units which have not been updated, and file hashes to avoid re-proving VCs that have already been proved. This is crucial when developing either the code or the associated annotations, to avoid unnecessary rework.

1.2   Ghost Code in SPARK

Sometimes the variables and functions that are useful for the implementation are not sufficient to specify a property in contracts. One approach is to introduce additional variables and functions, which will then only be used for the purpose of verification. But in a certification context such as EN 50128, the additional code will need to be verified at the same level as the application. This means performing structural coverage analysis, showing traceability to requirements, and demonstrating absence of interference between this verification-related code and the rest of the program if the verification code is to be deactivated in the final executable. A better solution is to use so-called *ghost code*.

Ghost code is identified through an aspect named Ghost that can be attached to variables, types, subprograms and packages to indicate that these entities are only used in verification code. The compiler checks that such code indeed only appears in contracts, assertions, and the definition of other ghost entities. As a benefit, any unintended interference between verification-related and application code is caught automatically, and the verification code can be removed when the final executable is built (hence the name *ghost code*).

Various kinds of ghost code are useful in different situations:

– Ghost functions can express properties used in contracts.
– Global ghost variables can keep track of the current state of a program, or maintain a log of past events. This information can then be referenced in contracts.
– Ghost types are types that are only used for defining ghost variables.

In a SPARK context, the GNATprove tool will check additionally that ghost code cannot have any effect on the behavior of the program. For an overview of the possible uses of ghost code in SPARK, see the SPARK User's Guide[4] and for the detailed rules defining ghost code, see the SPARK Reference Manual[5].

---

[4] http://docs.adacore.com/spark2014-docs/html/ug/spark_2014.html#ghost-code.
[5] http://docs.adacore.com/spark2014-docs/html/lrm/subprograms.html#
ghost-entities.

1.3   SPARK Library of Containers

Functional containers are part of the newly redesigned library of standard containers in SPARK. They consist in sequences, sets and maps. Functional containers are specified through a simple API with contracts, based on a few essential functions. For example, the API of functional sets is defined over its effects on the Mem function for membership. Here is the contract of function Inc that tests inclusion of set S1 in set S2:

```
function Inc (S1, S2 : Set) return Boolean with
   Post => Inc'Result = (for all E in S1 => Mem (S2, E));
```

Quantification over a container content is achieved by means of a generic mechanism in SPARK, which allows users to describe the functions used to iterate over a given datatype. Similarly, the API of functional sequences is defined over its effects on the functions Length and Get, and the API of functional maps is defined over its effects on the functions Mem and Get.

SPARK also comes with a library of imperative containers (lists, vectors, sets and maps). In the newly redesigned library, imperative containers are specified through an API with contracts based on functional containers. The benefit of this approach is that there is no need for a dedicated support for containers in the SPARK tools or provers, as they are specified through contracts like any other piece of code.

Naturally, client code that uses imperative containers can be specified using functional containers, and GNATprove can be used to prove that the code implements its specification. In this article, we aim at showing that functional containers can be used to express abstract specifications even when the implementation does not use imperative containers, and that the refinement proof can nonetheless be made automatically with GNATprove. Thus, we are using only functional containers in the rest of this article, in a way that is reminiscent of their use in the contracts of imperative containers.

2   Extracting a Model from the Implementation

As initial example, we consider a simple (inefficient) memory allocator that maintains an array of boolean flags to indicate whether the nth resource is allocated or not. For the purpose of better explaining how a given way of writing specifications is adapted to specific situations, we will present first the implementation and only then the specification. In actual software development, the order would be reversed.

2.1   A Simple Memory Allocator

In fact, in SPARK we can use an enumeration Status instead of a boolean, and an array Data over a precise range Valid_Resource with values in this enumeration as follows:

```
Capacity : constant := 10_000;
type Resource is new Integer range 0 .. Capacity;
subtype Valid_Resource is Resource range 1 .. Capacity;
No_Resource : constant Resource := 0;

type Status is (Available, Allocated);
type A is array (Valid_Resource) of Status;

Data : A := (others => Available);
```

Deallocating a resource consists in setting the corresponding status flag to Available when previously allocated:

```
procedure Free (Res : Resource) is
begin
    if Res /= No_Resource and then Data (Res) = Allocated then
        Data (Res) := Available;
    end if;
end Free;
```

Allocating a resource consists in searching for the first available resource if any, and then setting the corresponding status flag to Allocated before returning the resource position:

```
procedure Alloc (Res : out Resource) is
begin
    for R in Valid_Resource loop
        if Data (R) = Available then
            Data (R) := Allocated;
            Res := R;
            return;
        end if;
    end loop;
    Res := No_Resource;
end Alloc;
```

2.2   Model as a Ghost Function

In the simple memory allocator, we define a model of the allocator as a ghost function which will be used in the contracts of Free and Alloc. The *model* of the allocator data consists in two sets of resources: a set of resources available and a set of resources allocated.

```
package S is new Functional_Sets (Element_Type => Resource,
                                   No_Element   => No_Resource);
type T is record
    Available : S.Set;
    Allocated : S.Set;
end record;
```

Ghost function Model returns a value of this type, which additionally verifies additional properties relating the abstract model to the concrete data, expressed in function Is_Valid:

```
function Is_Valid (M : T) return Boolean;
function Model return T with Post => Is_Valid (Model'Result);
```

Ghost function Is_Valid expresses that sets Available and Allocated define a partition of the range of resources Valid_Resource:

```
function Is_Valid (M : T) return Boolean is
  ((for all E in M.Available => E in Valid_Resource)
     and then
   (for all E in M.Allocated => E in Valid_Resource)
     and then
   (for all R in Valid_Resource =>
     (case Data (R) is
        when Available => Mem (M.Available, R) and not Mem (M.Allocated, R),
        when Allocated => not Mem (M.Available, R) and Mem (M.Allocated, R))));
```

All the specification code presented so far in this section could be marked explicitly as ghost code. A better way of achieving the same result is to gather this code in a local package marked ghost as follows:

```
package M with Ghost is
   package S is ...
   type T is ...
   function Is_Valid ...
   function Model ...
end M;
```

With this model, is straightforward to express the functional contract of Alloc and Free as contract cases, using the function Is_Add from the functional set library, which expresses that a Result set is the addition of an element to an input set. The same property could be expressed by using Add and equality on sets, but using Is_Add results in fewer quantifiers being used, which facilitates automatic verification. The notation Result => Arg uses the named parameter passing mechanism instead of the positional one to clarify which call argument corresponds to parameter Result.

```
procedure Alloc (Res : out Resource) with
  Contract_Cases =>

    -- When no resource is available, return the special value No_Resource
    -- with the allocator unmodified.

    (Is_Empty (Model.Available) =>
       Res = No_Resource
         and then
       Model = Model'Old,

    -- Otherwise, return an available resource which becomes allocated

    others =>
       Is_Add (Model.Available, Res, Result => Model.Available'Old)
         and then
       Is_Add (Model.Allocated'Old, Res, Result => Model.Allocated));

procedure Free (Res : Resource) with
  Contract_Cases =>

    -- When the resource is allocated, make it available

    (Mem (Model.Allocated, Res) =>
       Is_Add (Model.Available'Old, Res, Result => Model.Available)
         and then
       Is_Add (Model.Allocated, Res, Result => Model.Allocated'Old),

    -- Otherwise, do nothing

    others =>
       Model = Model'Old);
```

Function Model is implemented as a simple loop that creates the two sets Available and Allocated by iterating over the content of the array Data.

2.3 Automatic Proof of Refinement

GNATprove can be used to prove automatically that the code of the simple memory allocator presented in Sect. 2.1 is free of run-time errors and implements the specification presented in Sect. 2.2. The loop-free implementation of Free is proved easily with the default minimal proof settings (only one prover called with a timeout of one second per proof). Indeed, setting Data(Res) to Available directly maps at model level with removing Res from set Model.Allocated and adding it to set Model.Available. The implementation of Alloc contains a loop searching for the first resource available in Data, which requires the user to write a loop invariant summarizing the effect of the loop on variables modified in the loop (here Data is not modified while looping) and accumulating the information gathered across iterations on all variables (here that no available resource has been encountered yet):

```
pragma Loop_Invariant
   (Data = Data'Loop_Entry
      and then (for all RR in 1 .. R => Data (RR) = Allocated));
```

Once the first available resource R has been reached, setting Data(R) to Allocated directly maps at model level with removing Res from set Model.Available and adding it to set Model.Allocated. Then, the implementation of Alloc is proved easily at proof level 2 (all three provers called with a timeout of 10 s per proof).

The proof of function Model also requires a simple loop invariant expressing that the property Is_Valid (from its postcondition) has been respected up to the value of resource for the current iteration of the loop. With this loop invariant, the implementation of Model is proved easily with the default minimal proof settings. Overall, the automatic proof of refinement of the simple memory allocator takes 12 s on a laptop with 2.7 GHz Intel Core i7 and 16 GB RAM (using a single core).

3 Maintaining a Model Within the Implementation

As a more involved example, we consider a more realistic memory allocator based on a free list. As before, we present first the implementation and then the specification, to facilitate exposure and understanding, in reverse order compared to the actual software development.

3.1 A Free List Memory Allocator

Compared to the simple memory allocator presented in Sect. 2.1, the free list memory allocator uses an array Data of cells consisting of a status (available or allocated) and a pointers to the next resource in a linked list. A variable

First_Available points to the head of the linked list of available resources (a.k.a. the free list).

```
Capacity : constant := 10_000;
type Resource is new Integer range 0 .. Capacity;
subtype Valid_Resource is Resource range 1 .. Capacity;
No_Resource : constant Resource := 0;

type Status is (Available, Allocated);
type Cell is record
    Stat : Status;
    Next : Resource;
end record;
type A is array (Valid_Resource) of Cell;

Data : A := (others => Cell'(Stat => Available, Next => No_Resource));
First_Available : Resource := 1;
```

Allocating a resource consists in extracting and returning the free list head:

```
procedure Alloc (Res : out Resource) is
    Next_Avail : Resource;
begin
    if First_Available /= No_Resource then
        Res := First_Available;
        Next_Avail := Data (First_Available).Next;
        Data (Res) := Cell'(Stat => Allocated, Next => No_Resource);
        First_Available := Next_Avail;
    else
        Res := No_Resource;
    end if;
end Alloc;
```

Deallocation is done by adding the deallocated resource to the free list head.

3.2 Model as a Ghost Variable

In the free list memory allocator, unlike the simple memory allocator, not every configuration is a valid configuration of the software, thus we cannot represent the model as a function. For example, the initial value of Data as seen in Sect. 3.1 does not define a valid free list. What is needed is to add the following code to the startup code of the compilation unit (the *package elaboration code* in Ada parlance):

```
for R in Valid_Resource loop
    if R < Capacity then Data (R).Next := R + 1; end if;
end loop;
```

Thus, it is necessary to define what configurations are valid, and to prove both that the configuration is valid at startup and that operations Alloc and Free maintain the validity of the configuration. This is expressed with a boolean ghost function Is_Valid:

```
function Is_Valid return Boolean;
```

Although it would be possible to express the specification of the free list memory allocator based on a ghost function as seen in Sect. 2.2, this would make it very difficult to prove automatically the refinement property. Indeed, the relation between the abstract model and the concrete data would rely on the reachability of resources in a linked list, thus making it necessary to reason by induction, something automatic provers are not good at. Instead, we define a model of the allocator as a ghost variable which will be used in the contracts of `Free` and `Alloc`. The *model* of the allocator data consists in a sequence of resources available and a set of resources allocated.

```
package S1 is new Functional_Sequences (Element_Type => Resource);
package S2 is new Functional_Sets (Element_Type => Resource,
                                    No_Element   => No_Resource);
type T is record
   Available : S1.Sequence;
   Allocated : S2.Set;
end record;
```

Ghost variable `Model` holds a value of this type:

```
Model : T;
```

The validity of the abstract model w.r.t. the concrete data at any given time is expressed by ghost function `Is_Valid`:

```
function Is_Valid return Boolean is
  ((if First_Available /= No_Resource then
      Length (Model.Available) > 0 and then
      Get (Model.Available, 1) = First_Available
    else
      Length (Model.Available) = 0)
    and then
   (for all J in 1 .. Length (Model.Available) =>
      Get (Model.Available, J) in Valid_Resource
        and then
      Data (Get (Model.Available, J)).Next =
        (if J < Length (Model.Available) then
           Get (Model.Available, J + 1) else No_Resource)
        and then
      (for all K in 1 .. J - 1 =>
         Get (Model.Available, J) /= Get (Model.Available, K)))
    and then
   (for all E in Model.Allocated => E in Valid_Resource)
    and then
   (for all R in Valid_Resource =>
      (case Data (R).Stat is
         when Available =>
           Mem (Model.Available, R) and not Mem (Model.Allocated, R),
         when Allocated =>
           not Mem (Model.Available, R) and Mem (Model.Allocated, R))));
```

This somewhat impressive (at least at first sight) function consists in a conjunction of four properties:

1. `First_Available` is the first available resource.
2. Sequence `Available` is an accurate image of the free list.
3. Set `Allocated` only contains valid resources.
4. Sequence `Available` and set `Allocated` define a partition of the range of resources `Valid_Resource`.

Like previously, all the specification code presented so far in this section is gathered in a local package marked ghost as follows:

```
package M with Ghost is
   package S is ...
   type T is ...
   Model : T;
   function Is_Valid ...
end M;
```

With this model, it is straightforward to express the functional contracts of `Alloc` and `Free` as contract cases, using the function `Is_Prepend` from the functional sequence library, which expresses that a `Result` sequence is obtained by prepending an element to an input sequence. The main difference with the contracts of the simple memory allocator is that property `Is_Valid` is required in precondition and in postcondition:

```
procedure Alloc (Res : out Resource) with
  Pre  => Is_Valid,
  Post => Is_Valid,
  Contract_Cases =>

    -- When no resource is available, return the special value No_Resource
    -- with the allocator unmodified.

    (Length (Model.Available) = 0 =>
       Res = No_Resource
         and then
       Model = Model'Old,

    -- Otherwise, return an available resource which becomes allocated

    others =>
       Is_Prepend (Model.Available, Res, Result => Model.Available'Old)
         and then
       Is_Add (Model.Allocated'Old, Res, Result => Model.Allocated));

procedure Free (Res : Resource) with
  Pre  => Is_Valid,
  Post => Is_Valid,
  Contract_Cases =>

    -- When the resource is allocated, make it available

    (Mem (Model.Allocated, Res) =>
       Is_Prepend (Model.Available'Old, Res, Result => Model.Available)
         and then
       Is_Add (Model.Allocated, Res, Result => Model.Allocated'Old),

    -- Otherwise, do nothing

    others =>
       Model = Model'Old);
```

Besides requesting that `Alloc` and `Free` maintain the validity of the configuration, we should also express that the configuration should be valid at startup with an initial condition on the package `List_Allocator` enclosing all the code of the free list memory allocator:

```
package List_Allocator with
  Initial_Condition => All_Available and Is_Valid
is
  ...
```

This initial condition expresses both that all resources should be available at startup and that the initial configuration should be valid.

3.3   Automatic Proof of Refinement

GNATprove can be used to prove automatically that the code of the free list memory allocator presented in Sect. 3.1 is free of run-time errors and implements the specification presented in Sect. 3.2. First, the implementation of `Alloc` and `Free` must be augmented to express how the ghost variable `Model` is modified in relation to modifications on concrete data. This is a difference with the simple memory allocator where this was not needed, as `Model` in that case was a function. In procedure `Alloc`, this consists in adding two ghost assignments (in the case where allocation succeeds) to components of ghost variable `Model` expressing that the sequence of available resources is stripped from its first element, while the set of allocated resources is augmented with that same element:

```
Model.Available := Remove_At (Model.Available, 1);
Model.Allocated := Add (Model.Allocated, Res);
```

In procedure `Free`, this consists in adding two ghost assignments (in the case where deallocation succeeds) to components of ghost variable `Model` expressing that the set of allocated resources is stripped from the element passed in argument to `Free`, while the sequence of available resources is prepended with that same element:

```
Model.Allocated := Remove (Model.Allocated, Res);
Model.Available := Prepend (Model.Available, Res);
```

Package `List_Allocator` contains elaboration code to set the initial value of array `Data`. Similarly, local ghost package M needs to set the initial value of the ghost variable `Model` in its elaboration code. This initial value needs to be expressed in M's initial condition so that it can be used to prove `List_Allocator`'s initial condition presented in Sect. 3.2. The code and contracts are not shown here for lack of space but can be found in a public repository (see reference in conclusion).

Despite the complexity of the `Is_Valid` function relating the abstract model to the concrete data, automatic proof is achieved as easily as for the simple memory allocator at proof level 2 (with an additional switch to prevent use of prover steps limit). Overall, the automatic proof of refinement of the free list memory allocator takes 18 s on a laptop with 2.7 GHz Intel Core i7 and 16 GB RAM (using a single core).

4   Related Work

B Method [2] has been used extensively in the railway industry over the past 20 years to prove that an implementation is a correct refinement of a specification [6]. While interactive proof was originally the main means to achieve proof, automation of proofs has steadily increased until now [3,11], as well as automatic refinement of abstract specifications [7]. The Isabelle Refinement Framework pursues a similar goal of facilitating the proof of a stepwise refinement in Isabelle/HOL from an abstract functional specification to an imperative implementation [16]. Our work aims at the same goal in the context of a programming language, with all the associated benefits in terms of strong typing, expressivity and tool support. Prior experiments in that directions have been performed in the context of the Eiffel programming language [22]. Our work achieves this goal in the context of a mature and industrially supported formal verification environment.

Automatic proof that code implements a specification expressed as a contract (precondition and postcondition) is the subject of active research, based on advances in the underlying proof technology and the intermediate verification languages, as visible from the activity in relevant workshops (in particular the SMT workshop and Boogie workshop) and tool competitions (in particular VerifyThis [14]).

Recent works [13,18] show how an abstract specification about mathematical quantities (real or integers) can be implemented efficiently in code (with floating-point numbers or bitvectors), and the refinement relation be proved automatically in Why3 or SPARK.

Automatic proof of refinement with more complex data has lead to the introduction of many concepts, some of which are used in this paper: ghost code, model code, alias management policies (such as ownership, permissions, separation logic) [9,23]. The difference in our approach is that the user can write contracts and intermediate assertions (like loop invariants which are needed in all these techniques) in the same programming language as the implementation. In particular, all contracts and assertions in SPARK can be executed and debugged, which greatly facilitates formal development. This was very useful during the development of the memory allocator examples presented in this paper, to catch bugs early on, before attempting automatic proof.

A recent work [15] examines which programming language features are useful in proofs of refinement, some of which could be included in future versions of the SPARK programming language.

5   Conclusion

This article presents two techniques to specify abstractly the behavior of a software component in terms of mathematical structures (sequences, sets and maps) and a methodology based on the SPARK tools to prove automatically that an efficient imperative implementation is a correct refinement of the abstract specification. The proposed methodology is illustrated with challenging concrete examples of memory allocators.[6] To the best of our knowledge, this is the first time such refinement proof is done automatically with both the specification and the implementation expressed in the same (executable) programming language.

In this article, we define two different abstract specifications for respectively the simple memory allocator and the free list memory allocator: the simpler specification based on sets is implemented by the simple memory allocator while the more involved specification based on sets and sequences is implemented by the free list memory allocator. One could object that, as both allocators deliver

---

[6] The results presented in this article can be reproduced with SPARK GPL 2016, which will be available in June 2016 at http://libre.adacore.com. The source code of the examples is available in the SPARK public repository at https://forge.open-do.org/anonscm/git/spark2014/spark2014.git, under testsuite/gnatprove/tests/allocators.

the same overall service (ignoring efficiency here), they could be refinements of the same specification. Indeed, it would be interesting to prove that the simple memory allocator is a refinement of the specification given in Sect. 3.2 and to prove that the free list memory allocator is a refinement of the specification given in Sect. 2.2. The latter would not be feasible in SPARK as it would require a notion of package invariant to hide property Is_Valid (although a sibling notion of type invariant will be supported in future versions of SPARK). The former should be already possible in SPARK.

Although we do not present it in this article, this abstraction also allows proving the correct use of the two allocators in client code, which would otherwise require to expose implementation details to the client. Effects of calling (de)allocation procedures on the concrete data and ghost model are visible from client code, and can be either left implicit (for the tool to generate) or explicitly stated. Note that if multiple allocators are needed in a project, the specification and code presented can be shared by making the package *generic*, in which case the automatic proof will be repeated for each instantiation of the generic.

Acknowledgements. We would like to thank Claude Marché, David Mentré, Piotr Trojanek as well as the anonymous reviewers for their useful comments.

References

1. EN 50128:2011 railway applications - communication, signalling and processing systems - software for railway control and protection systems (2011)
2. Abrial, J.-R.: The B-Book: Assigning Programs to Meanings. Cambridge University Press, Cambridge (1996)
3. Abrial, J.-R.: Formal methods in industry: achievements, problems, future. In: Proceedings of the 28th International Conference on Software Engineering, ICSE 2006, pp. 761–768. ACM, New York (2006)
4. Barnes, J.: Ada 2012 Rationale (2012)
5. Barnes, J.: SPARK: The Proven Approach to High Integrity Software. Altran Praxis (2012)
6. Boulanger, J.-L. (ed.): Formal Methods Applied to Industrial Complex Systems: Implementation of the B Method. Wiley, New York (2014)
7. Burdy, L., Meynadier, J.-M.: Automatic refinement. In: FM 1999 Workshop - Applying B in an Industrial Context: Tools, Lessons and Techniques (1999)
8. Chalin, P.: Engineering a sound assertion semantics for the verifying compiler. IEEE Trans. Softw. Eng. **36**(2), 275–287 (2010)
9. Clarke, D., Noble, J., Wrigstad, T. (eds.): Aliasing in Object-Oriented Programming: Types, Analysis, and Verification. Springer, Heidelberg (2013)
10. Comar, C., Kanig, J., Moy, Y.: Integrating formal program verification with testing. In: Proceedings of ERTS (2012)
11. Delahaye, D., Dubois, C., Marché, C., Mentré, D.: The BWare project: building a proof platform for the automated verification of B proof obligations. In: Ait Ameur, Y., Schewe, K.-D. (eds.) ABZ 2014. LNCS, vol. 8477, pp. 290–293. Springer, Heidelberg (2014)
12. Dross, C., Efstathopoulos, P., Lesens, D., Mentré, D., Moy, Y.: Rail, space, security: three case studies for SPARK 2014. In: Proceedings of ERTS (2014)

13. Dross, C., Fumex, C., Gerlach, J., Marché, C.: High-level functional properties of bit-level programs: formal specifications and automated proofs. Research Report 8821, Inria, December 2015
14. Huisman, M., Klebanov, V., Monahan, R. (eds.): Int. J. Softw. Tools Technol. Transf., special issue, VerifyThis 2012, vol. 17 (2015)
15. Koenig, J., Leino, K.R.M.: Programming language features for refinement. Submitted to EPTCS (2015)
16. Lammich, P.: Refinement based verification of imperative data structures. In: Proceedings of the Conference on Certified Programs and Proofs (2016)
17. Ledinot, E., Blanquart, J.-P., Astruc, J.-M., Baufreton, P., Boulanger, J.-L., Comar, C., Delseny, H., Gassino, J., Leeman, M., Quéré, P., Ricque, B.: Joint use of static and dynamic software verification techniques: a cross-domain view in safety critical system industries. In: Proceedings of the 7th European Congress on Embedded Real Time Software and Systems (ERTS^2 2014), Toulouse, France, 5–7 February, 2014
18. Marché, C.: Verification of the functional behavior of a floating-point program: an industrial case study. Sci. Comput. Program. **96**(3), 279–296 (2014)
19. McCormick, J.W., Chapin, P.C.: Building High Integrity Applications with SPARK. Cambridge University Press, Cambridge (2015)
20. Meyer, B.: Object-Oriented Software Construction, 1st edn. Prentice-Hall Inc., Upper Saddle River (1988)
21. O'Neill, I.: SPARK - a language and tool-set for high-integrity software development. In: Industrial Use of Formal Methods: Formal Verification. Wiley (2012)
22. Ostroff, J., wei Wang, C., Kerfoot, E., Torshizi, F.A.: ES-verify: a tool for automated model-based verification of object-oriented code. In: Formal Methods 2006. Poster (2006)
23. Tafat, A., Boulmé, S., Marché, C.: A refinement methodology for object-oriented programs. In: Beckert, B., Marché, C. (eds.) FoVeOOS 2010. LNCS, vol. 6528, pp. 153–167. Springer, Heidelberg (2011)

S3: Proving the Safety of Critical Systems

Nicolas Breton[(✉)] and Yoann Fonteneau

Systerel, Aix-en-Provence, France
{nbr,yfn}@systerel.fr
http://www.systerel.fr

Abstract. Systerel Smart Solver (S3) is a formal verification toolset built around a synchronous modeling language (HLL), and a SAT-based symbolic Model Checker developed by Systerel. It allows building efficient formal verification solutions specially fitted for a given mission in a given development process, with a built-in focus on trustworthiness. The architecture of such a solution is described, and its application to the proof of high-level properties unambiguously implying the safety of large industrial railway control systems is reported.

1 Introduction

The ever-rising use of software-based systems to fulfill safety-critical missions calls for methods to ensure the adequacy of these systems to their missions. Most industrial sectors have brought an answer in the form of standards such as EN-50128 for railways, DO-178C for aviation, ISO-26262 for automotive, or more generally IEC-61508 for critical systems. All these standards have in common the central role given to test-based validation techniques. However, alternate and usually complementary techniques, grouped under the banner of "Formal Methods", are gaining increasing attention for the development and validation of these systems. In particular, the "Model Checking" [1] technique has seen the multiplication of its application fields in the last decade. This renewed interest for a technique dating back to the 80 s has three major explanations:

- The emergence of efficient symbolic state space exploration techniques, particularly those based on solving the Boolean Satisfiability (SAT), and more recently the Satisfiability Modulo Theory (SMT) problems. The adoption of these techniques leads to a continuous increase in the power of model checking engines, enabling to tackle problems of increasing size and complexity.
- The largely automatic and *a posteriori* nature of the analyses, enabling a lightweight integration in existing development processes, and its relative ease of use.
- The multiplicity of missions than can be performed using these techniques: proof of safety properties, equivalence proof between various artifacts of a system, bug chasing, undefined code behaviors detection (division by zero,

---

Many thanks to the anonymous reviewers and to our colleagues Joël Allred and Laurent Voisin for their invaluable help in correcting and clarifying this article.

T. Lecomte et al. (Eds.): RSSRail 2016, LNCS 9707, pp. 231–242, 2016.
DOI: 10.1007/978-3-319-33951-1_17

overflow, use of uninitialized variable, out of bond array access, *etc.*), dead code detection, automatic test case generation, but also the resolution of routing, optimization, or planning problems.

To address its customers needs, Systerel has developed a formal verification solution, Systerel Smart Solver (S3), able to perform an *a posteriori* verification of the safety of critical systems. This solution, combining a specialized modeling language (HLL) with a SAT-based symbolic model checker, has shown to be particularly efficient in handling industrial-size critical systems coming from various domains such as railways or avionics. This article begins (Sect. 2) with an overly simplified introduction to formal verification concepts. Section 3 presents the generic S3 formal safety verification solution and the techniques used to make it trustworthy. Finally, Sect. 4 reports on its application to prove the safety of large industrial railway control systems, using a set of high-level properties unambiguously implying this safety.

2   Brief Introduction to Formal Verification

This section briefly presents some specific concepts of formal verification. To limit its size, the adopted point of view has been intentionally twisted toward that of SAT-based symbolic model checking, at the expense of generality.

Formal Verification: the act of mathematically proving that a system respects some properties under a number of hypotheses. When a property is proved to hold, it means that it is *impossible* to find an input scenario satisfying the hypotheses, in which the system would falsify this property (*exhaustivity*).

Safety Specification: this *formalized* specification contains both the set of safety properties that the system shall respect, and a set of hypotheses made on the environment, in a form suitable for mathematical reasoning.

Model Checking: a popular approach to formal verification, in which a model of the system, created manually or by an automatic translation of a design or software, is used to verify that some given properties hold. S3 falls into the category of SAT-based symbolic model checkers for a restriction of LTL to properties stating that some condition *always* holds, for every possible execution of the system model. These *system traces* are explored by translating the model to a number of combinational boolean problems, and using specialized algorithms to solve the problem of determining their *satisfiability* or *unsatisfiability* (*i.e.* the SAT problem). The S3 model-checker contains its own state of the art SAT-solver, but can also be used with other external SAT solvers.

Bounded Model Checking (BMC): a strategy searching for potential falsifications of the safety properties on traces of increasing length [2]. The outcome of this exploration is either an input scenario leading to the violation of the safety property (a *counter-example*), or the insurance that there exists no violating trace of length less than a given constant. With its ability to exhibit problematic scenarios, the BMC strategy is mainly used for debugging the system and the safety specification, or generating test-cases.

Unbounded Model Checking: a strategy able to prove that a safety property holds for any infinite trace. Several methods exist, but the most straightforward is *induction over time*. This is a two-phase procedure: in the *base*, the model checker verifies that the property holds initially, and in the *step*, it verifies that, for every state of the system in which the property holds, the property also holds in all of its successor states reachable in one transition of the system. If both the base and the step hold, it can be concluded, applying the induction principle, that the property always holds. Unfortunately, induction alone is sometimes insufficient for proving a property: it is not a complete proof method. Several solutions exist to overcome this problem, mainly exhibiting *induction strengthening lemmas* of some sort, either manually of automatically. Once proved by the model checker, these additional properties can be used to help prove the safety properties.

3   Systerel Smart Solver Workflow

3.1   Modeling Language

When designing a formal verification solution targeted at industrial users, it is important to offer a simple and clear language to express safety specifications. However, it is also important to have a rich and expressive language simplifying the task of developing specialized translators from system designs or code coming from various domains. The High Level Language (HLL) was created to answer both of these needs and keeps evolving to address new challenging problems.

HLL is a data-flow, synchronous, declarative language with formally defined syntax and semantics. It manipulates *stream* objects which are typed variables valued over an infinite sequence representing discrete time. It is similar to Lustre or Scade® but with a slightly richer type system (standard scalar and structured types, functions, predicates, hierarchical enumerations, *etc.*), a broad set of operators on these types (including the basic `next` and `previous` temporal operators), and specific constructs targeted at expressing generic safety specifications (quantifications over finite sets, constraints, proof obligations, *etc.*).

3.2   Typical Development Workflows

Even though this article focuses on software-based safety-critical systems, and specifically on the functional code of these systems, S3 solutions may also be applied to other kinds of systems, implemented using electro-mechanical devices such as relays, or IEC-61131 logic to be run on a PLC, or even implemented as a specific FPGA. This section describes idealized development processes of such systems, not meant to be representative, with only the level of detail needed to describe the interactions between the S3 tools and these processes.

Every process starts with some kind of informal specification, requirement, or even design document, most commonly in natural language. The development team creates a design of the system in a formally defined language. From this *formal design*, the code of the system is obtained either by a manual development, or by automatic code generation. Alternatively, the code can be directly developed from the informal specification. Sometimes diversified versions of the code are produced for safety, availability, and/or certification purposes.

The first alternative will be used in the following sections to illustrate the use of the S3 workflow. The usages for the other workflows are mere adaptations.

3.3   Safety Specification

In a typical S3 solution, the safety specification is expressed in HLL, bringing simplicity, clarity, and overall readability in the formalization of both the safety properties, expressed as *proof obligations*, and the environment hypotheses expressed as *constraints*. Additional *insulation* definitions can also be used to protect the safety specification against naming conventions changes in the system model, and *helper* definitions to define intermediate domain-specific "concepts".

Different "levels" of safety specifications exist. At the lowest level, loosely related to safety, the specification can be automatically generated based on the code structure and semantics. Such a specification allows to perform analyses ensuring the absence of undefined behaviors in the code or detecting dead code. At an intermediate level, the safety specification can be derived from the functional specification to show conformance of the code. However, such a safety specification does not give any insight on the correctness of the functional specification, nor on its ability to ensure the overall safety or mission of the system.

When applicable, better results are usually achieved by taking a safety-related point of view. A hazard analysis enables to identify the *safety hazards* leading to an accident. Refining these safety hazards enables to develop a set of safety properties which, when achieved by the system, ensures its safety. Being obtained using a method different from that used to develop the system, such properties are able to detect problems in the code, but also potential safety flaws in the specification. Once the code has been proved to respect such a safety specification, it may be used as a convincing argument in the demonstration of the overall safety of the system.

Depending on the level of refinement of the safety hazards, several levels of safety properties may be expressed. As a general rule, the closer to the safety hazards, the easier the modeling of the safety properties, and the more convincing that they imply the overall safety of the system. However, using high-level properties also complexifies the environment model, and makes these safety properties harder to prove.

Finally, for systems developed in a normative environment, or for which trustworthiness of the safety verification is required, the assessment of the *correctness* and *completeness* of the safety specification is usually achieved by reviews performed by an independent team. In this sense, having a clear and readable safety specification, unambiguously implying the safety of the system at the highest possible level, is clearly a plus. A drawback lies in the complexity of the environment model whose constraints have to be thoroughly checked for correctness. In particular, it shall be verified that this modeling does not over-constrain the input scenarios (*i.e.* the constraints are fulfilled by the real environment).

3.4 Uncertified S3 Workflow

When designing an S3 safety verification workflow, the first task is to build the part of the workflow needed to perform the analyses, without considering trustworthiness or certification. This workflow will be used to develop, debug, and mature both the generic safety specification and the system design. A typical uncertified S3 workflow synoptic is given in Fig. 1.

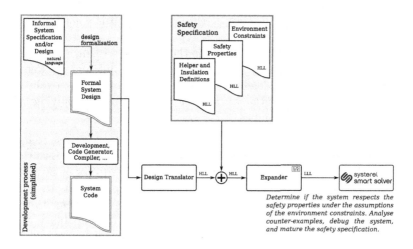

Fig. 1. Uncertified S3 workflow synoptic

Using a specialized translator from the design formal language to HLL, the solution creates a *formal model* of the system design preserving its execution semantic. This model is concatenated to the safety specification, giving an HLL file ready for analysis.

The S3 model checker does not work directly at the HLL level, and a further model transformation is needed: a translation, called *expansion*, from HLL to the Low Level Language (LLL), a restricted subset of the HLL language containing only boolean streams and a very limited number of core boolean operators (negation, implication, and equivalence), similar in essence to the AIGER format (see *http://fmv.jku.at/aiger*). An *expander* is used to inline HLL blocks, flatten structured types, expand quantifiers, bit-blast arithmetic, until the HLL model is transformed into a semantically equivalent LLL model.

This LLL model can then be handed over to S3 for analysis. When S3 reports that a property has been proved (using induction), nothing remains to be done.

However, when it reports a falsification it also generates a counter-example on the LLL model. After being translated back from the LLL world to the HLL one, counter-examples can be translated to scenarios to be run inside a simulator of the system. Another alternative is to use the why tool which loads a counter-example and guides the user from the violated safety property down to the root of the problem, displaying the values of the traversed HLL expressions, using powerful heuristics to choose what part of an expression shall be followed.

3.5   Certifiable S3 Workflow

The uncertified solution described in the previous section is used iteratively to correct the potential bugs in the safety specification and in the system, until all safety properties are proved. At this point, the problem of the confidence that can be granted to the formal safety verification solution shall be addressed. In particular, this is mandated by most certification standards when using such a solution in a verification process.

Starting from the uncertified workflow in the previous section, a hazard analysis is performed to build the comprehensive list of the different weaknesses in which a bug of a tool might lead to the erroneous proof of a non-valid safety property. Each of these potential weaknesses is addressed by applying specific and adapted protection techniques.

Protecting the Analyses: the first identified weakness is of course that of the model checker incorrectly reporting some property to be proved. Ensuring the correctness of a complete model checker using a standard mix of peer-reviews and tests is a very difficult task. A more pragmatic approach is to use an *a posteriori* technique called *proof logging/proof checking* for **every** run of the model checker. In this technique, S3 is enhanced with the capability, when it finds the proof of a property, to log this proof in a file which, starting from a reformulation of the analyzed LLL file, derives the proof as a deduction tree in a formally specified resolution-based proof system. After the S3 run, a specialized tool, the *proof-checker* checks that the reformulation corresponds to the LLL file given to S3, that the proofs are made of correct deductions, and that all properties have been proved. In SAT-based model checking, finding a proof is a complex task relying on error-prone algorithms, optimizations, and heuristics. However, checking a proof is fairly simple and can be done with a high degree of confidence.

Protecting the Translation Workflow: the next identified weakness is in the translation of the system design. An error in this translation could easily lead to an erroneous proof because the properties are analyzed on an incorrect model. Figure 2 gives a synoptic view of the protections used against this weakness.

The translation is protected using *diversification*. The translation is done twice, by diversified tools, developed by independent teams, using different programming languages and paradigms. When possible, and to increase confidence, the sources are also diversified by considering, on the one hand the translation of the system design, and on the other the translation of the system code.

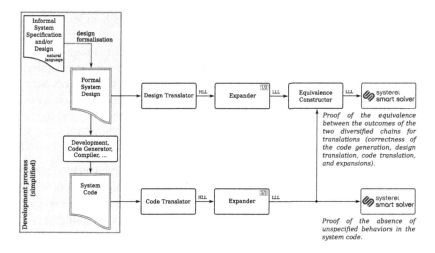

Fig. 2. Protecting the translation workflow

The obtained HLL models are then both expanded to LLL. The expansion is a complex model transformation in which an error could also lead to an incorrect model (*i.e.* when the semantic is not preserved between the HLL and the LLL models), and thus to an erroneous proof. To protect this transformation, the expansion is also diversified using two independent expanders. For each model transformation, a precise *logical foundation document*, describing the syntax and semantics of the involved languages together with the transformation principles, is used to specify this transformation, prove its *correctness* and *soundness*, and develop test-suites. This document is extensively reviewed by independent experts.

A second technique, called *sequential equivalence checking*, is used to compare the resulting LLL models. A tool, the *equivalence-constructor* takes the pair of LLL models and creates a third one, that encodes the fact that the two models, fed with the same input sequences, produce the same outputs. The resulting equivalence model is given to the S3 model checker to prove, using induction, that the equivalence holds. To make the equivalence system inductive, and simplify the model checker task, it is mandatory to provide a list of "suggested" intermediate equivalent points that will be proved and used to help proving the overall equivalence. When the equivalence holds, confidence is gained that the various model transformations (*i.e.* translations and expansions) have been correctly performed. There is indeed very little chance that a bug in one translator or expander is "matched" by another bug in the other tool chain.

Finally, sometimes an analysis of the produced LLL model of the code is also necessary to ensure some aspects of the correctness of the code modeling and translation. Some languages do not have a fully defined semantic and the modeling adds automatic proof obligations to the resulting model to verify that none of these undefined behaviors are triggered by the code. The modeling is thus considered correct, with respect to these undefined behaviors, *if and only if* these proof obligations hold.

Incidentally, the proof that the code is equivalent to the design is an interesting result in itself. First, it shows that the code generator, or compiler, has produced a correct code and thus enables to remove the verification activities usually performed to assess this correctness. This is not to be taken as a general correctness result of the code generator, but rather that, on this particular system, the code generation has been correct. Secondly, it shows that the safety properties that have been shown to hold on the design also hold on the code.

Protecting the Safety Verification Workflow: the last identified weakness is in the expansion of the overall system composed of the safety specification and the system model. The expansion of this element corresponds to the connection of the two parts, and the model transformation to LLL. Once again, an error in this transformation can lead to an incorrect model and thus an incorrect proof. As previously, this transformation is protected by expanding the system twice with independent expanders, and proving that the obtained pair of LLL models are equivalent. Finally one of the models is analyzed to prove that the safety specification holds on the system design.

Overall Solution: the various tools of the S3 toolset have been developed using a process involving a complete set of specification, design, and validation documentation, together with the necessary quality and verification activities. This process, associated to the described protection mechanisms enables an S3 formal verification solution to be used as a "verification tool". For example, it has already been successfully used as an EN-50128:2011 T2-class tool.

The expanders, equivalence-constructor, and the S3 model checker are generic tools proven in use on industrial-size systems. Generic translators also exist for Scade®, C, and Ada. These translators produce a bit-precise, exact HLL model of the system. For other languages, custom translators are developed.

4   Application to Interlocking Systems

An *interlocking* is a system commanding and controlling the signals and switches of a railway track layout, ensuring safe train operations. The S3 model checking solutions have been shown to be particularly efficient in proving the safety of Computer Based Interlocking (CBI) systems.

4.1   Interlocking Development Workflows

The vital code of CBIs is typically obtained through a process known as *instantiation*. In such a process, the *signaling principles* are captured by the engineers to produce the *generic design* in some suitable language. This design contains a set of generic code snippets that an interlocking system shall execute for each object of a given category, such as signals, switches, routes, *etc.* Each of these generic snippets is given in a parametrized form allowing to specialize it for the object to which it applies. For example, the generic code for a route will most probably be parametrized with the list of switches contained in the route. The generic design is thus specific to a set of signaling principles, but independent of a particular track layout.

To instantiate the interlocking system for a particular track layout, the geographical data representing this particular station topology is first processed by a *data-preparation tool* and gathered in some sort of database. This database contains the population of objects of the given station (*e.g.* signals, routes, switches, *etc.*) and the relations between these elements (*e.g.* starting signal of a route, switches contained in a route, *etc.*). An *instantiation tool* is then used to create "copies" of the elements of the generic design, called *instances*, for each object of the given station. Each instance is specialized by receiving the specific parameters values for the object to which it applies. The instantiated system is not necessarily produced as "code" in the common sense (a software in some known programming language), it can take many forms: boolean equations, ladder diagrams, automatons, or even mere data-tables. Such an instantiated system can then be interpreted by a generic software engine, or used as a design to generate the actual code.

In any case, when building an S3 solution to verify the safety of such a system, a translator (or a pair of diversified translators, see Sect. 3.5) is developed that will create a (usually) bit-precise HLL model of this instantiated system, preserving its execution semantic.

4.2   Generic Safety Specification

As an introductory remark, it is important to understand that, as the system is instantiated for a given station track layout, the formal safety verification performed on this system will only address the safety on **this** particular track layout. It is **not** a generic proof that the design is safe for **every** station track layout. In particular, the proof will have to be conducted each time a system is instantiated with a new track layout.

Having to prove every instance is however not a problem because for generic systems instantiated by data, such as an interlocking instantiated for a specific station track layout, the safety specification is also generic, and can be instantiated using the same data. Developing the *generic safety specification* is thus done only once, and proving that an instance on a specific station track layout verifies the generic safety specification instantiated on this same track layout is completely automated in the S3 solution.

Genericity is supported by three central elements of the HLL language: *sorts*, a set of types representing a hierarchical enumerated population, used to represent objects; *predicates* on sorts, used to represent relations between these objects; *quantifications* (universal and existential) used to "apply" an expression on every object instance of the sort over which it ranges. Sorts and predicates are first *declared* and used to express generically the safety properties and environment constraints. Later, when analyzing a specific track layout, the sorts are populated with the actual object instances on the track, and the predicates initialized with the corresponding relations. The generic safety specification applied to this description of the track layout becomes instantiated for this specific layout, and can thus be checked on the specific CBI vital code. As an example, an overly simple generic property (rather a lemma in fact), stating that two incompatible signals shall not be simultaneously opened could be written as:

```
ALL s1:SIGNAL,s2:SIGNAL (incompatible(s1,s2) -> ~(open(s1) & open(s2)))
```

where, for a specific track layout, the sort `SIGNAL` is populated with all the signals, the `incompatible` helper predicate is initialized, or defined using other lower-level predicates, and the `open` *integration* predicate is linked to the signals command outputs in the model of the code (`~` is the negation and `->` the implication operators).

As explained in Sect. 3.3, several levels of generic safety specification exist, and Systerel advocates the use of the highest possible level to unambiguously imply the overall safety of the system. This leads to the definition of three main safety properties (additional properties are also needed to ensure safety in the connection with other systems, but they are usually far simpler):

1. *Absence of Collision*: given two trains positioned on the track layout, no zone of the track is simultaneously reachable by both trains.
2. *Absence of Derailment*: given a train positioned on the track layout, no badly positioned switch is reachable by this train.
3. *Absence of Over-speed*: given a train positioned on the track layout that has been granted full-speed, no reduced-speed zone is reachable by this train.

A model of the environment is also needed to describe how a train can move, when it can cross a signal, when a switch can move, *etc.* This is done incrementally by analyzing the counter-examples, under the control of the safety engineers.

4.3   Analyzing Interlocking Systems

The S3 solution has been applied to an interlocking system obtained from a major railway company (undisclosed for confidentiality reasons). The specific application has been developed using the signaling principles used in an ongoing metro project instantiated on a test station designed to be representative of all the possible topological specificities to be found in the stations of the given line. This station is large from a metro standpoint, with 249 routes, 520 track segments, 69 switches, and 199 signals of all sorts. The instantiated code is given in an in-house format representing boolean equations and timers executed sequentially to compute the output actuators from the values of the input sensors. The code for this particular station contains 10 801 boolean equations, and 712 timers.

A custom translator was developed. Taking as inputs an application code containing the boolean equations and an XML file containing the description of the track layout, it outputs an HLL model of the code together with the representation of the track layout encoded as sort populations and predicates. An abstraction of the code timers have been applied stating that a timer can elapse at any time provided that it has been armed. The precise timer values are discarded, and the safety is thus proved under the hypotheses that these timers have been correctly dimensioned. Otherwise, the model is bit-precise. The concatenation of these models with a generic safety specification containing the safety properties described in the previous section is then given to S3 for analysis.

Four iterations were necessary to correct bugs in the application (it was handed over to S3 prior to validation), to express generic induction strengthening lemmas, and to adjust the environment model before reaching the proof of the safety of the CBI, totaling around four man·months of work including the development of the specific S3 solution. As all the generic parts have already been developed, subsequent runs on specific stations shall be largely automatic.

On this system, the analysis time on an Intel Core i5-4670 CPU is around 1 min for proving all the safety properties using induction, and around 2 h when searching for safety violations using a BMC up to 10 execution cycles of the system's logic. Both of these runs consumed less than a gigabyte of memory.

S3 has also been applied on two other families of interlockings of similar sizes, developed using different flavors of automaton-based languages with similar performances.

5   Related Work, Conclusions and Perspectives

Railway safety critical systems have always been a fruitful application field for formal methods. In recent years, the use of SAT or SMT based model checking to verify the safety of interlocking systems has drawn interest from a number of research teams and major signaling companies. The S3 approach to formal verification of interlocking systems is similar to the approaches described in [3–5]. A key point in these approaches is, starting from the design or the code of an interlocking system, to construct a "good" model of the system, its environment, and the safety specification. This is not only a matter of this model being sound, or easily capturing the generic safety specification in a clear formalism, but also of being well *conditioned* for the underlying model checker. In particular, it is important to ensure that the modeling doesn't introduce unnecessary additional complexity beyond that of the system itself. In this perspective, the use of a specific language to express this model together with a toolset controlling every translation-steps down to an in-house model checker powered with its own state of the art SAT-solver, is clearly a plus. Domain-specific knowledge in both railway critical systems and formal methods is also an important ingredient for building a successful formal verification solution.

S3 is the result of a successful technology transfer from state of the art research to an efficient industrially supported toolset. It is not to be seen as an off-the-shelf integrated solution, but rather as a collection of generic tools together with protection methodologies to ensure trustworthiness and certifiability. This toolset enables the engineering of custom and efficient formal safety verification solutions targeted at specific missions and system development processes. These solutions aim at automating the safety verification process and eliminating as much as possible the repetitive, time-consuming, expensive, incomplete, and error-prone human verification activities usually devoted to this task.

S3 solutions are routinely used to prove the safety of large industrial interlocking systems. Applying this technology to other safety-critical systems in the railway industry, or in other domains like avionics, is an ongoing challenge. Encouraging preliminary results have been obtained both on the support of floating-point arithmetic and in the handling of asynchrony and latencies when several interconnected systems are considered (*e.g.* multiple IXL, CBTC, *etc.*).

References

1. Clarke, E., Sistla, A.P.: Automatic verification of finite-state concurrent systems using temporal logic specifications. TOPLAS **8**, 244–263 (1986)
2. Biere, A., Cimatti, A., Clarke, E.M., Strichman, O., Zhu, Y.: Bounded model checking. Adv. Comput. **58**, 117–148 (2003)
3. Vu, L.H., Haxthausen, A.E., Peleska, J.: Formal modeling and verification of interlocking systems featuring sequential release. In: Artho, C., Ölveczky, P.C. (eds.) FTSCS 2014. CCIS, vol. 476, pp. 223–238. Springer, Heidelberg (2015)
4. Bonacchi, A., Fantechi, A.: On the validation of an interlocking system by model-checking. In: Flammini, F., Lang, F. (eds.) FMICS 2014. LNCS, vol. 8718, pp. 94–108. Springer, Heidelberg (2014)
5. James, P., Lawrence, A., Moller, F., Roggenbach, M., Seisenberger, M., Setzer, A., Kanso, K., Chadwick, S.: Verification of solid state interlocking programs. In: Counsell, S., Núñez, M. (eds.) SEFM 2013. LNCS, vol. 8368, pp. 253–268. Springer, Heidelberg (2014)

Increasing Proofs Automation Rate
of **Atelier-B** Thanks to **Alt-Ergo**

Sylvain Conchon[1,2] and Mohamed Iguernlala[1,3(✉)]

[1] LRI, Université Paris-Sud, 91405 Orsay, France
mohamed.iguernlala@ocamlpro.com
[2] Toccata, INRIA Saclay Ile-de-France, 91893 Orsay, France
[3] OCamlPro SAS, 91190 Gif-sur-Yvette, France

Abstract. In this paper, we report on our recent improvements in the
Alt-Ergo SMT solver to make it effective in discharging proof obligations (POs) translated from the Atelier-B framework. In particular, we
made important modifications in its internal data structures to boost
performances of its core decision procedures, we improved quantifiers
instantiation heuristics, and enhanced the interaction between the SAT
solver and the decision procedures. We also introduced a new plugin
architecture to facilitate experiments with different SAT engines, and
implemented a profiling plugin to track and identify "bottlenecks" when
a formula requires a long time to be discharged, or makes the solver *timeout*. Experiments made with more than 10,000 POs generated from real
industrial B projects show significant improvements compared to both
previous versions of Alt-Ergo and Atelier-B's automatic main prover.

Keywords: SMT solvers · B proof obligations · B method

1 Introduction

The use of formal techniques to assess that software components conform to given
requirements is gaining an increasing interest in the industrial world during the
last decades. Indeed, when software are deployed in critical safety domains such
as aeronautics, medical fields, and transportation, a high level of confidence is
required because a bug may cause very costly damage.

Among formal frameworks, Atelier-B [4] is an industrial software development tool that implements the B method, a method based on abstract machines
and refinement techniques. Roughly speaking, a developer starts a B project
by designing an initial and most abstract version of a program, called abstract
machine, that includes the formal specifications of the design's goal. Then, at
each refinement step, the machine is turned into a more concrete one by adding
more details about data structures or algorithms. At the end, a C/C++ or Ada
code is produced. Each refinement step generates a set of mathematical formulas,
called proof obligations (POs), that includes all the properties of the abstract
machine and of the refinement process. These POs have to be proven coherent.

© Springer International Publishing Switzerland 2016
T. Lecomte et al. (Eds.): RSSRail 2016, LNCS 9707, pp. 243–253, 2016.
DOI: 10.1007/978-3-319-33951-1_18

An industrial B project usually generates thousands of POs. Each PO is itself a big first-order formula that requires complex reasoning, such as Set theory and arithmetic, to be proved. In practice, proving manually the POs is a long and boring exercise. Therefore, the success and financial profitability of a B project strongly rests on the ability of proving resulting POs *automatically*.

Since its earlier versions, Atelier-B integrates a home-made automatic prover, which is mainly dedicated to B's Set theory [1] with some limited support for linear arithmetic. When a PO is not proved automatically, the user can either try to guide the proof interactively, or add some proof rules to the context of the solver, and prove the soundness of these rules later on. Consequently, to reduce the price of B software, a solution would be to increase proofs automation rate and to lower the number (cost) of manual proofs.

In order to increase proof automation, several research projects have started the integration of SMT (Satisfiability Modulo Theories) solvers. SMT solvers are recent and efficient automatic theorem provers built on top of a satisfiability (SAT) solver and a combination of decision algorithms for first-order theories of interest such as the free theory of equality and linear arithmetic over integers and rationals. In some application domains, these tools are extended with instantiation techniques to handle universally quantified formulas.

In recent years, we worked on the improvement of our SMT solver, called Alt-Ergo [3], in the context of the BWare ANR project [10]. BWare aims, among other things, at integrating SMT solvers as back-ends of Atelier-B. This relies on the Why3 [8] platform. Its main idea consists in translating Atelier-B proof obligations into Why3's logical language, combining them with a model of the B Set theory (also written in Why3's logical language) and feeding the result of the combination into different external solvers, among of which Alt-Ergo.

This paper presents our recent developments in Alt-Ergo that significantly improved its effectiveness in discharging POs coming from Atelier-B. Our enhancements include (1) new efficient data structures that boost performances of Alt-Ergo's core, (2) better heuristics for instantiating polymorphic quantified formulas coming from B model, and (3) a better interaction between the SAT solver and the decision procedures components. We also introduced a new plugin architecture to facilitate experiments with different SAT engines and provided a new experimental CDCL-based SAT solver. In addition, to be able to track and identify "bottlenecks" in our prover, we implemented a profiling plugin that allows us to observe the behavior of internal components of Alt-Ergo when a formula requires a long time to be discharged, or makes the solver *timeouts*.

We evaluated our improvements on a benchmark of more than 10,000 POs generated from four industrial B projects. The results are very promising and show a significant progression of current versions of Alt-Ergo compared to both previous releases of our solver and to Atelier-B's automatic main prover.

In Sect. 2, we present Alt-Ergo and its applications. Section 3 explains how B POs are enriched with a Set theory model and translated into Alt-Ergo. Section 4 details our benchmarks' characteristics and compares them with our existing test-suite. Section 5 describes some of our developments to improve Alt-Ergo for B POs, and Sect. 6 presents an experimental evaluation of these improvements. In Sect. 7, we conclude and discuss related and future works.

2 The **Alt-Ergo** SMT Solver

Alt-Ergo is an automatic solver of mathematical formulas designed for program verification. It is based on Satisfiability Modulo Theories (SMT). Solvers of this family have made impressive advances and became very popular during the last decade. They are now used in various domains such as hardware design, software verification and formal testing.

Alt-Ergo is used as a back-end of different tools and in various settings, in particular via the Why3 platform. For instance, the Frama-C suite relies on it to prove POs generated from C code, and the SPARK toolset uses it to check POs produced from Ada programs. Alt-Ergo is also used to prove POs issued from cryptography protocols verification and from the Cubicle model-checker. Recently, we started to use it to discharge POs coming from Atelier-B.

The simplified architecture of Alt-Ergo is shown in Fig. 2. The SAT solver interacts with the decision procedures to look for a model for the ground part of the input formula. If a fix-point is reached and unsatisfiability is not deduced, it asks the "Axioms Instances" part for some ground consequences of quantified formulas (axioms). Generated instances are added to the SAT's context and the interaction with the "Decision Procedures" part continues. The latter component provides a combination of decision algorithms for a collection of built-in theories including the free theory of equality with uninterpreted symbols, linear arithmetic over integers and rationals, fragments of non-linear arithmetic, and enumerated and records datatypes.

Alt-Ergo's native input language is a polymorphic first-order logic à *la ML* modulo theories, a very suitable language for expressing formulas generated in the context of program verification. For instance, the toy example shown in Fig. 1 declares an abstract polymorphic type 'a set, some function and constant symbols (add, mem, a, b and s), one axiom (mem_add) that specifies the meaning of membership over add, and a formula to be discharged (a goal) that involves arithmetic and uninterpreted function symbols.

```
type 'a set
logic add: 'a , 'a set → 'a set
logic mem: 'a , 'a set → prop

axiom mem_add:
  ∀ x,y: 'a. ∀ s: 'a set.
  mem(x,add(y,s)) ↔
  (x = y or mem(x,s))

logic a, b: int
logic s: int set

goal g: a = b+1 → mem(a-1,add(b,s))
```

Fig. 1. An example in Alt-Ergo's syntax   **Fig. 2.** Alt-Ergo's simplified architecture

3   From B Proof Obligations to **Alt-Ergo**

One of the objectives of BWare is to connect additional automatic provers to Atelier-B to increase its proofs automation rate and to lower the cost of manual proofs. This goal is achieved via the translation scheme given in Fig. 3:

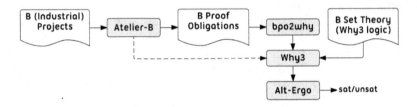

Fig. 3. Translating B proof obligations to Alt-Ergo's native input language

1. First, the POs produced by Atelier-B are translated into Why3's logic using bpo2why [9]. The latter tool has been extended during the project to cover a larger part of B constructs. A small PO and its corresponding Why3 translation are given in [9] (Figs. 2 and 4 respectively).
2. Datatypes and function symbols declarations, as well as the axioms of the B Set theory, do not appear in the original POs because they are built-in for Atelier-B's main prover. To make them explicit for Why3, a prelude that contains these information is written and appended to every translated PO. An overview of the content of this file is given in [9] (Fig. 7).
3. At this point, Why3 can be used to produce POs for a wide range of solvers in different formats (TPTP, SMT2, Alt-Ergo's native input language, ...).

Note that, a new proof obligations generator that is able to directly output POs in Why3's logic has been developed in Atelier-B during the project.

4   Benchmarks Characteristics

Quite at the beginning of the BWare project, we had a test-suite[1] of 12,831 POs obtained from four industrial B projects. The POs were previously discharged automatically or interactively in Atelier-B. They were translated to Why3 using bpo2why. Two benchmarks (called RCS3 and DAB) were provided by *Mitsubishi Electric R&D Centre Europe*. They are generated from B implementations of an automated teller machine and a software that controls a railway level crossing system, respectively. Two additional benchmarks (called p4 and p9) were provided by *ClearSy*, and were obfuscated.

Every PO is composed of three parts: the first one is a large set of declarations and axioms (universally quantified formulas). It results from the translation of

---

[1] A first release is available here: http://bware.lri.fr/index.php/Benchmarks.

the B Set theory prelude to Alt-Ergo's syntax. The second part is made of huge (in size) predicate definitions describing parts of the B state machines. It is part of the original B formula. The last part is the "goal" we would like to prove. It is a ground formula involving the predicates of the second part. The concatenation of the two first parts will be called "the context" of the PO.

A quick inspection of the POs shows that they are made of equalities over uninterpreted function symbols and atoms involving enumerated data types. A small portion of atoms contains arithmetic and records. Compared to our older benchmarks, the average number of axioms, as well as the size of the POs are much larger in this new test-suite, as summarized below:

	VSTTE	Why3	Hi-Lite	RCS3	DAB	p4	p9
Number of POs	125	4490	15993	2259	860	9342	371
avg. # of axioms	32	57	115	395	303	304	332
avg. size (KB)	8	12	36	907	252	258	420

At the beginning of the project, we ran state-of-the-art SMT solvers that can handle the POs of our test-suite. Those solvers have been running without any particular options or configurations. We used a 64-bit machine with a quad-core Intel Xeon processor at 3.2 GHz and 24 GB of memory. Time (*resp.* memory) limit was set to 60 s (*resp.* 2 GB) per PO. The results are shown in the table below, as well as the automation success rate of Atelier-B's main prover (denoted B-PR) for these projects. Note that, for the sake of equity, B proof obligations were first split to obtain one goal per file, before they were given to main prover.

prover	version	RCS3	DAB	p4	p9
Alt-Ergo	0.95.2	2226 (98.7 %)	822 (95.6 %)	8402 (89.9 %)	213 (57.4 %)
Z3	4.3.1	2191 (97.1 %)	716 (83.3 %)	7974 (85.4 %)	162 (43.7 %)
CVC3	2.4.1	2203 (97.6 %)	684 (79.5 %)	7981 (85.4 %)	108 (29.1 %)
B-PR	4.2	(90.1 %)	(95.7 %)	(83.0 %)	(96.2 %)

The evaluation shows that it is not immediate to obtain a substantial gain of performances by using SMT solvers to discharge B proof obligations. Without a specific tuning for B, SMT solvers compete equally with Atelier-B's prover on the test-suite. We describe in the next section the main improvements we made in Alt-Ergo to increase its success rate on these benchmarks.

5   Tuning Alt-Ergo for B Proof Obligations

We now provide a non-exhaustive list of modifications we made in Alt-Ergo to augment its proofs success rate on BWare POs. But, we will start by describing our profiling plugin that allowed us to quickly localize sources of inefficiency.

5.1   Spying the Solver

During our investigations to improve Alt-Ergo, we had to instrument several parts of its code to print some information and understand what is happening inside it. We ended by writing a profiling plugin that records relevant data and prints them in an appropriate way, with a negligible overhead when it is deactivated. Currently, information are printed in "text mode" and refreshed periodically.

When profiling, the user can switch between four views. The first view shows the progression of some global counters such as the current decision and instantiation levels, the total number of decisions and instantiations, the number of generated instances, the number of Boolean (*resp.* theories) simplifications and conflicts, the number of case-splits, etc.

The second one is a "matrix view" where the lines contain around twenty of the most used (time consuming) functions and the columns are labeled with the most important modules of Alt-Ergo. In every cell, the accumulated time spent in each function of every module is shown. This view allowed us to realize that, contrary to what we thought at the beginning of the project, arithmetic reasoning is very costly for some p4 proof obligations. In fact, arithmetic modules take more than 80 % of the solver's time on these POs. An enhancement of corresponding algorithms increased both the success rate and the execution time of Alt-Ergo.

The third view prints the stack of currently activated modules and functions. To differentiate successive calls to the same function, we associate a fresh stamp to every new call. This allows us to detect when a function is slow or looping thanks to the repetition of the same stamp ID after two successive prints.

Finally, the fourth view is dedicated to axioms instantiation. For every axiom, this view shows: the number of generated, kept and ignored instances, the number of instances that participated in a conflict, and the number of "consumed" and "produced" ground terms by the instances. Actually, an axiom that produces a huge number instances or terms may have a bad (*i.e.* too permissive) trigger, so choosing another trigger or completely disabling the axiom may alleviate the solver's context and permit to do the proof.

5.2   Improving Internal Data-Structures

During our first investigations to improve Alt-Ergo, we noticed that the representation of literals and formulas were not optimal, and that some normalizations were missing. This prevents the solver from making some straightforward simplifications, from getting the best from hash-consing techniques, and from doing some operations in constant time without allocating (*e.g.* computing the negation of a formula). To fix these issues, we reimplemented the internal data-structures for literals and formulas. In addition, we hash-consed internal data-structures of the decision procedures. This enabled the use of hash-consed based comparison to build sets and maps over these structures and induced an important speedup.

5.3   Improving the SAT Solver

In general, SAT reasoning is cheaper than theories reasoning. So, to improve the
interaction between the SAT and the theories, we made some modifications to
delay calls to decision procedures as much as possible and to make all possible
deductions at SAT level first. This is done when assuming unit facts, deciding
a literal, or when performing Boolean constraints propagation modulo theories.
A similar distinction is also made inside decision procedures: reasoning with
equalities is, in general, much faster than processing inequalities.

In addition, we modified Alt-Ergo's architecture to enable the use of different
SAT solvers provided as plugins, implemented a new CDCL-based solver, and
enriched the default SAT solver with some modern decision heuristics.

5.4   Better Axioms Instantiation Heuristics

During our investigations, we ran Alt-Ergo with profiling support on our POs and
noticed a large number of axioms instantiation, a high activity of the decision
procedures, and an important workload for the SAT engine. A further investigation revealed that this is due to the hundreds of axioms and the huge context
that implies thousands of generated instances, as shown in Fig. 4.

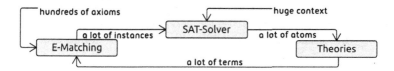

Fig. 4. Interaction of different components of Alt-Ergo on B proof obligations

In order to limit the number of generated instances at each matching round,
we modified Alt-Ergo to only consider terms that appear in the current active
branch (model) of the SAT engine when instantiating. We also added some
normalizations to detect and eliminate redundant (equivalent) instances.

Another improvement is related to E-matching technique: in SMT solvers,
matching process is performed modulo the set of known equalities. For instance,
if x is a variable, $f(g(x)), f(g(a)), g(b)$ are terms, and $g(a) = g(b)$ is a known
equality by the decision procedures, then E-matching a trigger[2] $f(g(x))$ against
$f(g(a))$ will produce two solutions $\sigma_1 = \{x \mapsto a\}$ and $\sigma_2 = \{x \mapsto b\}$, while simple
syntactic matching would only generate σ_1. Actually, the number of solutions for
the matching problem is directly related to the number of generated instances.
Consequently, we added the ability to disable the generation of new instances
modulo known ground equalities via a new option, called `-no-Ematching`. This
choice is justified by the fact that, while E-matching is not really mandatory to
discharge more POs for BWare benchmarks, disabling this feature makes Alt-Ergo
regress on our older benchmarks coming from Why3 and SPARK.

---

[2] Triggers are terms with variables that prevent the instantiation of quantified formulas
unless they "match" some ground terms present in the decision procedures.

5.5   Save (Replay with) the Context Used for a Proof

Another important feature we added in Alt-Ergo is the ability to identify and save, for a discharged PO, a reasonably small over-approximation of the names of axioms that are useful to do the proof. The overhead due to the activation of this feature (via option -save-used-context) is, in general, small compared to the benefits: saved information can be used to quickly replay the proofs (with Alt-Ergo via option -replay-used-context, or with another prover), as we demonstrate it in the next section.

6   Experimental Evaluation

In order to measure the impact of our improvements on BWare's test-suite, we considered two evaluation axes. For the first axis, we varied the time given to the solver for each PO: we used small timeouts that are adequate for an online integration (2 and 10 s per PO), and bigger timeouts, suitable for an offline integration (60 and 600 s per PO). For the second axis, we varied solver's options and resolution strategies:

1. the first strategy uses Alt-Ergo without particular options,
2. the second one uses the solver with the restricted options "-no-Ematching -nb-triggers 1": picking one trigger per axiom (default value is two) and disabling matching modulo equality will restrict the number of generated instances,
3. the third one is a portfolio approach that uses a dozen of configurations on a PO as long as it is not proved. This strategy is rather intended to be used offline, as timeout is set per configuration. Used configurations are listed in the figure below:

```
01 | '-nb-triggers 1 -no-Ematching'
02 | '-nb-triggers 1'
03 | ''
04 | '-no-tcp'
05 | '-no-theory'
06 | '-nb-triggers 10'
07 | '-greedy'
08 | '-sat-plugin satML-plugin.cmxs -nb-triggers 1 -no-Ematching'
09 | '-sat-plugin satML-plugin.cmxs -nb-triggers 1'
10 | '-sat-plugin satML-plugin.cmxs'
```

Basically, we restrict (*e.g.* -nb-triggers 1) or modify (*e.g.* -no-Ematching, -nb-triggers 10) some solver's capabilities, or use alternative implementations of some components (*e.g.* -sat-plugin satML-plugin.cmxs) to hopefully discharge a PO. Option -greedy enables the use of all the terms of the SAT solver when instantiating instead of those appearing in the current model only, option -no-tcp disables the simplification of disjunctions in the SAT modulo theories, while -no-theory completely disables theory reasoning.

For our experiments, we used the latest private release of Alt-Ergo (v. 1.10). The results are reported in the tables below (D = default strategy, R = restricted strategy, P = portfolio strategy, B = results of Atelier-B's main prover, and O = results of Alt-Ergo v. 0.95.2).

We can draw many conclusions from these results:

- even with a time limit of 2 s, the default strategy of Alt-Ergo 1.10 solves more POs than version 0.95.2 (which was ran in default mode with a time limit of 60 s),
- the restricted strategy is, in general, faster and solves more POs than the default one (except for RCS3, and for DAB with a time limit of 600 s),
- whatever the chosen timeout for Alt-Ergo, the portfolio strategy is always the fastest, and has the best resolution rate. This is as expected since the first and the second strategies are just particular configurations of the third one (in which timeout was set per configuration),
- more generally, we made substantial progress for both resolution time and the number of discharged POs compared to Alt-Ergo 0.95.2, in particular for projects p4 and p9,
- Atelier-B's main prover is still better on p9 even if we compare it to portfolio approach. The reason is that, contrary to p4 project that involves a lot of arithmetic reasoning, a substantial part of p9 POs necessitates lemmas superposition to be proven quickly. Unfortunately, E-matching is not suitable for that, and superposition calculus is currently lacking in Alt-Ergo.

	c.	RCS3	DAB	p4	p9
2	D	98.8%(2230/794s)	95.8%(824/ 138s)	94.7%(8849/ 1876s)	64.4%(239/ 126s)
	R	97.8%(2206/780s)	98.0%(843/ 135s)	98.8%(9230/ 1880s)	66.6%(247/ 124s)
10	D	99.0%(2233/811s)	95.8%(824/ 138s)	97.7%(9124/ 2940s)	67.4%(250/ 183s)
	R	97.8%(2207/783s)	98.0%(843/ 135s)	99.3%(9273/ 2126s)	73.6%(273/ 261s)
60	D	99.0%(2233/811s)	97.0%(834/ 518s)	98.3%(9179/ 4480s)	71.2%(264/ 691s)
	R	97.8%(2207/782s)	98.0%(843/ 135s)	99.3%(9274/ 2158s)	77.9%(289/ 547s)
600	D	99.0%(2233/811s)	99.0%(851/1789s)	98.8%(9231/13375s)	72.2%(268/1554s)
	R	97.8%(2207/782s)	98.0%(843/ 135s)	99.3%(9278/ 2542s)	82.8%(307/3064s)
60	B	90.1%	95.7%	83.0%	96.2%
	O	98.7%	95.6%	89.9%	57.4%

We also notice for DAB project that increasing timeout of the portfolio approach does not allow to discharge more POs. This may be due to two reasons: either the triggers computed for the remaining formulas are not suitable to do the proofs, or the proofs require superposition calculus.

	c.	RCS3	DAB	p4	p9
2	P	99.2%(2237/795s)	99.2%(853/ 138s)	99.4%(9289/ 1968s)	71.2%(264/ 142s)
10	P	99.2%(2237/795s)	99.2%(853/ 138s)	99.5%(9292/ 2204s)	81.7%(303/ 353s)
60	P	99.3%(2240/844s)	99.2%(853/ 138s)	99.5%(9295/ 2272s)	86.2%(320/1007s)
600	P	99.3%(2240/844s)	99.2%(853/ 138s)	99.6%(9303/ 4729s)	90.8%(337/3402s)

We made a second experiment to measure the impact of saving the "names of axioms" that have been used to discharge a PO, and of replaying the proof with the pruned context. For that, we used the default configuration of Alt-Ergo 1.10 and a time limit of 600 s. The results are reported in the table below. We notice that we have a small overhead when option -save-used-context is activated, compared to the results we got with the default strategy, and that around twenty POs are not proved anymore. However, thanks to the information saved when this option is activated, all proofs replay succeeded quite faster.

	RCS3	DAB	p4	p9
-save	99.0%(2233/821s)	99.0%(851/3015s)	98.7%(9216/15454s)	72.0%(267/1250s)
-replay	100% (776 s)	100% (124 s)	100% (1742 s)	100% (101 s)

7 Conclusion and Future Works

This paper describes our improvements in the Alt-Ergo SMT solver to increase its proofs success rate on formulas coming from the Atelier-B framework. Our experimental results show a substantial progression of Alt-Ergo 1.10 compared to older versions and to Atelier-B's main prover. It turns out that B proof obligations have some specificities that should be taken into account to obtain a good success rate. Note that, the integration of SMT solvers in the Rodin [11] platform to discharge proof obligations coming from Event-B [1] has already been investigated [7]. However, the translation scheme that has been employed is quite different from BWare's (static expansion of Set theory constructs before generating a PO for an SMT solver). It would be interesting to investigate the use of BWare's translation technique within Rodin. This could be achieved by adapting the investigations of [2] to use BWare axiomatization.

In the near future, we plan to investigate the integration of built-in support for a fragment of the B Set theory in Alt-Ergo via the extension of our rewriting-based frameworks AC(X) [5] and CC(X) [6]. This would improve resolution time and offer some nice completeness properties on this fragment. The extension of Alt-Ergo with superposition calculus would also increase proofs success rate. In addition, we identified some components of our solver that necessitate further improvements (*e.g.* triggers inference module). Other possible lines of work include the use of benchmarks coming directly from Atelier-B's new POs generator, and the extension of the B Set theory prelude[3]. Yet, a new project containing 60,000 POs has been recently translated to Why3's logic. It constitutes another interesting challenge for Alt-Ergo.

Last, but not least, a previous release of Alt-Ergo (version 0.94) has already been qualified for a usage in avionic area (DO-178B). It would be worth considering the ability to qualify a new version for a usage in the railway domain.

---

[3] The prelude is still under development, and some axioms may be missing to discharge a PO, or may be written in an "unsuitable" way for the solvers.

References

1. Abrial, J.-R.: The B-book - Assigning Programs to Meanings. Cambridge University Press, Cambridge (2005)
2. Adjepon-Yamoah, D., Romanovsky, A., Iliasov, A.: A reactive architecture for cloud-based system engineering. In: Proceedings of the 2015 International Conference on Software and System Process, ICSSP 2015, pp. 77–81. ACM, New York, NY, USA (2015)
3. Bobot, F., Conchon, S., Contejean, E., Iguernlala, M., Lescuyer, S., Mebsout, A.: Alt-Ergo version 0.99.1. CNRS, Inria, Université Paris-Sud 11, and OCamlPro, Dec 2014. http://alt-ergo.lri.fr/, http://alt-ergo.ocamlpro.com/
4. ClearSy System Engineering. Atelier B User Manual, version 4.0. http://tools.clearsy.com/wp-content/uploads/sites/8/resources/User_uk.pdf
5. Conchon, S., Contejean, E., Iguernelala, M.: Canonized rewriting and groundAC completion modulo Shostak theories: design and implementation. Logical Methods Comput. Sci. **8**(3), 653–683 (2012)
6. Conchon, S., Contejean, E., Kanig, J., Lescuyer, S.: CC(X): semantic combination of congruence closure with solvable theories. Electron. Notes Theor. Comput. Sci. **198**(2), 51–69 (2008)
7. Déharbe, D., Fontaine, P., Guyot, Y., Voisin, L.: Integrating SMT solvers in rodin. Sci. Comput. Program. **94**, 130–143 (2014)
8. Filliâtre, J.-C., Paskevich, A.: Why3 — where programs meet provers. In: Felleisen, M., Gardner, P. (eds.) ESOP 2013. LNCS, vol. 7792, pp. 125–128. Springer, Heidelberg (2013)
9. Mentré, D., Marché, C., Filliâtre, J.-C., Asuka, M.: Discharging proof obligations from atelier B using multiple automated provers. In: Derrick, J., Fitzgerald, J., Gnesi, S., Khurshid, S., Leuschel, M., Reeves, S., Riccobene, E. (eds.) ABZ 2012. LNCS, vol. 7316, pp. 238–251. Springer, Heidelberg (2012)
10. The BWare Project (2012). http://bware.lri.fr/
11. Voisin, L., Abrial, J.-R.: The Rodin platform has turned ten. In: Ait Ameur, Y., Schewe, K.-D. (eds.) ABZ 2014. LNCS, vol. 8477, pp. 1–8. Springer, Heidelberg (2014)

Author Index

Printed in the United States
By Bookmasters